THE CALL
of the
GREEN BIRD

ALBERTA HAWSE

MULTNOMAH BOOKS
SISTERS, OREGON

This book is a work of fiction.
With the exception of recognized historical figures,
the characters in this novel are fictional. Any resemblance to actual persons,
living or dead, is purely coincidental.

THE CALL OF THE GREEN BIRD
© 1995 by Alberta Hawse

published by Multnomah Books
a part of the Questar publishing family

Edited by Rodney L. Morris
Cover design by David Uttley
Cover illustration by David Frampton

International Standard Book Number: 0-88070-779-8

Printed in the United States of America

For information:
Questar Publishers, Inc. • Post Office Box 1720 • Sisters, Oregon 97759

95 96 97 98 99 00 01 02 03 04 — 10 9 8 7 6 5 4 3 2 1

To my son, Larry,
and my son-in-law, Nick,
my two most encouraging fans.

BOOK ONE

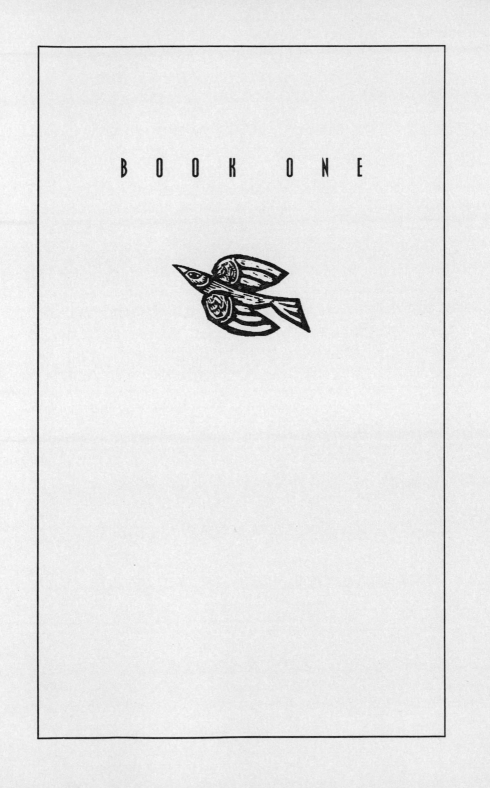

Spring 30 A.D.

T he Syrian oasis was as ancient as the wadi that fed it. Over a period of years, through wars and bartering, the oasis had become the summer camping ground for Prince Raaschid's Bedouin clan.

Gullies and hillocks, now bathed in early morning softness, would soon blaze with the brassy heat of noon. Palm fronds, now a shadowy green, would hang limp in the gilding of pale yellow.

Upon the ever-changing face of the flinty sand and gravel plain, the black goat-hair tents of the Jackal clan sprawled like huge caterpillars. From the center pole of the chieftain's long tent, the identifying brown and yellow banner flapped in the wind.

Beyond the tents, toward the east, the face of a limestone cliff pushed into the air. Behind it, an undulating ridge loomed like couched camels. Close to the outer edge of the tents, huge boulders had fallen from the face of the cliff and now formed a small arena of shade where the cooler air from the water courses seemed to linger.

Here, where the large stones helped to repel the sun, camp children came during the day to play. At night, lovers walked in the shadows, and friends exchanged confidences.

Today, two of Prince Raaschid's household played among the boulders. Kaleb, the eight-year-old prince, son of Gutne the first wife, was building a Roman "fort" on top of a flat rock. His delicate oval face, aquiline nose, dark eyes, and six black braids shiny with butter were typically Ishmaelite.

Mi'kal, the seventeen-year-old prince, was half-brother to Kaleb. His skin was much lighter and his braids shone with red-gold lights as he practiced with his sling trying to hit a small bronze bell hanging on a branch of a terebinth tree. His mother, Quintira, a captured Israelite, was the chieftain's second and favorite wife.

Above the boys, against the high white face of the limestone cliff, a bevy of birds was swooping and chirping in sheer ecstasy. Kaleb was the first to hear them. He glanced up, but the sun blinded him. He placed the last stone in the tower of his fort and looked up again, shielding his eyes with his hands.

"Mi'kal, look! Do you think they've found a rain pool?"

Mi'kal squinted upward. The cliff was a series of rough terraces hewn by centuries of weather. Halfway up, the birds seemed to be dropping into a rift.

"Maybe."

"Can we climb up and see?"

"We have no permission to go beyond the boulders."

"Nobody will know."

"I'm responsible for you. If anything bad happened to you, your mother would skin me alive." Mi'kal's sling whistled and the stone brought a listless clang from the bronze bell.

"Nothing bad can happen. I'm wearing my bead."

Above Kaleb's simple white loin-cloth, a blue bead hung on a leather thong about his neck. Gutne had put it there on the day he was born to protect him from the evil eye of the desert jinn.

Quintira, a Galilean Jewess, would never allow Mi'kal to wear such an amulet. Although only sixteen when she was kidnapped by the Bedouin sheik, she had struggled to hold fast to her Jewish faith.

"We do not put our trust in amulets. The Lord is our strength and shield."

When Mi'kal tried to explain that the other children thought she did not love him because he had no protection against the jinn, she took him into her lap.

"There will never be a son more loved than you. Never. Not until the mother of our Messiah holds God's Son in her arms."

Then as she playfully tied his two front braids into a knot under his chin, she laughed and kissed him.

Kaleb pulled impatiently at Mi'kal's tunic. "Brother, why don't you quit thinking and listen. Are the bird songs not like the flutes that call us to a wedding feast?"

Mi'kal smiled. It did seem as if the birds were inviting them.

"Kaleb, even if there is a pool, by the time we get up there the sun will have sucked up every drop."

"Oh, no. I'm sure it's a big pool. I think the water is as blue as one of your mother's pretty mantles."

"I really don't think—"

"Stop thinking. Everybody says you think too much about every-thing." Kaleb's voice was spiteful.

Mi'kal smiled with affectionate tolerance. He could understand Kaleb's excitement. A rain pool in the desert meant sun-warmed waters and a rare chance to bathe naked with the birds.

Mi'kal gave in against his better judgment because he truly loved young Kaleb. He felt no deep affection for Sa'ad, Gutne's older son. But then his older half-brother had never shown any love for him. Just the contrary. Sa'ad either ignored or tormented him, and at times he was actu-ally cruel.

Quintira had tried to ease his hurt by explaining it was because Gutne's son was jealous. Sa'ad seemed to think Raaschid might make Mi'kal leader of the clan because of his love for Quintira.

"Mother, Sa'ad is the first-born by five years! All the privileges of inheritance and clan leadership are rightfully his. I am glad it is so. I have no desire to be a ruler of men."

She patted his cheek. "My prince, you were born to be a leader of men. Wait and see."

Now he smiled as he remembered. He a ruler of men? He could not even control one small boy.

Kaleb was still pleading. "Mi'kal, take me up. See, I have ten thirsty camels." He lifted his foot and wiggled his toes.

Mi'kal pulled affectionately on the black braids. "All right. But remem-ber you must obey me in everything." He laid his sling beside the "fort" and said sternly, "You must not get one little scratch."

Ascending the cliff was not difficult because of the natural ledges, but they had to be careful where they stepped because the stones crumbled and spurs of volcanic lava were sharp as knives.

Kaleb was obedient and careful, but Mi'kal began to feel guilty. He should not have capitulated. The young prince was more like Sa'ad every day, arrogant and demanding.

Mi'kal was usually ignored by his young brother when Sa'ad was in camp. But many times Sa'ad was gone, as he was now, to negotiate for grazing grounds for the sheep.

While the camels and mares and milk goats could stay at the oasis, the sheep had to be taken farther north to the foothills of the Lebanon mountain range. Agreements had to be made before the migrating flocks could cross another tribe's grazing land.

Sa'ad was a good negotiator.

For several days now the camp had expected his return, but Gutne had boasted that he might stop in Damascus or Caesarea Philippi to select a suitable gift for his bride-to-be. A contract had been signed for him to marry his cousin Zalah, of the Boar clan.

Well known for her beauty, Zalah was the daughter of Raaschid's brother, Muktar. The marriage would reunite a tribe that had been split asunder in a family quarrel. Gutne had boasted that someday her son would be made leader of Muktar's clan instead of Zauf, Muktar's crippled son. And Sa'ad's camp would then be twice as big.

Quintira had expressed her worry when Mi'kal reported Gutne's boasting. "Zauf will not take the loss of his leadership easily. I have heard he is a breeder of fine horses and well able to rule his people even though he has been lame since birth."

Mi'kal's thoughts returned to Kaleb. He watched as his brother clambered up the last ledge to the wide shelf. The birds were not alarmed. They swooped and chirped. Water glistened on multicolored wings, and small rainbows fell as feathers shook themselves dry.

One larger bird had bright green on breast and wings. Something stirred in Mi'kal's mind, but Kaleb's excited voice put it to rest.

"Look! It's not very big, but it is blue."

Mi'kal looked down into a weather-carved cistern, no deeper than a man's height. At the bottom a deeper, rounded basin was filled with rain-water reflecting the cerulean sky. A narrow border of rotten limestone rimmed the pool. Shrubs and grass grew in isolated clumps. Small vines clung to the lower walls. Above the pool, the cliff face rose high and the sun shot white light.

Kaleb dropped his loin-cloth and teetered impatiently from one foot to the other. The blue bead blazed on his thin, dark brown chest.

Mi'kal pulled his olive green tunic over his head and stood in his matching loin-cloth. Kaleb watched him.

"Aren't you going to take that off? It's really too pretty to get wet." There was mischievous teasing in Kaleb's black eyes.

Mi'kal felt his cheeks warm. His loin-cloths had always been a source of amusement to the other boys. He had begged his mother to make them out of coarse plain cloth, but she insisted on bright cotton or silk.

He remembered the day he had complained and she had struck him lightly across the rump and laughed. "A prince should be a prince from the bottom up."

"Mi'kal!" Kaleb demanded in an imperious voice. "Are you going to stand there all day like a stupid donkey? If you are, I'm going to jump."

"No!" Mi'kal caught him about the chest with one arm. The blue bead bit into his arm. "Not until I see what's down there."

Kaleb tried to free himself. "Have you forgotten that I am a prince? And you have to do what I say?"

"I am a prince, too," Mi'kal reminded him. "And you will do as I say or I will haul you off this cliff and back to your Roman fort where we should be anyway."

Haughtiness vanished. Kaleb's small face quivered with entreaty. "Forgive me. I have spoken badly. All things you do for me are good."

The repentance was so false Mi'kal laughed. "Oh, come on. I will help you down." But a stubborn uneasiness tugged at him. "Our lord is going to be very, very angry with us when he finds out what we have done."

"I will take him a handful of the blue water to cool his anger." Kaleb's eyes twinkled.

11

"You are not a sand grouse that can carry water in the feathers of her breast," Mi'kal said.

Kaleb swung the blue bead to his back and held to Mi'kal's hands as he scooted on his stomach over the edge and found support for his feet.

"It's easy," his voice was excited and confident. "Just like steps. You can let loose now."

"Don't go into the water until I get there. The rocks might be sharp."

"I won't. I'm almost down."

Mi'kal leaned down and saw Kaleb standing with a triumphant smile on his face.

Mi'kal, still wearing his loin-cloth, started his own descent. He found his first solid foot-hold just as Kaleb screamed. The terrified cry was shrill, slashing into Mi'kal's ears and ripping his hands from the wall. He hit the ground hard, then he scrambled to his feet.

Beyond him, Kaleb lay face up by the pool, his eyes wide and staring. One arm was extended and the small palm filled and emptied as the water rippled over it.

Mi'kal had seen sudden death before. For a moment his world collapsed. Then he gathered Kaleb into his arms and sobbed.

When the sobbing ended the anger came...old anger he could remember as a child. Anger against death. Death should never have been. No matter how his mother tried to explain about Adam and Eve and their disobedience. God should never have put anything as ugly and final as Death into his beautiful world.

Nothing was as cruel as Death. Death took the very thing you loved the most. Death was a coward.

Death never did his own dirty work. He had servants: like the sandstorm many years before that had almost killed the Old One, the mysterious one, whom Mi'kal and Quintira had learned to love and call Grandfather; like the mad camel that had bitten his little friend, Rual; like the frightened mare that had kicked his dog.

And Death used men for his assassins, too. Men such as Sa'ad who had slain Haserah, Mi'kal's pet ostrich, all because of a necklace.

Which of Death's assassins had slain Kaleb? Which sly and deadly enemy could strike so quickly that the end came in a few seconds?

Here in the rain cistern there could be but one answer. A Palestinian viper! And it was still here, hiding among the clumps of dried grass or in the thorny shrubs that nested in the mounds of blown sand.

Mi'kal laid his brother down. He straightened the thin legs and the black braids and the blue bead, although he wanted to snatch the amulet and sling it into the pool. His anger was as much with God as it was with Death.

And Death was still here. He could feel the malevolent eyes upon him. He looked cautiously about. A coney sat in the sun on an open ledge and chewed its cud. A small brown bird with bright yellow legs walked stiffly about Kaleb's body.

He wiped the tears from his cheeks and began to search for a sharp-pointed rock. The serpent would be hard to find, for its green and brown striping blended with grass and sand. But he would stay here until he found it. An eye for an eye. A life for a life.

He had not expected to find it on his first circuit of the pool. He dislodged a scorpion from a hole in the wall and shivered at its dry rustle as it fell. A lizard raced across his feet and he jumped.

He felt the sweat of fear on his forehead. He crouched by the pool and washed his face, painfully alert for any movement. There was one last thing he could do for Kaleb. He would take the "ten thirsty camels" to the well. He stepped into the pool and eased Kaleb's body into the water. Slowly he pulled his brother into the pool. The black braids floated; the blue bead made strange patterns in the water; the small toes were like ten marching soldiers.

At the edge of the water, across the pool, a sudden movement caught his attention. The viper was taking the quickest way to reach sanctuary in the higher wall. Mi'kal dragged Kaleb out of the water and picked up the rock. There was a swirl of green and brown on the opposite side of the basin.

Mi'kal raced around the rim. He watched as the thick body whipped out of the pool and across the rotten limestone. The serpent went head-first into a break in the wall, but the hole was not deep enough. Instinct made him turn and face his enemy. The head lifted, the neck puffed.

Mi'kal felt sweat in his eyes again. Blood pounded in his temples.

He tried to remember what the Old One had told him about the snake charmers with hooded vipers in the Damascus bazaars.

He moved closer, his eyes trying to hold those of the snake. He found it hard to breath and his mouth was going dry. He lifted his left arm and began a slow sweeping motion. The viper puffed and reared, its head slowly followed the swaying arm.

Mi'kal's arm came nearer. The snake arched its neck. The front part of the heavy body lifted.

The arm made a sudden movement and the snake struck. It missed.

But Mi'kal's right hand came down with the stone behind the hooded head. The stunned snake slithered from the wall. The stone smashed down again and again.

High overhead a falcon cried. The drowsy coney ignored the warning. The falcon dropped down, then rose, the squirming victim in its talons.

Mi'kal watched as the falcon carried its prey high overhead. The black shadow of the wide wings fell against the white face of the cliff. To Mi'kal, the shadow was the symbol of Death.

He raised a clenched fist and shouted. "I hate you, Death! Someday, I, Mi'kal of the black tents, will have victory over you!"

A crow followed the flight of the falcon. Its raucous caws reverberated against the walls of the pool. To Mi'kal, it seemed that Death was laughing at his stupid challenge.

CHAPTER TWO

After tying Kaleb to his back, using the green loin-cloth, Mi'kal had managed to climb out of the cistern. On the ledge, he freed himself and stood up. Air currents rising from the pool cooled the skin he had chafed on the rough stones of the wall. As he rested and wrapped the loin-cloth about him, he looked out over the valley. The plain was part of the Roman province of Batanea, ruled by Herod Philip, one of the sons of Herod the Great.

Ancient, dried-up wadis criss-crossed the ancient valley, once known as Bashan, and faded into the distance toward the hills of Moab. To the northwest, the blue and purple ridge of the Lebanon mountains, dominated by Mount Herman, lay like mist on the horizon.

He lifted Kaleb and stood for a moment looking down at the camp. Raaschid's long tent marked the center of the encampment. The tent included private quarters for his two wives and separate rooms for both his chief steward Duag, an Egyptian, and Kwa, his favorite bodyguard, an African black man.

Both men had been purchased from slave caravans heading for Palestine. Duag had olive skin and a bald head. He had been intended to work in the mercantile warehouses of Phoenicia because he could read and write. He was intensely loyal to Raaschid, but Mi'kal considered him as cruel as the leopard whose skin he wore as a belt about his waist.

Kwa, an exceedingly strong man, was being transported to the asphalt pits in Judea when Raaschid bought him. His teeth had been filed and his chest showed ridges of a tribal initiation into manhood. Mi'kal and Quintira had always considered him a friend.

Mi'kal knew that if his mother were outside her tent now he would be

15

able to see her, for she always wore bright garments—every color except purple. He often wondered why she avoided the royal shade. He was sure it would emphasize the beauty of her dark hair and the touches of silver gray about her face and ears. Fortunately, Prince Raaschid loved bright clothing, too. He often came into Quintira's tent, his arms loaded with beautiful cloth that he had obtained through trading or raiding.

His mother would murmur a soft thank you, with scarcely a smile. But after Raaschid was gone, her eyes would glow with delight as she held the soft cottons or whispery silk to her face. Mi'kal often wondered why she would not let his father see her delight when he was so anxious to please her.

Perhaps the chieftain's love for Quintira would temper his punishment on her son. But Mi'kal knew the hope was foolish. The desert law of retribution was immutable. An eye for an eye.

Mi'kal tried to build up courage as he started down the cliff with Kaleb's body. Descending was more difficult than climbing. Some of the terraces crumbled beneath him and patches of sliding scree brought him down. Now and then the flash of sunlight on the crystalline deposits caused him to stumble. By the time he reached the foot of the cliff, his legs were trembling and his muscles knotting with pain.

He rested by the boulder that held his sling and the stone fort. Was it possible that only a couple of hours had passed since Kaleb had played there in perfect safety?

The camel bell swung in a gray haze and Mi'kal realized he was looking at it through tears. He laid his head against the stones. Somewhere in the distance a crow cawed.

"Are you sick?"

Mi'kal looked up. A small girl, holding a palm leaf doll, was staring at him. He shook his head.

"I thought maybe you are sick like Kaleb." She looked at the body propped up against the rocks.

"He isn't sick. He's dead." The words seemed unreal even to him.

Her eyes widened. "What happened?"

"A snake bit him."

There was terror on her face as she looked around. "Here?"

"No. Up there." He pointed. "In a rain pool."

"Oh!" She clutched her doll tighter. "Does his mother know?"

Mi'kal shook his head. "Nobody knows."

"I'll tell them."

"No, don't!" Mi'kal yelled at her, but she was gone. Numbness caused by weakness and heat was overcoming him. The boulders seemed to crowd upon him, suffocating him. He heard without knowing that he heard the low rumble running through the camp as the word spread.

He never remembered reaching the long tent. He was partly conscious of staggering and letting Kaleb roll into the sand. He thought he heard Gutne screaming.

He tried to focus on a figure he thought was his mother. Her blue mantle floated like haze before his eyes. He felt her arm about him, heard her voice crying, "Mi'kal. Mi'kal, what happened?"

Gradually the mists cleared. Gutne was on her knees holding her son and shrieking, "You killed him! You killed him!"

"No. No. A snake did it. A snake!" He tried to harness his stupid tongue. "I killed it. I did. I killed it."

Suddenly Gutne was on her feet calling for a knife. A skinner, who had been working on an antelope hide, threw her his blade. She started forward with wild anger.

Mi'kal lifted an arm to protect himself, but Quintira sprang between them. Under the force of Quintira's attack, Gutne dropped the knife. The women fought with primitive hatred, biting and gouging as they rolled in the sand.

Several of the women spurred Gutne to greater effort, for many of the clan's women often felt jealous of the Jewess. Some coveted her beauty and some hated her cleanliness. Many had been insulted by her contempt for their household gods and amulets. Others envied her, for while they were heavy with child year after year, her womb stayed empty.

Gutne ripped at Quintira's bodice. Quintira screamed. Mi'kal started forward. Raaschid laid a heavy hand on his arm.

Quintira finally rolled free, leaped to her feet, and put her foot over the knife. Her mantle was gone and her hair matted with sand, but her head was high. Her hands held the ripped bodice shut.

Raaschid released his hold on Mi'kal and walked toward the women. He pushed Quintira aside and picked up the knife. His face was unreadable. As he looked down at the body of his youngest son, grief took refuge behind narrowed lids. He clapped his hands for slaves to move Kaleb into Gutne's quarters. Some of the women followed to mourn and help prepare him for burial.

Then he spoke sharply to those who lingered. "Get you gone! Must you be as scavengers about a carcass?"

Mi'kal and his mother started to move away, but he said, "Stay!" They remained motionless as he went into Gutne's quarters.

Quintira spoke quickly. "How did it happen?"

He told her quickly.

"God help us. You will pay for your foolishness."

Raaschid returned, carrying the knife in one hand and Kaleb's black braids in the other. He pressed them against Mi'kal's face. The stench of rancid butter was nauseating.

"A prince has been shorn in sorrow because of you. Tell me—how did my son die? No, tell me *why* he is dead!"

The cold quietness of the chieftain's voice was more frightening than heated anger. He kissed the braids and passed them quietly to a girl who had come from Gutne to get them.

Mi'kal's words came awkwardly, like small things learning to walk. They staggered and fell.

Quintira tried to ease the awful silence. "Surely he cannot be blamed for what a serpent did."

"Are the serpents to be praised for being wiser than your son?"

"You know Mi'kal has loved Kaleb from the day Gutne birthed him in my tent."

"Love? Some love can be as a thistle under the blanket."

Mi'kal caught the familiar undercurrent of bitterness between them and felt guilty and confused, as he always did when they argued about him.

Quintira knelt. "My lord, I beg you, temper justice with mercy and I will be as one of your hired servants."

Mi'kal opened his mouth to protest. Quintira seldom asked favors from the prince, and even less often did she give him the title of lord, which she reserved for her own God.

Raaschid said nothing as he passed the knife from one hand to another. Then he spoke slowly. "Your son will be judged by the council within the hour when we meet around the judgment rug. If one should die and another live in a mutual act of disobedience, then let them say so. Until then—"

He moved so swiftly that neither Mi'kal or Quintira could react. His hands grabbed Mi'kal's braids and yanked them upward. The knife flashed and Quintira screamed.

Mi'kal expected to feel warm blood on his throat, but instead he felt the sawing of the knife into his braids. As they fell, one by one, Mi'kal suffered increasing shame. A Bedouin's braids were cut for only one of two reasons in Raaschid's camp—at the time of death as a sign of mourning, or when a man was judged unworthy to be a man.

Quintira moaned as she gathered up the braids and held them against her breast. Jealousy and pain crossed Raaschid's face. Mi'kal had often noticed that Raaschid could control his emotions before the camp, but in the presence of Quintira he was often vulnerable.

He is jealous of me, Mi'kal thought. Why would my own father be jealous of me?

"May we go to our tent?" Quintira asked softly, but there was no softness in her dark eyes.

"I am not finished," Raaschid said as he clapped for his attendants.

Mi'kal felt renewed dread as Duag and Kwa came.

Raaschid gave quick orders. "Unclothe him. As my young son came naked to me, so shall he be. Fasten him to the bar near the goat pen. Give him no food or drink."

Quintira screamed in protest. His voice grew more angry.

"Take him quickly. I am sick to death of the Jewish whelp!"

Raaschid's last words burned like a brand as Mi'kal watched him walk away. And yet he knew the angry words were more to hurt his mother than him.

Kwa laid a restraining hand upon Quintira and shook his head as Duag tore off the green tunic and the loincloth and Mi'kal stood naked in the middle of the camp.

Kwa and Duag caught Mi'kal under the arms and dragged him toward the goat pen. Only his toes brushed the ground. Cuts and bruises he had suffered during the day began to burn. Thirst promised to become a torment.

I am as a bustard, he thought. A stupid bird, trussed and ready for the pot.

Did the acacia tree, near the pen, shade the tethering pole? He couldn't remember.

If only his friend, the Old One, were here he would find some way to get water to him. But the Old One had left the camp as usual for a trip into Damascus to sell the leather skins and belts and palm leaf baskets he made. Then he would do a little gambling with his hard-earned coins. Already he was a day late.

As they tied him up, Mi'kal wondered if Kwa would consider that Quintira was his friend. Would he remember she had been as a physician to him in the time of hornet stings and thorn poisoning? Would he try to keep the fetters a little loose?

He tried to read the answer in the black man's face, but there was nothing written there. Overhead, for the third time that day, Mi'kal heard the mocking laughter of a crow.

CHAPTER THREE

The tethering bar was the place where the animals were hung to be skinned and dressed. Mi'kal was tied near one of the uprights. Stench rose in a sickening cloud. His hands were fastened over his head to the horizontal bar, and his ankles were tied to the bottom of the post. Some of his humiliating nakedness was hidden by the stanchion. By turning his head he could see portions of the camp and the edge of the goat pen.

The shade of the acacia tree did not reach him. Even though the sun was in the second half of the sky, the light jabbed through his closed lids. Hordes of flies settled on him, and his skin crawled with revulsion.

He tried to fasten his thoughts on anything that would make him forget his torment.

He remembered his mother's excitement when they saw the first flowers as they came northward from the red dunes. She had exclaimed over each tiny blossom. Mi'kal always marveled at the renewed life that sprang from a dead land.

Once when he had expressed his wonder, his mother compared the resurrection of spring beauty to the renewal of life that her father, Rabbi Ithamar, believed was the reward for every faithful Jew. A new life that would come when the Messiah came.

Mi'kal had asked her if the Messiah was like the Green Bird—the bird that the camp children sang about, the bird that knew the secret of coming back from the dead.

Quintira threw up her hands in horror. "Oh, no, little prince. The Phoenix is an Egyptian bird-god that the Romans and Greeks have deified. The tale of its dying and coming to life again is only a myth. Our Lord is the only true God. He is the one responsible for your every hour…your living and your dying."

Mi'kal was astonished. "You mean God wants people to die?"

"Oh, no." Quintira sat down on a stool and drew him near. "In the beginning God intended for everyone to live forever."

She told him of a beautiful garden where God put the very first man and woman, Adam and Eve.

"He made all things beautiful for them. He hung up the moon and the stars to shine by night, and he ordered the sun to give light by day. He gave Adam charge over everything—all the fish in the sea, all the animals on earth, everything—except one tree in the garden whose fruit they were not to eat. Just one."

"Why?"

"I don't know why. God had given Adam and Eve the right to make up their own minds, and I think he wanted to see if they would choose to obey or disobey. They chose to disobey."

"They should have left his tree alone if he had given them everything else."

Quintira laughed and hugged him. "I think so, too. But Eve looked at the tree and wondered about it. No other tree in the garden was as interesting to her as *that* tree. Surely, if all the other fruit was so delicious, *that* fruit must be more so."

Mi'kal thought of the fruits he liked. "Was it gold like apricots or red like pomegranates?"

"I don't know. Sometimes I think it might have been the olive tree. But let me go on. God put the Serpent in the garden."

"A snake?"

"Oh, this Serpent was not like the snakes in our desert. This snake walked upright like a man. He was one of the most beautiful creations in the garden. But he was jealous of God. He wanted to be like God. So he encouraged Eve to eat and told her nothing bad would happen.

"Now God had warned Adam and Eve that they would die if they ate the fruit of that tree. Eve had no idea what God meant. There was no death in the garden. No flower petals had fallen. Knowing nothing of death, she was not afraid. So Eve picked the fruit and ate it."

"Did she die then and there?"

"No. And the fruit tasted so good she wanted Adam to have some."

"It must have been an apricot."

Quintira smiled again. "If you say so. But when Adam saw that nothing happened to Eve, he decided to take a bite."

"Then what happened?"

"God said he would have to punish them. Thorns began to grow on the trees and flowers. Blossoms withered. Worms ate the fruit. Adam and Eve had to leave the garden and become as Bedouins. And one day they learned how terrible death can be when their first-born son killed his brother."

"Why didn't God just kill the Serpent and let Adam and Eve alone?"

"He did punish the Serpent, Mi'kal. But he had to punish Adam and Eve, too, because they disobeyed. They brought sin into the world, and sin will be here until the Messiah comes. Sin brought death, but the Messiah will take away the curse of death."

Mi'kal came back to unpleasant reality as a bee buzzed about his cheek. He jerked his head away, then looked down where a chicken pecked at a seed-filled gullet from a desert grouse. Small pellets hit his foot.

Death was here as well as in the tent of Gutne. Soon the children would be singing for Kaleb's burial. They would be singing the song of the Green Bird, the bird that could die and come alive again. If men could learn the secret of the Green Bird, they could have victory over Death.

Even though the Old One had told him long before that the Green Bird was a myth and all myths were like mirages, he was not convinced. Surely God had provided a way to escape the finality of death.

He understood why his interest in the Green Bird upset his mother. She had taught him the Jewish commandments, those given to Moses on a smoking mountain. One of them warned against heathen gods: "I am the Lord your God, who brought you out of Egypt.... You shall have no other gods before me."

Mi'kal noticed the awe in his mother's voice as she talked about the

God of Israel, but when she spoke of the Messiah, her voice grew wistful and gentle.

"Someday God is going to send us our King of Kings. He will be all powerful and yet more gentle than an evening wind. He will be holy, but we will be able to look upon him, and touch him, and talk to him. He will heal our sick and restore sight to our blind; he will sow righteousness in our fields and reap peace from our land."

He was little, and she lifted him to her lap. "Ah, Mi'kal, you dream of your Green Bird, but when our Messiah comes, he will bring what you desire. Set your thoughts upon the Messiah, darling. He is not a myth."

The smell of smoke from a revived cooking fire brought his eyes open. His thirst tormented him and the ankle thongs cut into his flesh.

Two children ran across camp, following a small cart pulled by a skinny greyhound. The greyhound made him remember his first dog. He had been very young when Grandfather brought the pup to him from one of his trips into a village outside the camp.

Men of the camp owned long-legged hounds that could bring down a gazelle, but the dog Grandfather brought was small and white, like a lamb. He had two round, black eyes and a cold, black nose. Feathery ears waved like the furry heads of the marsh grass. Mi'kal named his pet Brother, for he had no real brother. His older half-brother, Sa'ad, ignored him, and Kaleb was not yet born.

Mi'kal and Brother played on the tent floor together. He was scarcely more sure of his legs than Brother was. They grew together. Then one day as they played near a tethered mare, a desert rat ran under the mare and around its hooves. Brother scurried after it. The mare's hoof sent the small white body rolling.

Mi'kal held Brother for hours in spite of his mother's pleading. For the first time, Mi'kal understood death. No more licking tongue, no more twinkling eyes, no more warm comfort at night when the desert air chilled and the charcoal brazier burned low.

The children had a regular burial for Brother. They built a cairn and sang the song of resurrection:

O Green Bird, who sees you rejoices... Your father killed
you, your aunt put you in the cooking pot, but your sister, Bough
of Incense, laid you in the box of spices, and you came again to
life.

On the day of the funeral, Mi'kal lingered at the grave. Then he saw a
flash of green feathers in a clump of camel-thorn bushes. Maybe if he
asked, the Green Bird would help Brother. Mi'kal remembered following
the bird. When it rose high and flew away, he couldn't see the tents. He
was lost!

Thorns scratched his legs and he grew hungry. He found a bush with
some dried berries and tried to eat them. They were bitter. He began to
cry. Grown-up people died when they ate bad things. Maybe he would die
and be like Brother, cold and stiff.

He sat down under a bush and hugged his knees. Then he remembered what his mother did when she felt bad. He closed his eyes and
prayed.

A little later Quintira and Kwa found him. Kwa could always find the
lost children because he could read more in the sand and the stars than
anyone else.

Quintira switched him lightly for running away. Then she hugged
him and fed him raisins. He told her that when he was old enough he
would leave the tents to find the Green Bird.

"There is no Green Bird, Mi'kal, anymore than there are evil spirits in
the desert who are afraid of amulets."

Mi'kal pressed against the pole of the tethering bar and shuddered.
Certainly the evil at the rain pool had not been afraid of Kaleb's blue bead.
He opened his eyes and blinked against the sun. Thankfully, the heat was
abating. Activity in the camp was increasing. A crowd had gathered at
Gutne's porch, waiting for Kaleb's burial. Soon the desert pipes and the
tambourines would follow the wailing.

His mother would be on her knees praying for him, her face turned
toward the southwest, toward Judea and the Holy City, Jerusalem. Many
of her Hebrew customs had been forsaken, but a few clung like the

pleasant fragrances she always used.

God would also hear him if he prayed. Had his mother not quoted, "He that planted the ear, shall he not hear? He that formed the eye, shall he not see?"

Mi'kal closed his eyes and felt the surge of petition.

A warm hand touched his arm. "Hush," whispered Ne'ma, the daughter of Tullah, a concubine who had been cast out of the Boar clan by Muktar. She lifted a small pitcher of clabbered milk to his mouth. "Drink it, quick!" she ordered.

She tried to keep her eyes on the tents, but as usual the left one swung wildly from right to left. She was plump for a Bedouin girl, but light on her feet. Soon one of the warriors would take her for a wife. She was well past the marriageable age.

He choked on the thickened milk and part of it dribbled from his lips and splattered among the hairs of his chest. She lifted her skirt to wipe his chin. Ne'ma, who loved to play her tambourine and twirl until her skirts were high above her strong brown legs, never seemed to notice nakedness in herself or others.

"You shouldn't be helping me. You will be beaten."

"Maybe." Her lack of fear matched her lack of modesty.

Mi'kal spoke to her in a hoarse whisper. "You shouldn't be taking such a chance."

"Nobody noticed me. The women of the near tents are helping Gutne prepare for the burial. The men are fed up with the wailing and are dozing. Besides, nobody sees me unless I am playing my tambourine or dancing."

"Are you not afraid of our lord's anger? Did you not hear him deny me food or drink?"

"I do not think my lord would whip me very hard. Sometimes, when I dance before him, I think he really sees me. As my skirts whirl, I can feel his eyes."

"Ne'ma! Surely you know that even if he desired you, you would be nothing but a concubine. Someday he might discard you as Muktar discarded your mother."

She laughed as she brushed flies away from his chest. One hand touched him lightly.

"Sometimes, Mi'kal, one dip of honey is better than a dry cake." Then she laughed. "Much better to be your father's concubine than to be laid for one time in a gully by Sa'ad. Then I would be fit for neither concubine nor wife."

Ne'ma was right. Raaschid did not condone camp immorality. But he laid no punishment on his son for seduction or rape.

"Mi'kal." Ne'ma spoke quickly. "I have to go. Kwa is coming. If he suspects you have had food, tell him the ravens fed you. Your mother told me such a story one day." She went with the pitcher on her shoulder, her skirts swinging.

Mi'kal watched as she passed the slave. If Kwa noticed her he gave no sign. He said nothing as he checked the thongs and loosened the ankle bonds. Mi'kal was grateful.

"Is my mother all right?"

Kwa nodded.

"You won't let any harm come to her because of me, will you?"

The black raised expressionless eyes. He shrugged as if to ask what a slave could do. Then he broke his silence.

"The council is meeting. They will soon have a judgment." He gathered a handful of coarse grass and held it to Mi'kal's mouth. "Chew. It will take away the odor of the sour milk." There was a flash of affection on the black face.

When Mi'kal spit out the grass, Kwa caught it and rubbed it against the sticky spots on his chest where the flies were thick.

"Thank you, Kwa. But take care. I do not wish you to be beaten."

"Nor do I." For a moment the broad black hand closed tightly over his ivory necklace carved like crocodiles following one another.

As the slave left, Mi'kal felt encouraged. He had at least two friends. If Grandfather were here, he would have three. He should be here. Mi'kal glanced at the long tent and saw the elders departing, their chins low on their chests and their council cloaks swinging.

What had they decided? Was he to live or die?

Why did he feel so weak? Was he like Samson who had lost his strength after Delilah, the harlot, conspired to cut his hair? He closed his eyes and let the despair rise. He was as gullible as Adam and Eve, for Kaleb's entreaties had convinced him that nothing bad would happen.

He heard the rustle of a skirt and opened his eyes hoping to see his mother. But it was Gutne who stood there, wrapped in an aura of hate. Her black eyes were as malevolent as those of the viper in the wall.

"As the serpent bit my son, so shall the thorns of the desert bite you," she said, revenge thick on her tongue.

Mi'kal could not control his frightened gasp. He had never seen anyone beaten with thorns, but he had heard of it. Criminals were lashed; slaves were struck with rods; but the thorn beating was kept for those who had done abominable things.

Gutne left with her mourning mantle pulled over her head. Mi'kal felt his legs giving way. Fear had taken the last of his strength. He slumped. Excruciating pain plowed through his arms and shoulders.

He lifted his eyes to the acacia tree with its delicate leaves and yellow blossoms swinging gently. Hidden amongst the blossoms were the thorns. He shut his eyes and groaned.

CHAPTER FOUR

After Gutne left, Kaleb's funeral began. He had been dressed in his best and carried to the cairn on a brightly woven rug. The blue bead would be buried with him and his braids laid across the stones.

Ne'ma's tambourine blended with the beat of the ostrich-skin drums while the children sang: "O Green Bird…"

Mi'kal followed the words of the song. He was exhausted with pain, but he remembered the Old One had told him the Phoenix was reported to be alive again after five hundred years! In Damascus, gold and silver replicas of the bird-god were on sale at the bazaar. According to the gossip, Emperor Tiberius had erected a shrine for his own worship because the resurrection of the Phoenix promised prosperity for his kingdom.

When Mi'kal had told his mother what the Old One said about the Green Bird, she threw up her hands in aggravation. "Mi'kal, for the last time. There is no such bird! No such power!"

"But, Mother, you've said I must have faith in God even though I cannot see him or hear him."

Quintira turned in anger. "Do not say you cannot see God. Look to the sky! Look to the mountains! The whole earth speaks of him. Listen to the thunder and the wind and tell me you cannot hear him."

Later she spoke more calmly. "Mi'kal, the Green Bird has become an obsession with you. When you were little and ran away to find it, I could smile at you. But now you are growing up. You must put this idolatrous idea out of your mind. Someday, when death is conquered, it will be God who removes the curse from us."

He heard a camel bell, and he laid his check against the rough surface of the tethering bar. His thoughts were floating about like carob pods in a watering trough; they carried him to Rual. Rual had been his friend when he was Kaleb's age. They enjoyed playing warrior and riding the couched camels.

One day a male beast, mad with mating desire, singled out the she-camel Rual was riding. As the bawling male rushed her, the female rose to her feet in terror. Rual fell. He raised his camel whip to protect himself, and the camel grabbed his arm with large, yellow teeth. Flesh was pulled from the small arm and poisonous saliva filled the wound. Rual's mother came running as the boys screamed.

Quintira stayed with Rual night and day, but her medicines and leeches didn't help. Rual's arm swelled and turned black. He rolled in agony. One day he gripped his mother's hand, closed his eyes, and died.

Mi'kal carried stones for the grave and sang of the Green Bird. That night he asked his mother how old he would have to be before he could leave the tents and start looking for the bird.

All she said was, "Hush."

He was older when he talked with Grandfather about his desire. The Old One shook his head and called him a dreamer.

"Do you think your search for eternal life is something new? Men of all nations, all generations, have sought for the secret of unending days. The search is as ancient as the curse. I would not doubt that Adam and Eve went out of Paradise seeking such a bird."

Now as Mi'kal watched a desert mouse gnawing at the refuse near his feet, he realized his faith in the Green Bird was slowly fading. A second dream was forming. He longed to see the world outside the goat-hair tents, the world the Old One seemed to know so well. He remembered the day he boasted he would see all the things his old friend told him about.

Grandfather laughed at him and pulled at his red-gold braids. "It will be many years before you can leave the camp."

"Not too long. I am growing taller every day. See." He stretched high by the tent pole where Grandfather had marked his height, month after month, for many years. "See, you must make a new mark." He laughed in triumph as his friend expressed surprise and cut another notch over his head.

Then the Old One made another mark high over Mi'kal's head. "When you reach this, it will be time to talk of leaving your mother."

"I'm not leaving my mother. I want her to see everything, too. We will go to Greece and Rome and Egypt. I want to see the big face with the lion paws that you've told me about."

The Old One rubbed his fingers through his "goat's" beard and squinted his eyes. "Let us see what the fates have to say about your journeys." He began to draw circles and triangles and stars in the sand with a tent peg. He crossed and recrossed the lines, pursing his lips and murmuring.

Mi'kal watched, fascinated. Later, he understood that the squinting and the murmuring meant nothing. Nor did the circles and the stars. Only what his friend was saying was important, for his prophecy had come from the wisdom within him.

"You will see much. But many of the things you wish to see you will not see."

Mi'kal protested. "Yes, I will. Nobody can stop me."

The Old One drew the boy into his arms. Mi'kal could not see what his friend saw; shining, dark-gold locks, a childish chin waiting to be molded into stubbornness; green eyes with flashing yellow and black fire in them.

"There will come a time when your future is laid before you. Different paths that you might take. The choice will be yours," Grandfather said.

Memory of the Old One brought back the nagging worry. Where was the gray donkey and her weary rider? Quintira would need him if Mi'kal did not survive the beating.

Grandfather never spent more than one day disposing of his palm-leaf baskets and dolls, his tanned leather and elaborate belts, and at rare times, a bag of mandrake roots. Allowing two days to come and go, Grandfather should be home. Empty of purse, from gambling, but with gifts for Quintira and the children.

Mi'kal looked up. The sun was poised on the rounded hills of Moab far to the southwest. The day was ending but the camp was coming to life. He watched as those who had been appointed to take part in his punishment came to the acacia tree for branches and sought for other thorn bushes and thistles.

Duag passed him without looking and cut a large branch from the acacia, probably for Gutne.

Mi'kal laid his head against the pole. "Surely God is my salvation; I will trust and not be afraid." But he was afraid—sickly, whimperingly afraid.

Duag came back with Kwa, and together they carried him, again like a trussed bustard, to Kaleb's grave. They threw him down, spread-eagled, over the rocky curve of the cairn. He thought he felt Kaleb's braids under his chest. Four minor slaves held his arms and legs.

Mutterings and murmurings increased as men and boys came with the thorns. Few women took part in camp punishments.

Somewhere he heard the desperate moaning of his mother. Later, he learned Kwa and Duag had been ordered to restrain her. He tried to yell, to tell her to go away, but the yell merged with his first scream. Gutne brought her acacia branch down on his back. The branch was shorn of leaves and flowers. She dragged the thorns across shoulders and buttocks, bringing the pain of a hundred fiery pokers. As the others stepped forward, thorns raked through his hair and snagged in the short curls. Blood mixed with the hair. Blood dripped over his face and chest and matted the braids beneath him.

Long before the scourging ended, he fainted.

His last remembrance was of a shadow, a threatening darkness, hovering above him. He was running, like a coney, for the rocks. Racing ahead of him was a green bird.

CHAPTER FIVE

When Mi'kal awoke, he was lying face down on his sleeping mat. He wasn't sure of the day or hour, for he had floated in and out of consciousness. He turned his face enough to see the morning mist creeping in under the tent flaps and evaporating in the heat of the fire bowl where the camel dung burned with blue and yellow flames.

Aromatic steam rose from the ointment pot. An oil lamp hanging from the roof pole cast a moving shadow on the linen curtains that concealed Quintira's bedroom.

Mi'kal shifted his position and groaned softly. His mother was beside him instantly with a shallow bowl of hot oil and a sponge. The sponge felt as rough as lava rock on his back, but the warmth of the oil brought relief.

"What time is it, Mother?"

"Dawn of the second day. You have slept many hours, and that is good.

"Did I scream?"

"No."

Was she telling the truth? He seemed to remember screaming, but maybe it was the coney that screamed. His memory fluttered. What coney? Oh, yes, he was running like a coney from the rocks, terrified. But something or someone was running ahead of him. Who or what, he could not remember.

She washed his back again, and he shivered. "Mother, did you know his braids were under me? Kaleb's braids were under me." His voice broke. "I am ashamed to cry, but when I think of Kaleb…" Quintira leaned over and kissed his cheek.

33

"When a man can't show grief, he is less than a man." She rose from her knees. "Everyone must be acquainted with tears in order to know true joy."

"Is that why you weep so often?" He knew the question was too intimate, but surely she must know that he had noticed and cared when she wept.

"Women cry for many reasons. Even when they are happy."

She turned away and dropped the sponge into hot water. Mi'kal closed his lips. She had evaded his question again, as she so often did.

Quintira rolled up the eastern curtains, and the brighter light of dawn came in, stealing the strength of the lamplight. She picked up her hairbrush and sat cross-legged on a rug in the doorway. Her hair, so dark it could be called black, fell to her waist. Above her ears and over her forehead it had turned silvery white.

The wings of white reminded Mi'kal of the hedgerow birds, the black and white magpies. His mother was like them. She seldom rested, and she liked to talk—but not enough about the things he wanted to know. There was much about her that remained a mystery.

The thorn slashes were hurting again, but Mi'kal kept silent as his mother chose her outer garment for the day. It was a soft rose color, with a mantle of light blue and a girdle of interlocking circles of blue and white wool.

Now, Mi'kal thought, she is no more the magpie, but the tender singer of songs; the small bird with the rosy breast that flashed blue wings among the branches of the young oaks.

She lifted her hands to twist her hair into a long coil.

"Mother, let it hang loose."

She smiled. "I can remember my father saying the same thing. He would lift my mother's hair against his face and peek at me and say, 'Is she not beautiful...my Deborah?'"

She changed her brush for his. "Mi'kal, do you think you could sit up? The wounds are still open but none are festered. I spent many hours picking out the pieces of thorn."

Her hand touched his head, and he knew she had washed his hair and mourned the loss of his braids.

Every movement brought a different pain, but Mi'kal bit his lips and leaned back against the sheepskin rug Quintira had draped over a camel saddle. Little by little, the pain diminished.

"I am glad Sa'ad wasn't here," Mi'kal said. "He would have killed me with his whip."

During a raid, Sa'ad had found a whip made from the barbed tail of a sting-ray from the Persian gulf. About two feet long, the whip resembled a snake. Barbs, as long as a finger, extended from the end. Mi'kal had seen Sa'ad flay the skin from a young goat that had chewed the toes out of a pair of his favorite boots.

"You are alive, darling, and that is all that matters now. But do not trust him in the dark. He was fond of Kaleb."

"Have they heard from him?"

"One of his scouts came in and said he had gone on to Damascus to find a wedding gift for Zalah. Mi'kal, do you remember anything about our visit to your Uncle Muktar's camp many years ago? You said you never wanted to go back because every time you played with Zalah, Zauf threw horse dung at you."

Mi'kal started to laugh, but the effort brought pain.

She patted his leg, sympathizing with his discomfort. "I've heard Zalah has grown into a beautiful girl."

"I hope her disposition has improved. As I remember, I didn't dare win any of the games we played."

"Her father is the same. He would rather fight for pasture than negotiate. There were always arguments and jealousy between him and Raaschid. Fortunately there has been nothing more destructive than ill-will between them."

Mi'kal knew she spoke of blood-feuds. Many times in the desert, tribes and clans took revenge on one another for real or imagined insults or injuries. Brother could still spill the blood of brother without remorse or censure during such a raid.

Quintira formed a few red-gold curls across his forehead as she continued. "Ill-tempered or not, they say Zalah is very much in love with

Sa'ad. I am not so sure it's the same with him. He may be more interested in the restoration of the tribe."

"Shouldn't Zauf lead the clan?"

"Yes, but his father and the elders hold his lameness against him." She rose and threw some charcoal on the fire.

Mi'kal remembered what she had told him about the lameness. Shelah, his mother, had been gathering fire brush when her time came. She delivered Zauf and Zalah behind a sleeping mare. As she gave birth to the girl, the mare rolled on the boy. Now it was seldom mentioned.

As Mi'kal watched, Quintira dropped a handful of raisins into water to plump them and set a cup of honey by the fire to warm. While the meals for Raaschid and the others in the long tent were prepared by slaves in the main kitchen, Quintira had always made her own, except on feast days. Many times the Old One would share the meal with them.

"Has Grandfather returned yet?"

"No. I'm worried. I keep telling myself he is well able to take care of himself."

"Then why do you predict dire calamities every time I suggest going with him?"

She laughed. "Maybe I just don't want to admit that you are growing up. Think on that for awhile." She picked up a milk pitcher.

He winced as he tried to ease his back against the sheepskin. "I don't think I will." He spoke to her back as she left the tent. "Everybody believes I think too much anyhow."

He stretched carefully, testing the pain. His hand touched a small, cool object, and he lifted a delicate pair of silver tweezers. He remembered the day he had first seen them. He had been very little. His mother was cleaning a melon on the shaded pavilion. He tottered about in the tent looking for amusement, and a small box in a low, open hamper intrigued him. With effort he pulled the box out and spilled its contents on the floor. There were rings and bracelets, ivory combs and earrings, small boxes with pretty lids. He remembered how the tweezers twinkled in the sunlight.

At the bottom of the box, he found a piece of tightly folded cloth and he pulled it out. He loved the color. Later he knew it was purple. The edges were ragged and sun-faded, the embroidered silver threads dull. But the scarf, or mantle, was softer than anything he had ever held. He put it over his head. He slipped the bracelets over his feet and went to show his mother how splendid he looked.

He never forgot what happened.

Quintira leaped to her feet. The melon rolled from the platter and splashed wet seeds across his legs. She snatched the scarf from his head and shook him until the tent spun upside down.

"Don't you ever, ever get into my things again!"

Mi'kal recalled his frightened and insulted wails. His mother had let him scream while she put the box and the scarf away.

And from that day to this, she had never apologized or explained why she was so angry. Or why she seemed to think more of the purple scarf than she did of him. Jealousy and hurt had faded, but curiosity remained. What was the story behind the purple scarf?

Quintira had often mentioned her childhood in Galilee. In the city of Sepphoris, her father, Ithamar, had been a rabbi. His wife, Deborah, was a midwife and had trained her young daughter in the art of oil and herbal medicines.

Mi'kal knew his grandfather was named in honor of the son of Aaron, the first high priest of Israel. He was sorry he had never known his Galilean grandparents. He liked to think of them—Ithamar, gray-haired and stooped; Deborah, plump, with lovely hair.

Quintira had told him that his grandmother had a famous name too. Deborah had been a judge when the land was ruled by judges, before the time of King Saul. She had explained how she had so much knowledge of the history of her people.

"I had to recite a portion of Scripture every day for my parents. But I didn't mind. I loved the scrolls. They were full of exciting stories and beautiful poetry. I wanted to be a teacher." She threw back her head and laughed. "My father informed me in no uncertain language that no woman could be a rabbi or a leader of men."

"What about Deborah? Didn't the judges direct the people?"

"I think I asked my father the same thing." She squeezed him again before she released him. She was always spontaneous in her love for him.

He often wondered why she could not be the same with his father. Raaschid loved her. There was no doubt about it, and yet Quintira never showed any affection for him. Mi'kal knew she had been kidnapped as a young girl by him and a small band of his raiders, but she never talked about it.

One day, when he was very young and equally unwise, Mi'kal had said, "Our lord loves you. Why do you not love him?"

She held his face between her hands and stared for a moment into his eyes. Her own eyes glimmered with tears.

"When you have heard the song of the lark, little one, you cannot be enticed by the voice of the crow." Her voice was as sad as a night bird's cry.

He had not understood then; he did not understand now. The lark was part of the enigma, as was the purple scarf. But surely he was now old enough to know.

Quintira returned with the goat's milk and began to mix flour and raisins and spices. They would break the cakes and dip them into a sauce of warmed honey with a small amount of goat butter floating in the bowl.

Mi'kal gathered his courage. "Mother, where were you when you heard the song of the lark?"

For a moment her hands were still. Trespassing sunlight made shadows under her eyes.

She began slowly as she dipped a wooden spoon into the batter. "I heard the song of the lark one day in the desert." She dropped the batter onto the hot griddle. The olive oil sizzled. "I was a happy child for many years in Galilee. Only once have I known greater happiness. Only once!"

Her voice faltered. Her hands took up the speech. Mi'kal was always fascinated with his mother's hands. They were not dainty, but they moved with rhythmic cadence.

"When that joy came, every grain of sand became a golden pebble; the desert wind held eastern perfumes. And the nights—" Her voice broke. "The nights were as canopies of purple and blue laced with moonlight."

Mi'kal listened. All the burning hurt in his body was gone. Here was the source of the beautiful things he sometimes wanted to say, and did not, for fear of ridicule.

She paused for a moment, and then, as though dropping a curtain on the conversation, she turned the browning cakes and began to pile them on a brass platter. She put another blanket behind him and stuffed a pillow beneath his knees. Then she placed a small ebony table with brass legs over his lap.

Mi'kal remembered the day she had bargained for the table. The leader of a caravan had refused all her offers of woven goods—cloaks and girdles; rugs and saddle bags. She returned to the tent, tears of frustration in her eyes. Then Raaschid came bearing the table. He had given the caravan leader a better bargain—three pregnant camels.

Mi'kal could not believe his mother did not jump with joy. She accepted the gift without smiling. She bent one knee and said, "Thank you, my lord." There was something of the obsequious servant in the tone.

Raaschid started to remonstrate and then turned and strode from the tent, his face dark with anger.

That day Mi'kal was also angry with her and sorry for his father. Once before he had felt the same confusion.

Raaschid had brought her a pair of red leather slippers with a jeweled design over the instep. In spite of herself, Quintira's eyes flashed with pleasure.

"A gift for you from the city of Petra," Raaschid said, and this time the bite was in his voice.

After he left, Quintira held the slippers to her breast. Then, snatching up her scissors, she cut them into pieces and fed the pieces, one by one, to her fire.

Mi'kal protested. "Mother! Why? They were beautiful."

She did not answer.

Now, she was silent again as she placed the bowl of honey and breakfast cakes before him and poured his milk. A basket made of marsh reeds held dried apricots.

She sat down, cross-legged, before him. He waited for the blessing.

Mi'kal was always amused as he watched her hands from half-closed lids. Even in prayer she could not hold them still.

"The eyes of the LORD are upon those who fear him, on those whose hope is in his unfailing love.... In him our hearts rejoice, for we trust in his holy name. May your unfailing love rest upon us, O LORD, even as we put our hope in you."

After dipping her first cake, she looked at him with thoughtful eyes. "So you wish to know about the lark?"

He nodded. He was afraid to speak for fear he might say the wrong thing.

"Tonight, when the moon is young, we will walk to the boulders. That is, if you feel that you can."

Mi'kal took her hand in his. Their fingers were sticky, but he didn't care. "I would walk to Galilee if necessary."

Her other hand touched his cheek. "Since you are old enough to shave, you are old enough to know."

CHAPTER SIX

In the mingled hours of starlight and moonlight, which the tent-dwellers loved, Mi'kal heard his mother's story. They talked among the boulders, far enough away from the marshes of the wadi to escape the night insects. Frogs croaked softly in the reeds. Above them, the bowl of the sky captured the stars and held them close to the earth. Among the tents strung over the plain, the cooking fires burned down to embers.

Quintira sat on a low rock with a white woolen shawl over her head. Mi'kal, sat opposite her. He wore a loose cloak that touched lightly on his wounds.

His mother began slowly. "I promised to tell you about the lark, but first we must go back many years to when I was a child in Galilee, in the beautiful walled city of Sepphoris. You know something of my life there, but not all. I chose to speak only of the happy days, but now you are no longer a child to be confused or embarrassed."

Mi'kal warmed with pleasure.

"My father, Ithamar, was a devout man of strong convictions. Stubborn and determined, as you often are. He was a man of peace, but he found it irksome to remain passive under Roman oppression. He particularly hated the appointment of the high priesthood of Israel as though it were a political post rather than a spiritual inheritance for the sons of Aaron. Consuls and governors ordered us to give reverence to the emperors, as though they were gods. As Jews we can be ruled only by the Lord God."

"But Mother, you have told me of your kings. Saul and David and—"

"Yes. Kings we have had. Good and bad. But we were supposed to wait for the King of Kings. Our Messiah. We became impatient. We were as Abraham who could not wait for Sarah to conceive according to God's promise. She shared in his lack of faith, for she offered him her hand-maiden, an Egyptian slave. And like one who eats green fruit, Hagar and her son, Ishmael, became a pain in Abraham's belly. Enmity between Isaac and Ishmael will continue until our Messiah comes."

When she spoke again, Mi'kal knew she was quoting from one of her father's scrolls. Her voice was musical and soft.

"For to us a child is born, to us a son is given, and the government will be on his shoulders, And he will be called Wonderful Counselor, Mighty God, Everlasting Father, Prince of Peace."

Mi'kal knew her praise was for her promised Messiah, but he was growing impatient. "Mother, I want to hear about you."

She laughed. "I'm sorry. Sometimes I am like the crow that takes the long way around rather than cross water." She rose. The moonlight seemed to move with her.

"I have told you of our four religious groups. The Pharisees, the Sadducees, the Essenes, and the Zealots. The Zealots are the militant ones. Rebels against Rome. They want Israel for Israel, and one king only—our Lord God Jehovah." She drew her shawl tight about her as she stood in front of him.

"My father sympathized with the Zealots, but he did not belong to any organized band. He helped when he could by collecting money and supplies. One room of our house was used as a storeroom.

"One day, very early, before we had risen, mercenary troops under a Syrian commander marched into our city. They searched every suspected home. We had no chance to rid ourselves of the crates of weapons and blankets in the storeroom.

"They dragged my father into the courtyard. My mother followed in her night garment. I remember it had rained. The cobblestones were wet and shiny. I could smell the roses before I began to choke on the smoke from our burning house." Her voice thickened with tears as she sat down again on the low boulder.

"They shoved my father to the ground by the oleander bush my mother had just planted. She ran to help him. A spear went through her from back to front as if she were a ripened pear. My father grabbed the garden shovel and smashed the murderer's face. Then a sword slashed into him. I was not quite eleven."

She sat for a moment with her hands over her face. Mi'kal rose and knelt beside her. "Mother, did they harm you? I mean, did the soldiers..."

"No. They herded us like sheep. We were sent in exile to a city called Bathyra. It was built during the time of Herod the Great. He was afraid of the raiders who lived in Trachonitis and gave permission for a Babylonian Jew, named Zamaris, to settle there. Zamaris had come into Palestine with many horsemen who were famed for their archery. They brought their families with them. They promised help to Herod, and so he let them build a city in which there would be no tribute or taxes required." She took him by the hand and he rose and sat beside her.

"Things went well. People came. Some were bribed to move to the new city. Some joined us in exile there. I was sold to a Jewish couple, Huldah and Jacob. I learned to love them. After seven years, I would be given my freedom according to the laws of Moses.

"Jacob went about the countryside buying up crafts made by artisans. Huldah sold them in the bazaar. I had learned about herbs and healing ointments from my mother. Our booth was almost as popular as the apothecary."

The moonlight washed over her face. Beyond them the gray mist was beginning to rise about the marsh grass, and Mi'kal thought of the burning home in Sepphoris. He put his hand on her shoulder. She was shivering.

"You are cold. We should go back to the tent."

"No. I am almost to the part you wish to know. After Herod the Great died—I was born about that time—his son, Herod Philip, took over the rule of several provinces, including Trachonitis. He was, and still is, an able and just ruler. He decided it was not fair for his other cities to be taxed and Bathyra to go free, so he put a small tax on us, both Gentiles and Jews. This angered many of the Gentiles and, of course, the Jews were blamed. For some reason, we are always blamed for everything.

"Those who were dissatisfied began to plague us. They hired outside people to come in and terrorize us. One day four shouting horsemen came against our booth. Huldah was knocked down. I don't know if she was hurt or not. Fire was taken from under our pan of roasting squash seeds and used to ignite the curtains. The leader, who seemed to be drunk, picked me up and hauled me into his saddle. I was terrified. I knew what would happen to me. I was sixteen and men called me beautiful."

As she spoke, something in her voice told him she was telling him things she had never told anyone before, things she had kept locked up in a secret recess of her heart.

"The horse reared. My captor held me firmly while he reached for a purple scarf hanging on our booth."

Mi'kal stared at her. The shaft of moonlight was hitting his face, and she could see his amazement.

"Is that the purple scarf you keep in your box?" he asked.

"Half of it."

She appeared puzzled at his reaction. Evidently she did not remember the day he had never completely forgotten. He wanted to laugh. He had been jealous of a purple scarf for fifteen years for no reason. No wonder she cherished it. It was the only thing she had from her days in Bathyra.

"I'm sorry I interrupted, Mother. Go on."

"The men who raided us were Nabateans. The assault had nothing to do with taxes. For many years there has been smoldering hatred between the Nabateans and anything connected with the Herods.

"But I had no idea who they were when that man lifted me to his horse. I fought. I bit his arm. He laughed. When he set his horse into a gallop I had to hang onto its mane. My hair was loose and blew in his face. He tied the scarf over my head and yelled into my ear, 'Beauty for the beautiful.' I turned to look at him, hoping he could see my anger and disgust. I found myself staring into two eyes such as I had never seen before—green, with flecks of burning topaz and brilliant black. I knew then he was not drunk, only heady with the exhilaration of the raid."

Quintira paused. "Mi'kal, I hated his mocking laughter, but there was something about him that made my pulses leap. He rode as a god would ride, and I told him so. He laughed and said I would have to settle for a prince. I thought he was jesting, but he wasn't. He was a son of Aretas, king of Petra. His mother, Mumtaza, was a favored concubine. He told me his father loved her very much and she would have been queen were it not for politics. The next day I was riding my own mare."

Mi'kal stood. "Mother, are you telling me that you fell in love with him?" She nodded and rose with him. "I could have played a woman's game with him, but I am glad I did not. One night, in moonlight such as we have tonight, we spoke our wedding vows. There was no one to witness our marriage, for he had sent his men ahead, but I knew God approved." She was using her hands now to help with the story. The shawl fell loose about her, making her seem more than ever like an alabaster statue.

"We used the purple scarf as a canopy. My heart threatened to burst with happiness as I heard him claim me as his wife before the very stars of heaven. Early the next morning we heard a lark singing as though it had been sent of God as a benediction on the consummation of our love. Before the end of the month, I knew I was with child."

She stopped suddenly and Mi'kal knew she was crying.

"Mother, am I the child?"

She lifted her head and her eyes, though wet, were filled with love. "Yes, Mi'kal, you are."

He drew her into his arms. A moment passed before he could speak. "That explains why I am so different from Sa'ad."

"You are the image of your father, except his hair was darker. His name was Myndus." Her voice seemed to caress the syllables.

"Myndus," Mi'kal repeated softly.

"On the very morning that I told him I was pregnant, Raaschid came with three of his warriors. They found us bathing in a pool at the base of a lava cliff. We were naked and without weapons. There was nowhere to run. I knew, as if it were shouted from heaven, that I would live and Myndus would die.

"The lance whistled over my head. Your father fell. I tried to run, but

Raaschid caught me by my hair. He raped me without even spreading his blanket beneath us.

"Later, I asked if I might look upon my husband. I tore the purple scarf in half and bound one piece about his arm. I asked God to let the scarf go with his soul so that he might know I would always love him."

She sat down again on the stone. "Mi'kal, Raaschid is not a man who rapes. Perhaps there was contrition in his soul when he made me his wife."

"Does he know that I am not his son?"

"Yes. From the day you were born."

"Is that why he seems to hate me and is jealous of me?"

"I do not think he hates you. He is jealous of you, yes, for he would like to believe that you are from his loins. I am sure he wanted you to be. I remember the morning you were born. You came hard. Several of the midwives came to help. Gutne stayed away, hoping you would be born dead. The prince paced back and forth before my door. You came, squalling like a hungry calf. Your wet hair looked black at first, but I could see the red in it. Your eyes were blue but, little by little, the green came, and finally the yellow and black lights."

"Does anybody else know about me? Gutne or Sa'ad?"

"I am sure she suspects, but she does not dare to mock you, for Raaschid accepted you as his own. He laid his war mare's bridle across your bed and placed his curved sword at your feet. He carried me out for a celebration as though I had indeed borne a prince for the clan. I know how much he loves me, Mi'kal. But I left all my love with the purple scarf on your father's arm.

"Even as our lord acknowledged you before the clan and boasted of other sons to come, I knew I would bear no more children. I knew God had closed my womb."

CHAPTER SEVEN

Sunlight flooded the doorway as Mi'kal woke to the sound of flapping curtains. He sat up with feelings of relief and loss. He was not Raaschid's son. He was free to find his own destiny beyond the desert, though there was much about the black tents that he loved.

There was no thought of claiming a relationship with Aretas of Petra. He had no more desire to be a prince in Petra than he had to be the leader of the Jackals. Besides, what proof did he have except his mother's story and a piece of purple scarf?

Beyond the tent door the pebbles were changing color under the morning sun, and Mi'kal knew that in some way he was changing too. He no longer felt the guilt of Kaleb's death. Perhaps his punishment had won him relief.

The scabs pulled on the healing wounds as he rose and stretched. He decided against a top for his wrap-around skirt. The sun would be good for his back.

Quintira came in with the pitcher of goat's milk. Her face was bright under the red mantle that matched the sash tied about her white garment.

"I think Grandfather is returning to his nest. Some of the hunters reported a small dust cloud such as might be raised by a donkey."

"What do you think he's been doing?"

"Gambling. What else? You know he is never happy unless he comes home with an empty purse and a head full of gossip."

As Mi'kal poured himself a mug of milk, he told Quintira how Ne'ma had brought him a drink while he was tethered and burning up with thirst.

"She is a good girl, Mi'kal. She might be plain of face and have a contrary eye, but her bosom is full of love."

"There must be quite a lot of it," Mi'kal said, controlling his smile.

"So you have noticed?" She grinned, and as usual, the dimples went deep. "I have told you of Leah who was equally plain and of her love for Jacob?"

"A dozen times. I think it is one of your favorite love stories."

"My father always said it was better to have crooked eyes than a crooked heart like her sister, Rachel. Jacob must have thought so too, for when he died he asked to be buried next to his plain wife."

Mi'kal thought of his mother's beauty and of Ne'ma's plainness and her impossible dream.

"Mother, do you know that Ne'ma believes that someday our prince will—"

Mi'kal was interrupted by yelling children and barking dogs.

"It must be Grandfather!" he exclaimed. "Come on." He grabbed her hand and they rushed out.

A tired and dusty duo came to a halt outside the central tent. Mi'kal helped the Old One dismount and relieved him of the shoulder pack he carried his most precious purchases in.

Quintira embraced him and scolded him with affection. "Where have you been? We have worried about you." She unwound his dusty turban and beat it against her knees.

The Old One was bald, but a rim of dirty gray hair hung over his ears and neck. Blue, watery eyes squinted at Mi'kal. "What happened? Why are you shorn?"

"I brought terrible trouble to our camp."

"And to yourself, I see." The Old One touched the wounded back.

Quintira spoke quickly. "We will tell you everything after you rest and eat."

"First, I must talk to our lord. Then I would like some water. After that we will see what I have for you and the children."

Quintira and Mi'kal exchanged puzzled glances as Grandfather walked toward Raaschid's pavilion. What business could he have with the prince?

Duag, at the doorway, detained the Old One until Raaschid gave orders to let him enter.

The children crowded about the donkey, investigating the strange lumps of the saddle bags. Now and then the donkey bared her teeth at them.

Mi'kal recalled the day the Old One had brought the half-starved animal into camp. The two strays had formed an unlikely friendship. Grandfather insisted on calling her Astarte, in honor of the Phoenician goddess of love and fertility. But the donkey was neither lovable nor fertile.

The Old One didn't stay long with the chieftain. Raaschid followed him to the door and watched as Quintira brought out a pitcher of water. She was oblivious to Raaschid, but she could not hide her curiosity from her old friend. He grinned at her as he lifted the pitcher to his lips.

"If you must know, I had to inform our lord that he is getting company."

"Company? From outside?" Quintira's eyes glowed. Any word of the world beyond the tents was as food and drink to her.

He nodded. "There is a Roman toll-house with a small garrison a little over a day's camel ride from here. On a road that goes eastward to Damascus. The soldiers buy my saddle skins. The men need fresh meat. There was a retired centurion by the name of Quintillius visiting at the garrison. The captain asked him to come and bargain with Raaschid for livestock and trapped game."

"And he's coming?" Mi'kal's excitement matched his mother's.

"Will he know anything about Galilee?" Quintira asked.

"He should. He lives in a villa near Capernaum on the Sea of Galilee."

"My father used to take me to Capernaum. We bought salted fish for our friends in Sepphoris."

"Will there be others with him?" Mi'kal asked.

"Aurans. A young lieutenant." The Old One grinned at Mi'kal. "His hair is light red but no gold in it like yours. And he has brown dots all over his nose and cheeks."

"When will they be here?"

"Probably this week. They will have a mule cart and a camel boy in case Raaschid parts with some of his calves."

"Now," Quintira said as she took the pitcher away from him, "tell us why you were so late."

"There was much to hear and see in Damascus. The city is preparing for a meeting of several important men. Herod Philip has come over from Caesarea Philippi. Governor Lysanias is down from Abila, and King Aretas is up from Petra."

Mi'kal threw his mother a quick glance.

"They are saying that Damascus will soon be given over to the Nabateans again. Many think Rome is working on behalf of Herod Antipas of Galilee to soothe Aretas. He suffered a family insult several years ago. His daughter was married to Antipas, but while Herod was visiting in Rome, he fell in love with his brother's wife. He brought her home and sent the Nabatean princess back to her father with divorcement papers."

"Oh," Quintira exclaimed in quick sympathy. "Even if her heart wasn't broken, she would feel socially disgraced."

The Old One nodded. "His rejection of her was politically stupid. Antipas and Aretas have been fighting over boundary lines and broken alliances for years. The Roman surrender of Damascus would be a small price to pay for peace."

"Grandfather, maybe you should rest and tell us everything later," Mi'kal said.

Quintira agreed. "Mi'kal will go with you to take care of Astarte. Tonight you will share our meal and tell us more about your trip."

"Yes, but first I must take care of my little ones."

The children were becoming impatient. They milled about, cajoling and begging. The Old One threw up his hands in surrender and took one of Quintira's small rugs to lay on the sand. He lifted a cloth bag from the donkey and poured out a pyramid of brightly colored marbles. The children shrieked with delight. They grabbed up handfuls of the Old One's gift and raced away to show their shining wonders.

He gave Astarte a slap on the rump and ordered her to go home. She plodded away toward the small tent on the far edge of camp, near the make-shift horse corral. Then he rummaged through the pack Mi'kal had taken from him. He lifted out an alabaster vial, rose red, with streaks of light green. The stopper was shaped like a rose bud.

Quintira took it with delight. "Perfume! Oh, my dear friend, may God bless you." She threw her arms about him.

Mi'kal was aware of Raaschid standing on his porch, his hands thrust into the sleeves of his white tunic. A sign of agitation.

Quintira shook the bottle gently and pulled the stopper. "Damascus roses!" she exclaimed. She touched the stopper to her throat and temples and then ran it over the Old One's dusty cheeks. He grinned with pleasure.

In an impulsive act of joyous pleasure, she lifted the vial over her head and began a slow turning. Her red sash swirled as her movements quickened.

Mi'kal could sense Raaschid's rising displeasure. Quintira was unaware of the gathering storm. She pulled off her mantle and swung it in slow, undulating waves as her feet beat the hard gravel. Ne'ma came running with her tambourine. Women from the nearest tents began to clap. Quintira's skirts flared.

Raaschid's shout cut through the gaiety. "Enough! Get you to your tents. All of you. I will not have my wife dancing like a Babylonian harlot."

Quintira stopped in red-faced embarrassment. She stepped forward and her foot tangled in the mantle that was dragging on the ground. She fell to one knee.

Raaschid grabbed the perfume from her hand and poured it over her head. Tantalizing fragrance turned sickening sweet. Quintira scrambled up with anger flashing from her eyes. Her hands rubbed through her wet hair and she wiped her fingers on her bodice. His eyes followed the movement and something ignited in his face.

"Cleanse yourself and come to me."

Mi'kal spoke under his breath, but the Old One heard him. "Sometimes when he is humiliating her I want to kill him."

"You do not have what it takes to kill anyone."

"They think I killed Kaleb," Mi'kal said bitterly.

While they walked to the small tent, Mi'kal told him of the rain pool and the serpent and the thorn punishment.

"I was certain I would die."

"Some men have. But I believe the stars have promised you a long and happy life."

"Really?" He looked to see if the Old One was smiling. He was, but his face was gray with weariness. Mi'kal wanted to tell him about Quintira and Myndus too, but he knew his friend was too tired to listen.

At the tent, Mi'kal unrolled a sleeping mat and laid out a pillow. The Old One stretched out with a heavy grunt and a drawn out sigh, and in a few minutes he was snoring.

Mi'kal worked while his friend slept. He fed and watered and brushed Astarte. He gathered firewood. He washed the dirty sleeping rug and the saddle skin the Old One had used on his trip. Then he softened the ibex leather with his hands and feet.

The sun was dropping when the Old One woke. Mi'kal brought out Grandfather's black leather stool and a rush-filled cushion for himself. Mi'kal told him about Myndus and the marriage under the purple canopy.

"It is hard to realize that I am not Raaschid's son. I have thought of him as my father for seventeen years. I will probably always think of him so."

"I do not find it difficult. I never understood how you and Sa'ad came from the same seed pod."

Mi'kal laid his hand on the stool made of black rhinoceros leather with oryx horns for legs. He had always thought it must be the most beautiful stool in the world. Even Raaschid did not have such a stool. He remembered the first time he had seen it, years before when he was very small. He remembered looking up into the wind-wrinkled face and the scanty beard that reminded him of a goat and asking, "Whence did you come from, Grandfather?"

The Old One took his time in answering. His arms folded across his chest and his eyes looked into the distance. "I am like the birds that fly overhead as the seasons turn. Where do they belong, little one? Tell me, is it north or south, east or west?"

"I don't know, Grandfather. Perhaps it is wherever they were born. My mother says you came in out of a desert sandstorm a long time ago. Are you a spirit from the dunes?"

"I am no jinn. I had a mother and a father, just like you. I had a sister and a brother and a half-brother. My parents are dead. Perhaps all of them are gone now." The Old One's voice quivered. "How sad, little one, when children have enemies who wish them dead."

"Why would anyone want to kill you?"

"Even a child can stand in the way of an ambitious man. I owe my life to a faithful friend. He had been my father's friend until the winds changed. He had to flee for his life. He knew I was in danger, too, so he took me. I thought he was kidnapping me out of my bed, but he was saving my life. We lived as the birds live. Here, there, everywhere."

His scant beard rested for a moment on his chest. Then he looked at Mi'kal with a hint of humor in his eyes.

"Would you believe me if I told you I sat on a throne with my mother when I was your age? That I rode the great ships with my father?"

Mi'kal wanted to laugh, but as he watched, Grandfather changed. His shoulders stiffened. His chin lifted. Authority showed in his face.

"Grandfather, if you are a prince, why do you not dress like one? Why do you have no gold pieces or fine raiment?"

"Do you think gold and fine clothing make a king?"

"You should have a little gold. And at least one silk aba, and maybe two slaves."

"Wait," the Old One said as he went into his tent, which was scarcely high enough for him to stand. He came back with a small mother-of-pearl box. When he opened it, a golden object glistened. Mi'kal picked it up. It was round, like a coin, but it had two sections fastened together with a hinge. There was a place to attach a chain or strap. Something had been written on both sides, but Mi'kal could not read it.

"What is it?"

"The Romans call it a *bulla*. Fathers or friends usually give them to the babies when they are born or christened. Boys wear them until they are thirteen. Girls use them as jewelry. Inside there is a space for a good luck amulet."

"Like Kaleb's blue bead?"

"Yes. The inscriptions on front and back are Latin. Someday I will teach you to speak and to read and write Latin and Greek."

"Good. I wish to learn all things that you know. You are very wise, Grandfather."

The old man smiled.

Mi'kal's hand closed about the *bulla*. Gold felt good. No wonder Raaschid desired gold pieces when he sold mares or camels. No wonder his mother hoarded her few golden coins in a secret place.

"Grandfather, are you a Roman?"

His friend pointed to the small clouds moving slowly across the sky. They were as sheep grazing. "Tell me, little one, are those clouds Arabian or Syrian?"

Mi'kal thought for a moment. "They never stay in one place long enough to belong to anyone."

"Then you will understand why I say I am not a Roman. I have had to move from country to country to stay alive."

"Wouldn't you like to be a king?"

"No. A king has two cups he must drink from eventually—war and politics. Sometimes he has a choice, but there is death in either cup."

"But don't you have important friends somewhere?"

"I have you and your mother."

"But you are poor."

"Oh, no. I have many riches. Here and here and here." The calloused fingers moved from lips to chest and then to brow. "I have memories. I go into the city to play the games, and I come back without money but with many memories. I talk. I laugh. I argue. I bring back something more precious than gold. Knowledge."

Mi'kal had not understood everything that day so long ago. And now as he sat on the cushion in front of his friend, he still did not understand all things about him. But Mi'kal was older now, and he knew that sometimes it is necessary to live with mysteries.

"Mother will be anxious to hear everything you know about Galilee and everything else you have learned."

"I am as anxious to tell it as she is to hear. For I have something for her more precious than essence of roses."

The Old One rose from the stool as Mi'kal rose. There was a twinkle in the faded blue eyes. "Peace go with thee, O Prince of Petra."

Mi'kal shook his head. "I have no desire to be a prince. I only wish to be an ordinary man."

The gray head shook. "That, my golden-haired one, you will never be."

As Mi'kal drew near his mother's tent, he caught the faint scent of roses. Far to the west, out of sight, lay the great rift of the Jordan River and the green hills of Galilee. How and when would he be able to take his mother back to her beloved country? Someday it would happen. For as surely as the birds had enticed him to the pool, voices of lands beyond the desert were calling to him.

CHAPTER EIGHT

Twilight lay like a lavender shawl over the shoulders of the hillocks, shading to deeper purple in the cleavage of the gullies. Oil lamps sputtered as they swung from the center roof pole of Quintira's quarters, even though the western flaps were still rolled up. Charcoal glowed in the fire-bowl, but the meal was finished.

Quintira passed a tray of the Damascus figs Grandfather had contributed to the supper of roast partridge stuffed with crushed wheat soaked in milk and garlic, and fried onions made golden with saffron.

Kwa had brought the red-legged bird and some eggs earlier in the day. Mi'kal had cleaned the fowl while the Old One slept, and had remembered he had never told his mother how Kwa had helped him while he was tied up.

"He is a good man, Mi'kal. He has served Raaschid fairly, but I have often thought he might run away."

"Raaschid would send Duag after him, and Duag would gladly kill him. They work together, but they hate one another."

"Kwa has never forgiven Duag for what he did to him, even though it was Raaschid's order."

Once, Mi'kal had asked Quintira why Kwa did not grow fat and soft as eunuchs often did. She told him the African used several plants whose juices helped him avoid enlarged breasts and other feminine traits.

After hanging the cooking pots, Quintira settled on a thick red cushion and faced the two sitting on the sheepskin rug. "Now, Grandfather, it is time for you to tell us all that you heard and saw on your trip."

The Old One spit a fig stem into his hand and tossed it out into the deepening dusk. "There was much going on I spent most of my time in

Damascus, but I did not neglect the villages scattered like small flocks of sheep around a tree or well. Sometimes the small villages are built on top of ancient ruins, and as I pass them I seem to hear the tread of boots—the armies of Alexander the Great and Marc Antony, darling of Rome. Sometimes, while I rest beneath the tree or by the well, I close my eyes and hear a woman's voice bargaining, pleading, demanding."

His voice grew stronger with passion, deeper with hidden knowledge.

"A woman?" Quintira asked. Mi'kal also was curious.

"She wanted more and more of the riches of this land. There was no satisfying her, but he tried."

"Who, Grandfather?"

"Antony. Marc Antony. She was as a leech, bleeding the riches of this land through his veins...Cleopatra of Egypt."

Emotion fleshed out the old man's words, emotion that throbbed like the pulse of the heart.

Mi'kal found himself studying his friend as though he would need to remember him. His short garment was hempen, with holes for head and arms. As always, he wore an ornate worked belt of rare leathers about his middle. He delighted in making and wearing elaborate belts. He would part with many things at the market or wager them at the gaming table, but never his belt or his donkey.

"Grandfather, when you go into the cities how do you know what men to talk to?"

"I walk slowly. I listen to the voices. One can always tell a Galilean. I often butt into a group as if I were a calf seeking the udder. I find it easy to agree or disagree on any subject. I am fortunate to know both Greek and Latin as well as the languages of the desert.

"Arguing in the forums or the streets is like children quarreling. Sometimes of no importance at all except to speed the passing of the hours. But in the arguments I find bits and pieces that I can fit together as I do a pattern for the cutting of my leather. This time I was interested to learn that young Salome has come to Damascus with her husband, Herod Philip. They say Philip is happy with his marriage to her, in spite of the age difference. I have heard there has been a great change in her since she left Jerusalem. But the girl is still ill-spoken of by the Jews who cannot forget she and her mother were responsible for the death of their prophet, John the Baptist."

Mi'kal could not remember hearing anything about a girl called Salome. "What did she do that was so terrible?"

The Old One explained quickly about a birthday party for Herod Antipas.

Mi'kal shook his head. "How could a girl's dancing cause a man to do such evil?"

Quintira waited for the Old One to answer.

"Antipas is not a strong man. He is as a donkey yoked with an oxen. His wife, Herodias, has all the cruelty and avarice of her grandfather, Herod the Great. Marc Antony can be blamed for elevating Herod to the position of king of several Palestinian territories."

"Tetrarch Philip has been honorable, hasn't he?" Quintira asked.

"Yes, even though he is brother to Antipas, he is a moral man with fair judgments. That brings us back to the news. Everyone is sure that Damascus will be put under Aretas because Governor Lysanias wants to retire and visit Rome, and Philip is reported to be ailing."

Quintira leaned forward and touched Mi'kal's knee. "Just think, your grandfather is going to be within two days' journey of you. While he is in Damascus, it would be good for you to meet him."

Mi'kal protested. "I have no intention—"

"But he should know what a wonderful grandson he has."

"It is more important that you meet him, Mother."

"He would never believe me unless he saw you."

The Old One was amused as his eyes glanced from one to the other. Cooler currents of air moved about him and the lamps flickered. He rose and dropped the curtain.

"May I continue?" he asked with dry humor.

The two of them murmured apologies.

"I will tell you a little of the bits and pieces before I begin on the Galilean gossip you will be most interested in."

Quintira started to plead, but he shook his head.

"No. You have to wait, for what I tell you at the end, you will still be thinking about tomorrow."

He began with descriptions of the new theaters and shops, new songs, and new heroes of coliseum and stage. He told of improved methods of weaving and dyeing, of foreign fruits and delicacies to be found in the bazaars. He recounted tales of the foolishness of the rich and powerful and of the sufferings of the poor.

Quintira and Mi'kal feasted on the Old One's words as they had feasted on the partridge. His voice grew a little husky, and she poured him a cup of wine.

"And now for the news of Galilee."

Quintira leaned forward, and Mi'kal knew her gaze would never leave Grandfather's face as long as he spoke of Galilee.

"There is great unrest in your land, Quintira. In fact, all through Palestine and into Perea."

"Are the Zealots rising again?"

"Here and there. But most of the unrest is based on the contentions between the authorities in the temple and the public acceptance of a Nazarene prophet. He is a carpenter who claims to be a spokesman for your God."

"A Nazarene carpenter? My father knew a carpenter from Nazareth, but I have forgotten his name. It might have been Joseph."

"This man is called Jesus. They say he has more followers than John the Baptist."

"And he claims to be a prophet sent of God?"

"More than that," the Old One said, his eyes beginning to twinkle. "Listen now. Don't get excited. This man from Nazareth—this carpenter—claims to be the Messiah of Israel!" He sat back as if waiting for her reaction. It came swiftly.

Quintira jumped to her feet. "The Messiah!" There was a moment of silence. Then she burst out, "But it couldn't be. Not a carpenter from Nazareth. He blasphemes!"

"Mother!"

"Mi'kal, when our Messiah comes to reign, the whole world will know it. The priests will not argue about him. He will be ringed with fiery chariots and angels with blazing swords. He will sit on the throne of David and rule from the holy temple."

Mi'kal laid a hand to his head. "And she thinks my dream of finding the Green Bird is foolish. Chariots and angels indeed."

The Old One smiled.

"Well, there are ways we can prove he is not the Messiah," Quintira declared. "Has he done the deeds of our Messiah?"

"Such as?" the Old One asked, still amused at her excitement.

"Isaiah has said—"

"Sing it, Mother, as you sometimes do."

She smiled and began to sing. Her voice was melodious, her phrasing dramatic. "Say to those with fearful hearts, 'Be strong, do not fear; your God will come....' Then will the eyes of the blind be opened and the ears of the deaf unstopped. Then will the lame leap like a deer, and the mute tongue shout for joy."

The old man touched her hand as she finished and said softly, "All those things has the Nazarene done, according to the word in Damascus."

Quintira stared.

"All of them?" Mi'kal asked the question for her.

"All." The Old One rose. "I am tired. May the stars appoint you a peaceful night." At the curtained door he paused. "The next time I am in Damascus I will get you more perfume."

Quintira was unusually quiet as they prepared for the night. Mi'kal spread his sleeping blanket and watched as his mother brushed her hair in front of the dying fire. All but one of the lamps had been quenched. The white wings of her hair were like small ostrich plumes, and Mi'kal thought of Haserah.

The Old One had brought him the ostrich chick for his twelfth birthday. Mi'kal had been delighted. While ostriches were familiar to the camp, they were used for food, seldom for grown pets. Mother suggested the Jewish name of Haserah. The ostrich grew rapidly on a diet of seeds and red caterpillars.

When it developed plumage, Mi'kal traded the black and white feathers for favors from his friends or from women in the camp. He received sweetmeats, firewood, and camel dung. Quintira was amused with his bartering, but she warned him.

"Don't be surprised if someone does your friend evil. Haserah gets more obnoxious every day with his prancing and preening."

One day her prophecy came true. Mi'kal was fourteen. Sa'ad came into camp on El Gamar, his new silver stallion, and the children ran to meet him, especially the girls. Sa'ad rode bare-chested, proud of the black hair that ran from neck to navel. About his neck he wore a chain with a carved ball of Phoenician brass. Inside the ball, a large clear crystal blazed with white light. The necklace had been given to him by Zalah when the marriage contract was made in his Uncle Muktar's tent.

Sa'ad reared his horse to make the girls scream. Then he took both hands from the bridle and used his heels and thighs to control the stallion. With one hand he began a game of catch with the girls, throwing the necklace to one after another. His other hand rested lightly on the scabbard that held his short, curved sword.

Mi'kal had come to watch. Haserah ran awkwardly beside him, his long neck stretched.

One of the girls missed the necklace. The ball passed over Mi'kal, the crystal gleaming like a falling star. Haserah's neck swiveled, the wide mouth opened, and the brass ball began to descend.

The children screamed as the bulge went lower and lower. The chain dangled from his beak, and Haserah sensed he had done something foolish. He took off at a lumbering gallop.

Sa'ad laid his heels to his horse. The ostrich could not win in a short run. Sa'ad leaned to the right and the sword slashed. Haserah's head flew off and bounced over and over on the gravel. The body wobbled and plopped into the sand.

Sa'ad dismounted and dragged the necklace out of the severed neck. He wiped the blood on a hummock of grass.

Mi'kal was furious. He jumped on Sa'ad's back, pounding with both fists. Sa'ad shook him off and knocked him to the ground. Both mothers came running. Quintira held her screaming son while his fists beat the air.

"I hate you," Mi'kal screamed. "I hate you! Someday I'm going to kill you."

Years of repressed dislike poured out with the words. Many who heard shook their heads. Quarrels between clan brothers often meant trouble for the camp.

As Quintira laid her brush aside and quenched the lamp, Mi'kal turned on his sheepskin mat. He tried to rid himself of the unpleasant memory. He had no desire to do harm to his brother, but he was sure Sa'ad would seek vengeance on him for Kaleb's death. Kaleb was the only person Sa'ad loved, except himself.

Quintira was right. He must be careful to stay alert in the dark.

His mother lifted the edge of her curtain and called to him. "Do you think there could be any truth in the Nazarene's claim to be the Messiah?"

"The son of a carpenter? I would as soon believe my Green Bird is roosting with the chickens."

"Be serious! Do you suppose the Romans will know anything more about Jesus?"

"Maybe. Go to sleep now, Mother." He pulled his blanket over his head, yawned, and closed his eyes. He heard a fervent murmur ending in a sigh.

"I hope so."

CHAPTER NINE

Sa'ad rode into camp at midmorning astride El Gamar. The brass necklace hung as usual on his chest. Black tassels danced from the bridle of his silver stallion.

He swung from his horse, loosened his striped cloak, and bowed low before Raaschid. "Father, I bring good news. The flocks in the foothills will double with lambs. And all the summer grazing is secured with payments of gold and pledges of salt."

Slaves scurried to take care of the sweating stallion and to deposit the saddlebags in Sa'ad's quarters. Mi'kal and Quintira moved forward to greet him. He acknowledged them briefly, and they withdrew to their own porch.

Sa'ad embraced Gutne. "Mother, I have brought many beautiful things for you."

Her dark face, with its sharp nose, lightened with pleasure.

Mi'kal waited for the inevitable. Kaleb always came running to meet his adored brother and ride while the stallion was cooling.

"Where's Kaleb?"

Gutne threw Mi'kal a venomous look as she started to answer, but they were distracted by loud shouting. A richly ornamented camel litter was entering the camp. Two of Sa'ad's companions, on weary mares, accompanied the swaying carriage. Long, gold-colored horns curved up from the four corners of the conveyance. Curtains of red and yellow cloth protected the passenger from sand and sun. Red tassels swung beneath the belly of the camel.

Sa'ad forgot Kaleb and turned an excited face toward his mother.

"This that comes is my wedding gift for my black-eyed bride." He lifted Gutne off her feet and swung her around. "For this gift, my Zalah will ravish me with love."

Gutne regained her balance as she stared at him. Raaschid narrowed his eyes and watched with his arms folded. The mares and the camel stopped before the tent, and the men dismounted. They brought the caparisoned camel to her knees. Sa'ad laid his hand on one of the curtains. "Behold," he exclaimed, "a virgin slave for a virgin bride."

Women pushed to see. Men exchanged glances. Sa'ad pulled the curtain aside and draped it over one of the horns. He extended his hand and slender fingers came out to meet his. Nails glowed like pink petals. One slim leg was revealed as the girl stepped to the ground. Green sandals were as bright foliage about the flower tips of her toenails.

She was slender and tall. Her gown, falling in folds from her shoulders, was the color of unripe grapes. Hair, light as silver, was caught by a sparkling circlet into a folded loop on the crown of her head. Mi'kal opened his mouth and drew in a whistling breath. She was the essence of moonlight.

Sa'ad spoke to his father. "This is Leyla. She will serve Zalah night and day."

Mi'kal was not surprised at the wedding gift. He remembered the day Sa'ad had asked some of the marriageable girls what they would desire as a gift from their husbands.

They shouted many things: "Silver bracelets." "Copper pots for my kitchen." "A silk coverlet for our bed."

But one girl had screamed louder than the others, jumping up and down and pulling at Sa'ad's arm. "A slave! A slave for my very own. But she must be ugly so my husband will not leave my couch."

Mi'kal remembered that Sa'ad had laughed and slapped the girl on the rump and sent her away giggling. But he had followed her advice and bought a slave for his future wife.

Mi'kal noticed that the girl was giving a quiet but determined pull to free her fingers from Sa'ad's clasp. Gutne stood silent, jealousy riding high on her dark cheeks. Once before, beauty had come into camp and she had lost her husband. Now she was about to lose her son. Zalah would have been competition enough. But now this!

Quintira, also, felt the sharp prick of motherly jealousy. Only once before had she seen such admiration on her son's face—the day she had traded for his red stallion.

Gutne advanced toward the girl, her sharp face stern. The girl drew back, but her chin remained high.

"Stand up straight! I want to examine you."

"I am not slouching. I never slouch. I am a dancer."

Blue eyes rimmed with silver lashes challenged black eyes.

Gutne turned to her son. "Are you sure the merchandise is flawless?"

"I'm sure. I was guaranteed," he said sharply.

"Was she on the open market?"

"No. I would not have gold enough to bid for her against the rich. As she told you, she is a dancer. Rekha, the owner of the entertainment group, allowed me to buy her after I convinced her the girl would have a respectable place in my wife's tent. I paid plenty, but you can see she is worth it. Zalah will be pleased."

Gutne stared at him. "You fool." Sa'ad flinched under his mother's scorn. Raaschid remained silent, but his eyes had missed nothing—neither the amazing beauty of the slave nor his son's fascination with her. His hands slid into his sleeves.

Gutne was giving orders to the girl. "Until such time as my son is married, you will have your own tent. If you are caught fornicating, you will be stripped and staked out to perish. You will dress as my slaves dress, and you will cover your head."

Leyla was fighting to control her anger. Her body shook as she stepped around the carriage and spoke to someone inside.

"Come, Grandmother. We are to have our own tent."

An old woman in a dark burnoose descended slowly. Weak eyes surveyed her new world.

Gutne turned on Sa'ad. "What is this? Are we to furnish food and drink for bones that should be buried?"

Raaschid spoke. His words were for all who listened. "These women are our guests. Keep your tongues quiet and do what needs to be done to make them welcome."

He turned and went into his chambers.

"This is my grandmother," Leyla announced with a hard ring to her voice. "Her name is Ammoni. She is part of the agreement. We are not to be separated. If anyone tries to harm her, I will kill them."

A surprised murmur ran though those who heard. Her unexpected threat was as unusual as thunder in the summer sky.

Slaves began to work putting up a tent. Children helped by bringing furnishings from their mothers' tents. Some of them deprived themselves in order to give, for their chieftain had made it plain that Leyla and Ammoni were to be treated with respect. While the slaves worked, Ne'ma used her tambourine to make them forget the oppressive heat.

As the hours passed and the work was done, Leyla and Ne'ma found it easy to talk to one another while the grandmother dozed. Leyla was curious, excited, and somewhat fearful as she asked questions about the people she had seen. She was particularly curious about the woman with the bright mantle and the broad-shouldered boy with the short hair and the marks on his back and legs.

Ne'ma answered the questions and more. She told about the thorn punishment, and Leyla was horrified.

"Many times the judgments are cruel and quick," Ne'ma explained. "That is the way of the Bedouin. But we can be generous and kind, too. My lord is not unkind. He took my mother and me in when she was cast out by his brother. My mother was a concubine." She dropped her voice a little. "Some day I will be my lord's concubine."

"But, Ne'ma—" Leyla's instinctive protest was cut off as she stared across the camp. A cloud of dust was rising over sandy hillocks. "What is it?"

"Our horsemen are returning with the horses. The mares and the stallions have been resting and feeding in a valley far away from here."

The sound of galloping hooves grew louder. Leyla and Ne'ma watched as the horses were herded past. Ne'ma said, "See the big red. That is Mi'kal's. Someday you must ask him to take you for a ride. You can trust him, but never, never leave the camp with Sa'ad."

Mi'kal, too, saw the horses come in, and he ran to meet the powerful chestnut stallion. He threw his arms about the high arched neck and kissed the narrow nose.

Three years before, Quintira had bargained for the horse from traders. He had scolded when his mother offered to part with so many of her precious woven things. She had laughed. "Mi'kal, you should see your face. You are coveting him."

He knew in his heart she was right. Every line of the stallion was perfection. Surely he must be the reincarnation of the magnificent red horse Ishmael was believed to have found in the desert of Arabia.

That day he had said, "Mother, I will accept him as a gift if you will take the first ride with me."

Quintira agreed and gathered up her skirts. He lifted her to the stallion's back. The horse's small ears flicked. Large sensitive eyes rolled backwards. Soft nostrils flared.

Mi'kal laid his hand on the high rump and vaulted into place. There was no bridle, only a nose halter. He could feel the quivering of the muscles as the animal waited for a command. Mi'kal put one arm about his mother and touched his heels to the stallion's flanks. The horse began to move, lifting its hooves high and sniffing the wind.

"What shall we call him, Mother?"

"You must decide."

"We will ride first."

He gave a second command with his thighs. The horse broke into a gait that carried them forward with the awkward sway of an ostrich. Mi'kal tightened his arm on Quintira and dug in his heels. The stallion stretched into a full run.

Quintira grabbed for the black mane. Wind snatched her head scarf away. Her skirts billowed, blocking Mi'kal's view. He pressed them down and held them with his knees. Ahead of them, a huge boulder loomed in their path. Quintira screamed and Mi'kal gave the stallion his head. The chestnut soared over the rock and came down without breaking stride.

Now Mi'kal knew how the eagles felt as they rode the air currents.

The boulder was only the first of the hurdles. The stallion took gullies and thorn bushes with the same high lift.

When they dismounted, breathless and flushed, Mi'kal wiped the foam from the shining flanks. He laid his hand against the soft lips and said, "You are a horse, but you think like a man. I shall call you Centaurus. Welcome to our tent."

He laid his face against the long cheek, and the horse and boy became as one.

As Quintira waited for Mi'kal to return from the stables, she remembered the day, almost eighteen years before, when she had been brought into camp. Tongues had wagged about her as they would wag about the virgin gift. But all the snickering and whispering ceased when Raaschid declared she was to be his wife.

The clan had given her a good wedding. There had been music and dancing and feasting. She wore a garment of shimmering crimson silk that Raaschid had confiscated from a shipment going to some noble lady in Tiberias. Several young girls worked with her long hair, braiding it into plaits laced with white ostrich plumes.

Older women showed curiosity about her virginity and offered her the fleece which would prove that she had never lain with a man. Others, who felt they could read her face, were sure that Raaschid had already claimed that which belonged to a husband.

Quintira remembered how the roof of the nuptial tent slanted and was lowered over them to show that a groom had taken his bride to bed. Beyond that she had no memory of her wedding night. She had willed herself to forget it.

Now she felt tears on her cheeks. She was crying both for herself and the slave girl. She cried for Zalah, the princess bride.

Quintira had hoped Zalah's personal slave would be an older woman, a woman who could understand when a young wife wished herself dead. And yet, perhaps Zalah was not the weeping kind. Rumors said she was as hot-tempered as her father.

Darkness was coming, and Quintira moved to the pavilion. Where was Mi'kal? He had gone to give the stallion the usual evening treat. But he should be back. She seldom worried about him, but tonight she felt uneasy.

In the corral, darkness settled down softly as Mi'kal curried Centaurus for the second time. The stallion's coat was shiny. The few weeks of rest and grass had been good for all the horses.

His final act of love was the offering of an apple, a precious thing in the desert. Fresh fruit was seldom seen in the caravans that passed. But sometimes it came packed in snow, destined for the royal palaces in Galilee and Judea as well as the provinces on the eastern side of Jordan.

Mi'kal patted the soft nose as the horse's teeth crunched on the love gift. He did not hear the footsteps until he felt an arm about his neck and the touch of a cold blade under his ear.

He was too frightened to struggle.

He heard Sa'ad's quiet but furious voice. "I should slit your throat. But I won't. My father says you have paid for Kaleb's death. I am not going to kill you, but someday I will lay you open with my whip."

Mi'kal shuddered as Sa'ad released him and disappeared like an evil dream. He put his hand to his throat expecting to feel blood. He leaned against the stallion and shivered.

At last all the ill feeling between them had come to a head. Sooner or later Sa'ad would do as he threatened, and Mi'kal would have to defend himself. He wound his fingers in the black mane.

The Old One was right. He was not born to kill. He wondered if God was trying to tell him it was time for him to leave the black tents. He had long since passed the notch on the Old One's tent post. He did not want to tell his mother about Sa'ad's threat, and yet he needed a good reason, beyond his own expressed desire, for leaving.

As Mi'kal returned to his tent, he passed Leyla's. He presumed she and her grandmother were already asleep, but as he came near he heard soft singing. He lingered. The song was a love song, a tribute to a cherished grandmother.

Mi'kal felt a tender sorrow. He had never had a grandmother. But maybe, someday, if Mumtaza, the beloved of Aretas, were still alive... He shook his head. No, he would probably never see her, for he had no intention of visiting the Nabatean court.

The words of Leyla's song came clearly. She must be making up the melody as she sang, as Quintira sometimes did with the Scriptures. "O thou, with the wrinkles of time, like blossoms dropped from the almond tree; most precious, art thou. O thou, with the white wool on thy head and the marks of dark toil on thy hands, softer are they than the kiss of a lover. More to be desired are they than the singing of birds. Sleep, sweet mother of my mother, sleep."

Mi'kal moved into the shadows as the song ended. He could hear Leyla unfastening the curtains. She came out, stretching her arms. The moonbeams braided themselves into her hair and were lost in its brightness. She began to dance barefoot over the ground. The moonlight laid a carpet beneath her feet.

Mi'kal did not move until she reentered her tent. Then he went slowly, grateful that he had heard and seen something beautiful—something that would help erase the memory of the ugly scene with Sa'ad.

CHAPTER TEN

On the second day after the return of Sa'ad, scouts reported the approach of two Roman soldiers. They were escorting a driver of a mule-drawn wagon and a cameleer with two baggage beasts. Neither soldier was heavily armed.

"Is the wagon covered?" Raaschid asked the scouts.

They assured him it was not. The bed held only empty crates. Raaschid growled. "Why should I provide meat for Roman pens?" He spat to show disdain.

"For gold, Master," Duag answered him.

A few of the men who heard the tone of unease in their chieftain's voice smiled behind their hands. Their prince was plagued with fleas of doubt. Romans had no cause to love the Bedouin chief. Their caravans were often waylaid to provide him with the leathers, the cloth and spices, and the provisions that ensured the prosperity of the clan.

Kwa brought out the prince's black wool *aba* and a white headpiece with a crimson *agal*. Freya, his black mare, was saddled. Raaschid mounted and Kwa draped the bottom of the cloak across the horse's rump.

At the far edge of the camp, barking dogs announced the Romans' arrival. Centurion Quintillius and Aurans, his young lieutenant, dismounted. They laid their sword belts on the bed of the wagon.

As Raaschid drew near, the centurion lifted his hand in a peaceful and respectful salute. His gray eyes appraised the black-cloaked figure on the black mare.

Raaschid drew rein and sat for a moment studying both men. The officer was a seasoned warrior with old wounds. The crinkled eyes held to his without awe or fear. The young one had strange brown spots over his nose and cheeks, and his knees were painfully sunburned. He moved as if saddle sore.

Raaschid bowed slightly and raised his hands, palm against palm. Quintillius returned the bow and spoke. Although his greeting was slightly elaborate, Raaschid could hear no overt sarcasm. He was equally elaborate in return.

Finally, Quintillius introduced his aide. "Aurans is my lieutenant." There was a twinkle in the gray eyes. "I find if I give a man a title, I will get more work and loyalty out of him."

Raaschid nodded. Here was a man he could enjoy after he made certain of the Roman's intentions.

Quintillius removed his flapless helmet as he talked. "If I may, I would like to explain why we are imposing on your hospitality. I am visiting the custom post that sits on the caravan route leading northward to Antioch and eastward to Damascus and Palmyra. The garrison needs meat. I would like to stock the pens and larder for the captain out of courtesy."

"Is there no meat in Damascus?"

"The old man from your camp—the one who sells us leather goods—convinced us that we should throw ourselves on your mercy rather than deal with the thieving merchants in the cities."

Again there was no false note in the voice or betraying flicker about the eyes. Raaschid found himself admiring the adroit flattery.

"What exactly did you have in mind?" He laid his hand on Freya's nose, for the mare was growing restless.

"We have brought gold to pay for whatever your warriors can bring in with nets and snares. We would like domesticated stock, too. Young camels, milk goats, chickens, pigeons, and ostriches. If possible, we would like to have the wagon and camels loaded by tomorrow afternoon."

Raaschid nodded, pleased again. How much easier to deal with a man who knew what he wanted, and when, than to do business with a merchant Jew.

"Mount," he said, "and follow me."

Aurans had never been in a Bedouin camp. He smiled at the dark-skinned children. Many of them ran naked, but almost all wore small tinkling trinkets on ankles or necks.

The centurion did his share of close observation also. He saw bed mats covered with rich materials that had probably been shipped to Roman matrons. Pieces of fine Cypriot copper pans, now fire blackened, hung on notched stakes beside the cooking fires. Wine flagons of Corinthian bronze lay beside goat-skin water bottles.

No wonder Romans were not welcome in Bedouin camps. Raaschid must know that he was notorious as a common brigand. Perhaps not so common. He had an elegant way of sitting the mare. Such a cloak of Laodicean wool was not sold in the ordinary markets. And the boots must be soft Moroccan leather.

Raaschid's arm raised, and the horses stopped.

A few lengths from the canopied pavilion of the main tent, the three men dismounted. Quintillius, with his eye for perfection, saw the woman on the adjoining pavilion. She was unveiled, garbed in flower-yellow. Amber combs held a long, dark-brown mantle to her black hair. Quintillius knew he had seen far less beauty in the Roman courts.

His gaze shifted to the boy beside her. Taller than his mother, with golden fuzz on his chest and legs, he looked as the young Alexander of Macedon might have looked on the day he rode Buecephalus.

Often when he saw boys such as this one, or the merry-eyed Aurans, he experienced a sense of loss. Encounters with women he had experienced many times, in many places, but as far as he knew he had never sired a son.

Raaschid clapped and a bald-headed attendant in a short white tunic brought a sea shell holding a mound of coarse salt. Raaschid lifted a pinch and offered the shell to Quintillius. The centurion lifted some between forefinger and thumb. They put the salt on their tongues, bowed slightly, and swallowed.

Quintillius relaxed. The "covenant of salt" insured his safety as long as he stayed in camp. Raaschid passed the salt to the younger officer. Aurans looked at Quintillius who nodded at him. He too took a pinch of the salt and swallowed. He choked a little and apologized in embarrassment.

Quintillius said, "You are excused for now."

Aurans saluted and stepped back from the pavilion. Quintira and Mi'kal were watching and saw him leave looking undecided and ill at ease.

"Mother, could I ask him to share our shade?" Mi'kal said.

"Of course, darling, and he may know something about Galilee." Her eyes were shining.

On Raaschid's porch, Quintillius asked for permission to remove his leather *cuirass* and accepted a seat on a camel saddle covered with an antelope hide. He had sympathized with Aurans and was relieved when he saw the golden-haired boy invite his lieutenant to join the woman on her pavilion. Behind his relief was a prick of envy.

The man who had brought the salt now ordered a lesser slave to bring cups of sour camel's milk. Quintillius found it remarkably refreshing.

On the adjoining porch the woman in yellow was pouring a drink for the lieutenant and the boy. The three of them were in animated conversation as they disappeared into the cool shelter of her private quarters.

Aurans had accepted Mi'kal's invitation with relief. He felt awkward with the Bedouin prince, but he was soon at ease with this woman and her son. Evidently there were no younger children in her tent. Aurans had been the first-born of his mother, who had given birth eleven times in twenty years.

Quintira touched his shoulder. "Would you like some wine and nuts? We will not eat for several hours."

She poured rose-amber wine into three cups and set a tray of salted pistachios before him.

Mi'kal straddled a brass-legged stool. "Mother thinks her wine is good, but we hear that your Falernian wine is the best."

Aurans grinned and Mi'kal was fascinated by the small brown dots all over his nose and cheeks. "Beer we see; wine seldom. Our post rations are just one step removed from swine slop."

"Have you complained to Tiberius?"

"Oh, yes." His brown eyes twinkled. "And he has promised to send us bottles from his own cellars as soon as the sea loses its salt."

Mi'kal laughed and then asked, "Are you going to be in Syria long?"

"No. We are returning to Capernaum soon. I expect to get orders to report to the garrison at Jerusalem. They are reinforcing the Antonia troops."

"Are they expecting trouble?" Quintira asked.

"Maybe. In a few weeks the Jews have a festival. A feast of some kind and—"

"The Passover."

"I understand they usually have trouble with religious fanatics during that time."

"The Passover celebrates Israel's release from slavery in Egypt, but sometimes it reminds my people they are still slaves to Rome."

"My village in Britain is subject to Roman occupation also," Aurans said. "Julius Caesar brought the first invaders to our coast, but he did not find the landing easy. Later they tried again. It will be years before all the tribes are subdued."

Mi'kal looked at him with awe. "The Old One has told me Britain is very far from here. How did you get to be a Roman soldier?"

"Things were hard in my village. I had an opportunity to work my way on a vessel to Rome. I had to become a citizen in order to join the army."

"Someday my people will be free," Quintira said. "You may have guessed that I am not an Arab. I am a Jew." There was pride in her voice as she stood outlined against the light of the doorway. "Someday our Messiah will put Rome to the prod and Caesar to the goad."

"Mother!" Mi'kal spoke with warning and embarrassment. He turned to the young Briton. "She believes we have been promised a Redeemer—the Messiah who will bring peace to the entire earth."

"No one desires peace more than I," Aurans said, "but as long as men fight, I am pledged to fight for Rome." There was determination in his strange accent. He turned to Quintira. His voice was softer. "As for your Messiah, have you heard the rumors from Galilee?"

Quintira turned quickly. "That there is a man called Jesus claiming to be the Messiah, Son of David? Do you know anything about him?"

"Only that there is a lot of argument, with much to be said for both sides. People in Galilee and Judea have seen him do miracles. He has restored the blind and the lame and the deaf. Even the lepers."

"Have you seen these things with your own eyes?" Mi'kal heard the spark of hope in her question.

"No. But Captain Quintillius has told me about a miracle Jesus performed for him. He has a servant, Dolmicius, who has cared for him and tutored him since birth. One morning Dolmicius woke up and could not move or speak. Quintillius walked into Capernaum to get Jesus, and Jesus offered to return with him. Quintillius told him that he did not have to visit a Gentile's house. He believed that if Jesus but said the word, his servant would be healed."

"But surely Jesus would have to see the servant and touch him in order to heal him," Mi'kal argued.

Aurans shook his head. "He said the captain's faith in him was enough. When Quintillius got back to his villa, Dolmicius was entirely well."

"You can swear to this?" Quintira asked.

"Yes. I have visited with them. But he did something even greater that I know about for sure." He stopped to spit out a piece of pistachio shell. "Jesus raised a little girl from the dead. I've seen her."

Mi'kal's stool fell over as he jumped to his feet. "From the dead? Where?"

"In Capernaum. She was the daughter of the ruler of the synagogue. She was sick and she died. The doctor said she was dead. When Jesus saw her, he said she was sleeping. The doctor was furious. A lot of people were there when Jesus went into the house. They heard him say, 'Maiden, arise!' And she got up and ate her supper."

"And you believe she was really dead?" Quintira asked.

"My centurion has no doubts, and he is not an easy man to fool."

Quintira's eyes glowed and her hands moved like excited birds. "Mi'kal. It might be true that Jesus is our Messiah!"

Aurans went on with emphasis. "Those who believe she was dead are calling Jesus the Son of God. Those who don't call him a sorcerer. So there you are."

Mi'kal turned to his mother. "If he isn't the Messiah, he might be the Green Bird. At least he knows the secret of resurrection." He felt foolish even as he said it, and yet he knew he was halfway serious.

Quintira moved her arms in exasperation, shoving his remark aside.

"The green bird?" Aurans asked.

Quintira sighed. "Ever since he was little he has been obsessed with the idea that there is a bird that knows the secret of resurrection. Our children of the tents sing of such a bird. Mi'kal refuses to admit it is just a legend."

Mi'kal turned to Aurans for support. "Do you think my belief in the Green Bird is any more fanciful than her belief in a Messiah who will cure the ills of the entire world?"

Aurans held up his hands. "I can't take sides. I've never thought much about death. I believe when you're dead, you're dead, and others come to fill your space."

Quintira stared. "But don't you believe your soul lives forever?"

"No. What is there about me, or any man, that deserves to live forever? We come. We go. That is the way of all things."

Mi'kal shook his head. "We say the sun dies, but it comes again the next morning. The moon wanes, but it comes into full circle again. Flowers wither and come again in the spring. Aren't we more important to God than these things?"

"Mi'kal is right, Aurans. We are made in God's image. Therefore we must be important to him."

"I hope you are right."

"Mother, why don't I go to Galilee and find Jesus of Nazareth and see if he is your Messiah?"

She started to protest and Mi'kal hurried on. "We both know it is time for me to leave."

She tried to control her tears. "Please, Mi'kal. Not yet."

"Raaschid has never loved me. And I am as vermin under Sa'ad's shirt."

Aurans turned away. He looked without seeing the camp outside the tent door. He was remembering his own mother's tearful entreaties.

Kwa came and broke the painful silence. Prince Raaschid was inviting Mi'kal and the lieutenant to join him and the centurion. Quintira and Mi'kal exchanged glances. Personal invitations from Raaschid to Mi'kal were rare. Today the prince must be in good humor.

Before they followed the servant, Aurans wanted to know if the old man who had sold them the leather goods was in camp.

"He is out looking for wood for tent pegs," Mi'kal said. "He said to tell you he was sorry to miss you if you came."

"May I leave some money for him? We were gambling, and I was short and—"

"You mean he won?" Quintira asked.

"Is that such a surprise?"

Mi'kal and his mother laughed. "Nothing less than a miracle," she said.

CHAPTER ELEVEN

Mi'kal and Aurans found the older men deep in an avid discussion of wild game hunting. Raaschid greeted them, invited them to sit down, and then went back to his conversation with the centurion.

"Does it take the sons of Esau to fill your larder? The hills near your post are full of red deer and aurochs."

"But we have no hounds fleet enough to bring down the bigger game." Quintillius seemed completely at ease as he lounged against the camel saddle.

"You need falcons to peck out their eyes."

"Some of the men own hawks, but there is none as splendid as yours." The centurion motioned toward the hooded hawk tethered inside the entrance of Raaschid's rooms.

Mi'kal knew Quintillius could have done nothing better to gain Raaschid's favor. The falcon seemed to sense the Roman's admiration and puffed its feathers.

"Ah, you speak the truth. There is none like my shining meteor. My Anaga."

Duag offered Aurans a low bench laced with thick strips of zebra skin. Mi'kal sat cross-legged on a floral-patterned rug. They held their own quiet conversation as the dialogue between the men turned to politics.

Aurans was interested in the life of the black tents. He tried to count the roaming camels and mares. When he noted the absence of sheep, Mi'kal told him that most of them had been sent to the Lebanon foothills.

Mi'kal tried to appear at ease, but he dreaded his meeting with Sa'ad who would be joining them soon. This was the usual time for him to let the falcon fly. What would they have to say to one another after the unpleasant encounter in the corral?

Raaschid and Quintillius were arguing in a friendly way about the latest Roman tollgate tax for pregnant camels when Sa'ad came. He barely acknowledged the guests and his eyes avoided Mi'kal. He wore a heavy leather wristlet on his left arm. The bird moved its claws on the perch and rustled its feathers.

"Give him his wings," Raaschid said. Sa'ad untethered Anaga and carried the bird on his wrist to his father. The chieftain's fingers smoothed the marbled plumage as he crooned. "My beautiful one! My beater of the wind!"

The falcon cocked its head and opened its beak.

"Father, he is anxious to dine."

Raaschid agreed. "Order the pigeon."

Sa'ad motioned for a small boy and sent him to the coops. He came back with a gray and white bird.

Anaga's hood was taken off. "Up! Up!" Sa'ad cried. The wide wings beat as Anaga launched into the air. Raaschid's cry ascended with him. "Away my pretty one!"

The falcon soared and circled. The pigeon was tossed into the air. The killer's cry echoed faintly from the face of the white cliff. The pigeon beat its wings, trying to find a refuge, but the falcon came down like the meteor for which it was named, wings folded, legs close to its body, until its breast almost touched the back of its victim.

The talons closed down. Feathers flew. The camp cheered. On the ground, the falcon pranced from leg to leg while it tore open the pigeon's breast to get to the heart.

Though Quintillius applauded the victor, he had not watched the uneven battle. His eyes were on Sa'ad. "A bad one," he thought. Sa'ad's black eyes were as cold and hard as the crystal that blazed from the brass ball on his bare chest.

Aurans watched as Sa'ad used one of the pigeon's feathers to stroke the ruffled pinions of the killer. He had cleaned the beak and claws with water. The bird's eyes continued to blink maliciously as the jeweled hood was slipped over its head.

As Sa'ad tethered the falcon, Aurans was the first to see the girl with the tambourine coming toward them. Mi'kal leaned toward Aurans. "She is Ne'ma, the daughter of my uncle's discarded concubine."

Ne'ma walked with long strides, a blue skirt swirling about her. Her black hair was unbound and held in place with a band woven from her own locks. Before she reached the long tent, she lifted her tambourine and began a light shaking. When she was directly in front of the men, she raised both arms and, with one hand beating the instrument, began to stamp her feet.

Her anklets tinkled as she circled and spun with long-legged grace. The circles diminished until she reached the vortex. Then she began to kick. Her toes touched the tambourine over her head. Women, looking up from their cooking pots, growled under their breath.

"She is like a grouse beating for a mate."

"Shameless! O foolish one, what could our lord see in you?"

As the dance ended, Ne'ma dropped to her knees and smiled into the face of her lord with adoration. Only then did Quintillius notice the crooked eye.

Raaschid motioned for her to stay. At his order, Duag fetched a silver coin. Raaschid gave it to her. He smiled, as a fond parent might smile, and dismissed her. While the Roman and his aide applauded, Raaschid's mind moved swiftly. He could feel Gutne's jealous gaze burning the back of his neck. He would have to find a husband for Tullah's girl.

Ne'ma entered her mother's tent and wiped the perspiration from her face. She tucked the coin away after kissing it. If prayers to a hearthside god had any value, someday her lord would invite her to his couch.

Tullah said nothing. Ne'ma was as plain as she herself had been when Muktar raided her clan and took her as a concubine. Later she was cast off. Raaschid took her in, but she had never been to his tent. As long as the Jewess lived there would be no other woman for Raaschid. Stupid Ne'ma!

Sa'ad was furious. How crude of Ne'ma to give such an open invitation. Men usually had no use for fruit ready to fall into their hands. He thought of Leyla. He had not seen her for many hours. He shook his head. He must stop thinking about her—at least until after his wedding.

Mi'kal's thoughts were still on the pigeon. This game with the falcon was just another way to glorify death. Bird against bird. Man against man. The Old One had told him of a world where orator competed against orator, poet against poet, musician against musician. A world where scientists and physicians struggled to be the best in order to produce the most good for the most people. Not the most harm.

Mi'kal remembered his first experience with senseless death. He had been very young. His mother had taken him to a secluded pool to bathe. Willow trees hung down like tent curtains. He splashed naked while she bathed in her white shift.

An inquisitive boy, not old enough to be a warrior, climbed into one of the date palms that rose high over the willows. A woman doing her washing in the stream saw him, and when she decided he was watching Quintira bathe, she yelled for him to come down. Raaschid heard and came to see. He was furious. He ordered his wife out of the pool and the boy out of the tree.

"He has done nothing evil my lord," Quintira protested. "I was not unclothed."

"He has looked upon you with lust in his heart."

Quintira gasped. "My lord, he doesn't know the meaning of the word!"

Her protests were useless. Raaschid ordered the boy to kneel. He lifted his sword. Quintira held Mi'kal's face against her legs. He heard a swish and then a thud, as if a melon had rolled into the sand.

As he thought about it now, he wondered if that was when he began to hate death.

The afternoon of conversation ended when Quintillius ordered Aurans to check on the wagon and see that the driver and the cameleer were fed. Raaschid invited the centurion to share his evening meal.

Mi'kal went back to his tent and was surprised and excited to learn that Quintira had sent for Leyla and her grandmother to share their meal with them. "I am doing this against my better judgment," she said half-seriously. "But God has told us to be kind to strangers. Especially needy neighbors. The grandmother has the look of death about her. And the girl is to be pitied. She is—"

"As Sa'ad's pigeon," Mi'kal finished as he prepared to trim his growing beard.

For the evening, Mi'kal chose a dark green tunic with a wide panel of embroidery down the front. He fastened it about him with a bronzed link belt.

He was glad his wounds were healed and the scabs fallen. He ran a comb through his hair. He no longer missed his braids. When he traveled into the world of the Romans and Greeks he would want short hair.

The sun was setting and the rays flowed softly over the distant plain as Mi'kal escorted Leyla and her mother to his mother's tent. The old woman was dressed in heavy black, but Leyla seemed to float in a dove-gray garment with a purple sash. Today her hair was in a heavy plait down her back and her eyes were a violet hue. Perhaps it was a reflection from the purple cord that closed the neck of her garment, letting the folds fall softly across her shoulders.

Raaschid and Sa'ad were on their pavilion with Quintillius. Gutne was in her doorway and she yelled sharply, "Go back, slave, and dress as you were told to dress."

Raaschid growled and motioned his wife to silence. "Pork, not beauty, turns a man's stomach. The girl will dress as she pleases."

Gutne retreated to her quarters.

Sa'ad showed his chagrin as Leyla brushed past him to take Quintira's outstretched hands. "Welcome to our tent," Quintira said.

Mi'kal brought a large feather-filled pillow for Leyla and a tapestry stool for Ammoni. Quintira set out low tables. A mixture of lamb and vegetables was roasting on the coals of the fire bowl.

Leyla smiled at him. He warmed with pleasure. Quintira expressed admiration for Leyla's garment and fingered the purple sash. "No wonder kings want to keep this color for themselves."

"It is my favorite."

"Mine, too." Quintira caught her son's eye and her dimples danced.

Both of them were thinking about her new garment she had cut from a bolt of lustrous purple silk that morning.

Ammoni and Quintira were talking around the cooking fire, and Mi'kal grew uncomfortable. What did a boy talk about with the most beautiful girl he had ever seen?

"Would you like to take a walk?" he asked.

The question was abrupt, but she didn't seen to mind.

"I would like to. Everything here is so strange to me." She extended her hand.

Mi'kal's fingers closed about it. The sensation was exciting and new. He called to his mother. "Do we have time to walk to the boulders and back?"

"Yes. But be careful."

He knew what she meant.

As they walked, Mi'kal knew there had never been a more beautiful evening. They could feel the moister air from the springs in the oasis and hear the night birds and the early croaking of the frogs. As they passed Kaleb's cairn they stopped.

"I am sorry about your little brother."

"You know about Kaleb?"

"Ne'ma told me. She is often in our tent. She has told me much about you."

"Then you know why I have no braids."

"I like your hair short. It is much nicer than Sa'ad's. He doesn't like you, does he?"

"No."

"Why not?"

"He took in jealousy with his mother's milk. She hates my mother."

"Because she is your father's favorite?"

"You know that too?"

"Ne'ma says your mother is a Jew and your father kidnapped her."

"Is there anything she hasn't told you?"

"Yes. Why are you so different from your brother?"

"You mean there is something she doesn't know?" Mi'kal lifted her to a boulder.

"Yes, and I'd like to know more."

Incredibly, he found himself telling her about his mother and Myndus and the purple scarf. She clapped lightly when he ended. "You're a prince of Petra!"

He put a finger on her lips. "Sssh. This is our secret. I don't ever intend to do anything about it. I want to live my own life."

"As you wish, my lord, we will say no more. Do you know that Ne'ma is passionately in love with your fa— I mean with Raaschid."

"She has told me."

"I feel sorry for her, she is so plain."

"Every girl cannot be as beautiful as you, but Ne'ma is a good person. And she has a right to dream of her heart's desire. As long as I can remember I have had dreams of doing things that may be impossible."

"Me too."

Silence fell between them. Shadows lay in pools near the cliff. Finally, Leyla said, "Ne'ma has promised she will always be my friend."

"She will keep her promise."

"Will you promise to be my friend too?"

"Of course."

"Who is your best friend?"

"The Old One." Mi'kal explained about the man who had come into the camp mysteriously a long time ago. "Mother loves him too, but she would disagree about the best friend. She says my best friend is the Lord, our Hebrew God."

"I have a household god that I pray to. She protects me."

"I hope so. Mother and I do not believe in the desert gods of wood and stone, but with Zalah and Sa'ad, perhaps any god will help."

Her blue eyes grew luminous in the shadows. "I wish you were going to be my master instead of Sa'ad."

"I'm not going to be anybody's master."

She slipped from the boulder and raised herself on tiptoe. Her lips touched his cheek.

Sa'ad came quietly through the boulders just in time to see the kiss. He had tried to leave the porch when he saw the two of them walking away, hand in hand. His father had detained him by sending him to find the younger Roman officer and invite him to the evening meal.

Now, as he watched from the increasing shadows, he clinched his hands in frustration. Someday he would do what he had threatened to do. He would settle the score with Mi'kal with the sting-ray whip. The red-gold curls would be scattered like caterpillars on the ground.

Soon he would be the one Leyla was kissing. Until then, he would go back to the tent and drink some of his father's wine waiting to be served with the evening meal.

CHAPTER TWELVE

The next morning passed quickly for Quintillius. The night's fast had been broken behind a thin curtain in Raaschid's quarters. Slaves served goat's milk, barley cakes, and fresh dates and early figs.

Hunters returned with the game they had captured in snares or nets. The centurion measured out coins to pay each man. He poured the remainder into Raaschid's palm to pay for the young camels hitched to the baggage animals and the goats tied to the wagon. Crates were already loaded with domestic fowl. Water and fodder enough for a twenty-four-hour journey were loaded on camels and cart.

Mi'kal listened as they spoke of their return. They might bivouac for a couple of hours during the night at a small oasis. But the route lay straight north on an ancient road, after they passed a high plateau of black basalt. With the help of the gods, the mule driver thought they should be at the custom house by afternoon of the following day.

Quintira packed the young Roman a pouch of dried fruit and nuts. His carrot-red hair touched her cheek as he kissed her.

He turned to Mi'kal. "Perhaps we shall meet again if you come to Galilee."

"I will be there. Maybe sooner than you think."

When the Romans had departed, the usual afternoon quiet descended on the camp. Children played with their marbles inside, out of the sun. Ne'ma visited with Leyla, who was teaching her to do more than twirl and kick when she danced.

Mi'kal walked among the boulders. He looked up at the cliff, but there were no enticing birds. The sun must have drained the pool. He wondered what the coneys and the lizards were doing. He saw a flash of green wing and thought of the Green Bird.

He passed his hand though his hair. The curls were getting longer. He felt his cheeks. His beard was thickening and growing soft. He was no longer a boy.

He was feeling sadness and gladness. When the Romans left the camp he realized he was ready to leave also. Ready to do all the things he longed to do. See all the things he longed to see. Ask about Jesus, find knowledge, and yes, even look for the Green Bird that was still calling him.

Why hadn't he planned to go back with the Romans today? If he left immediately in the morning, he might catch up with them. He could travel to Galilee with them.

Quintira was sewing on her purple garment when he entered the tent. He sat on his haunches beside the hamper where she stored her sewing things.

"Mother, we have to talk."

"Is it the girl? I know she is enticing, but you must remember she is not yours."

"I would never do anything to dishonor her or you."

"I suppose I am worried because I know you are growing up." She shook out one of his outgrown tunics. "My little boy is gone, and like yesterday, he will never come again."

"That's what I want to talk about. Being gone. I have decided it is time for me to leave the tents."

She wrapped her hands in the purple cloth to keep them from trembling. "Are you sure, Mi'kal? I have prayed about it. I have always known you would want to go someday. But are you sure?"

"Yes. For several reasons I know it's time to go. Since I am not Raaschid's son, I have no real obligation to stay."

They held each other tight. He looked down into her face. "Is there no way you can come with me? I will see Galilee first."

"Raaschid would follow us to the ends of the earth."

He released her. "I want to leave early and maybe catch up with the Romans."

She began to move with purpose. "That would make it safer for you. I will help you pack."

"The first thing I will do, Mother, is search for Jesus. If he is your Messiah, I will come back and tell you."

They spent the rest of the day selecting what he would need. She insisted on giving him a bag of coins she had saved, and he took them knowing he would need them until such time as he had found a way to make a living.

At the last she opened her citron box and handed him the piece of purple scarf. "If you ever visit Aretas..."

He said nothing. He knew he had no intention of trying to meet his grandfather. In the morning he would tie the scarf around his waist under the tunic. He would put his coin pouch there, too. Someday he would give the scarf back to her.

Ammoni rolled on her mat. Something had wakened her. Maybe it was the pain inside her. Something heavy was sitting on her chest. Her left arm hurt. She closed her eyes. A jolt of pain took her breath.

On the other side of the curtain, Leyla was mending a tear on the bottom of the gray garment. Perhaps she had caught it on a briar while walking with Mi'kal the night before. She laid the scissors down and was bending over her rolled blankets when she heard something brush against the tent flap.

She listened. A dog? A stray goat? She leaned forward to quench the oil lamp when she saw fingers working at the door laces.

"Grandmother," she whispered softly, "Grandmother!" Her heart sank as she realized Ammoni had fallen asleep.

She was holding the gray garment in front of her when Sa'ad lowered his head and entered. He dropped the curtain behind him and stood, unsteady on his legs.

She tried to control the panic in her voice.

"Go away. You're drunk. Go away."

He continued to advance. She backed against the pile of blankets.

"I'm going to scream."

His tongue was thick. "Go ahead. Nobody is going to keep me from taking what I have paid for."

"I'm not yours. I'm a gift for your bride. Remember?"

"After I am married, I will move you into a tent next to mine."

"No. I won't be a concubine."

She tried to slip past him and hit the lampstand. The lamp fell, splattering the oil. The wick flickered and smoked.

Sa'ad grabbed her, and she could smell the wine. He forced her backward. Her body arched and his chest pressed against hers. His necklace bit into her breast and she screamed.

Her hand grasped the scissors she had left lying on the mat. As she twisted away, she slipped and fell backwards. The breath went out of her as she hit the mat, the blades of the scissors pointing upward. Sa'ad laughed and started to push them away. His foot slipped on the oil-soaked skin in front of the mat and he fell. The scissors pierced his chest. He groaned and slid sideways.

Leyla pushed him away, and he rolled onto the floor, face up. A ray of moonlight came through the swinging flaps, and she saw the blood and the scissors, upright a hands-breadth above his navel.

A scream rose in her throat, and she clapped her hand over her mouth. She must be quiet. She must find someone to help her.

She grabbed up one of Ammoni's dark shawls. Outside, the wind was cold, the stars sharply white.

She kept to the moonless shadows as she ran to Quintira's tent. She beat frantically on the flaps but kept her voice low. "Quintira! Quintira!"

Mi'kal heard her and woke his mother. Together, they opened the curtains and pulled her in.

On the edge of camp, near the acacia tree, a man moved awkwardly in the darkness. His mare had been tethered far enough away so she would not encourage neighs and snortings from the stallions in the corral.

He had been watching the camp for many hours. He had seen the Roman supply wagon pull away in the late afternoon. He saw Sa'ad carrying a large wine flagon into his own quarters. The necklace blazed in the late sun and hatred filled the man's belly.

He remembered the day his twin sister had bargained for the heavy neckpiece from a desert vendor. "A gift for me," he rejoiced to himself, for it was their twelfth birthday.

But Raaschid and Sa'ad had come, and a marriage contract was signed. The necklace was put over Sa'ad's head, and Zalah kissed him.

Hatred had sprung up like a thistle that day. Later, it had flourished as a thorn hedge.

Now was the time to act. If he waited it would be too late. The wedding would occur before the clans gathered for the winter migration back to Arabia.

He knew what he had to do. For years he had been slighted, considered less than a man because of his affliction. Now the leadership of the clan was slipping away from him.

But the loss of the clan was the smaller part of his anguish. The real cause must not be spoken aloud. No, not even in the secret places of his heart.

He limped closer, staying with the shadows.

He watched as Sa'ad moved with drunken steps to the small tent. He heard his cousin's fingers fumbling with the laces. He saw a shaft of oil lamp light. He heard the girl's frightened and angry voice. He waited. There was a clatter and the light went. He imagined the struggle, then saw the girl running away. He moved closer. Surely Sa'ad would follow her. This was going to be easier than he had thought.

Sa'ad came out, his hand pulling at something tangled in the chain of the necklace.

The limping shadow advanced into the moonlight. Sa'ad blinked and stared with drunken eyes. His confused welcome to his cousin changed to sudden soberness as he saw the lifted knife.

He turned to run. The blow caught him between the shoulder blades. He fell forward. Strong hands removed the knife and rolled him over. The brass necklace was yanked off over his head.

In the tent, Mi'kal lit a lamp while Quintira helped Leyla to a stool. Between sobs, she gasped out her story.

Quintira said, "I don't understand Sa'ad. He knows his father would never condone it. This brings dishonor to Muktar's daughter, and Raaschid is never anxious to anger his brother."

Leyla shivered. "He was drunk. But he knew what he was doing."

"Are you sure you killed him?" Mi'kal asked as he lit one of the lamps from embers in the fire hearth.

"He groaned and fell over. And there was blood."

"Even if he isn't dead, Mi'kal, she can't stay here."

"What can we do?"

"You are packed and ready to leave in the morning. Take her and go now."

He stared. "What am I supposed to do with her? I don't even know where I'm going."

"If you could get me to Damascus, Rekha will take me back."

"Can you ride?"

"Horses, not camels."

"Take El Gamar," Quintira said. "Sa'ad won't be needing him."

"But that makes me a horse thief!"

"God understands. Trust him. Now we must get the things you will need."

Leyla stopped at the doorway. Her words were anguished. "What about my grandmother? I can't leave her."

"I will take care of her," Quintira said quietly. "I will need someone after Mi'kal is gone. Come on."

Although the moon was covered with tattered clouds, Quintira and Leyla could see the body lying in the thin shreds of milky light. Quintira paused.

"I thought he was inside your tent."

"He was. On the floor."

Leyla shuddered. Quintira knelt. The scissors had fallen loose near him, but a small pool of dark blood filled the navel and smeared his chest. He was definitely dead.

"We have to get him inside. The longer it is before they find him, the more chance you have to escape."

As they dragged Sa'ad into the tent, Leyla pointed to the dark path of blood they were leaving on the white gravel. "Where did all that blood come from?"

"Be quiet and help me."

They laid his body on the oil-soaked mat and stepped around him as they gathered what Leyla would need: a cloak, sturdy sandals, a heavy blanket, and one of Ammoni's dark burnooses to protect her from sun and sand. Leyla added a small wicker box to the other things.

"I must kiss Grandmother." She lifted the thin curtain. Ammoni was sleeping like a curled kitten on her mattress. One hand lay open on the floor, the fingers curled. Leyla knelt and lifted the fingers to her lips. Then she sat back, as if she had been pushed, and called faintly for Quintira. When Quintira came, Leyla pointed mutely. Quintira put her head down on the thin chest.

"Is she...?" Leyla murmured.

Quintira nodded.

Several hours later, Quintira lay awake, crying. Suddenly she sat up. Would Raaschid think Mi'kal had something to do with Sa'ad's death? Would everyone think Sa'ad and Mi'kal had fought over the girl? The horror of the thought brought her out of bed and to her knees.

CHAPTER THIRTEEN

Mi'kal and Leyla rode out of the camp with the horses' hooves wrapped in camel hide. Starlight softened the low shrubs and outlined the thin trunks of the struggling trees. They rode for several hours, the plain lighted by sharp pointed stars and a listless moon that drifted slowly through hindering clouds.

He was thankful she knew how to ride. If all went well and the Romans bivouacked at the water hole as they had planned, he should be able to join them sometime tomorrow. If he and Leyla succeeded in reaching the Romans, it would be impossible for Kwa and Duag to take them back.

Perhaps Quintillius would be kind enough to delay his return to Galilee for a few days—at least long enough for Mi'kal to deliver Leyla to Damascus. He would be glad to be rid of the responsibility. He didn't know anything about handling a girl. He turned, aware that she had been silent for some time, and saw her dozing in the saddle. He halted the horses, and she woke with a start.

"What is it? Why are we stopping?"

"We're going to rest. There is a small oasis ahead. It may be the water hole the centurion mentioned."

The horses stepped gently through tall grass that swished their legs as they entered the area of palm trees. Night insects expressed annoyance. Mi'kal began to have his first misgivings. There was no evidence that anyone had stopped at the oasis for days. The Romans must have decided to go on since they had forage and water with them.

The water hole was dry, but he took off his sandals and moved about, searching for the dampest spot. He found it and began to dig with the small shovel his mother had packed. The ground grew moist and then muddy. A puddle formed. The horses drank before the water cleared. He had water skins on each stallion, but he intended to keep them for emergencies.

Leyla walked away into the shadow of the thicker trees.

"Where are you going?" Mi'kal yelled.

"None of your business."

"Here, take this." He tossed the shovel toward her.

He was grinning as he untied their sleeping rolls. He piled her mat and blanket by itself. She could make her own bed. He would be doing enough to get her to Damascus.

Later, as he was almost asleep, she called to him. "Mi'kal, the rocks are hurting my back."

"Next time we'll bring a feather mattress. Go to sleep." He turned over and shut his eyes. He heard her moving toward him and looked up.

"What is it?"

"I keep hearing things. Listen."

He listened. The movement was slow and rustling and he laughed. "Just a porcupine. He won't bother you if you don't bother him."

"But I keep feeling crawly things."

"Only centipedes, scorpions, and spiders."

"Mi'kal!"

He realized she was really afraid. He turned back his blanket and moved over.

"Come on. We'll never get any sleep if you don't."

She slid in beside him. "Are you angry with me because I killed your brother?"

"You know Sa'ad wasn't my brother."

Her hands touched his cheeks and slid over his chin. "You don't look like an Arab. Your face is all corners."

Her hands made him uncomfortable, and he drew back.

"Tell me again how you came to be. Tell me again about your mother and her Nabatean prince."

He told her the story again. She sighed when he told about Quintira

95

tying the piece of purple scarf around the arm of her dead husband.

"I hope someone will love me that much someday."

"They will. You are very beautiful."

"Do you think so?"

Her breath was warm on his cheek. She was much too near. He pushed her away.

"Go back to your bed. I'd like to get some sleep. I'm sure the crawly things are gone."

"You're mean," she said, but she went.

How graceful she was in her white shift as she moved through the luminous silver-gray grass. Beside her crumpled blankets, Leyla stretched her arms upward as she had stretched outside her tent after singing to her grandmother. Mi'kal watched again.

Moving slowly, as wind through the tufted grass, she began to dance. Without tambourine or flute she made music with hands and feet. She began to sing, composing as she sang a song of love, of longing, of consummated rapture, of sadness, separation, and death.

She was singing of Quintira and Myndus.

Mi'kal watched as she sank to the ground, wrapping herself in her own arms. And for the first time, he wanted to hold her close.

He laid his hand on his waist where the purple scarf was tied. No. He would wait until he was sure. Wait until he found the love that would remain forever.

He fell asleep with his hand upon the scarf.

A faint line of pink showed on the horizon as he woke. He threw off his blanket and walked out of the grove to relieve himself. Centaurus heard him and whinnied. El Gamar lifted his nose and answered the call.

The morning was a world of silver mist. Mi'kal experienced a feeling of unreality, as though what he saw was part of a dream. Was he really fleeing from the black tents with a girl he scarcely knew? How was it possible for him to save her from Raaschid's revenge? By now he was in danger, too. All the camp would believe that he had something to do with Sa'ad's death. The trackers, under Kwa, would be on their way to bring them back.

A feeling of sympathy for Raaschid swept over him. He knew he was struggling with old feelings. He had wanted to love the man he had called "Father" for seventeen years. Though he knew he came last in Raaschid's affection, he had never doubted that he was the chieftain's son.

He looked down at Leyla. She was still sleeping, her shining hair spread out on the dark blanket. He touched her gently with his foot. "Get up. Time to go."

Leyla opened her eyes and stretched. He moved away, something inside him flashing a warning. He was not sure what he might do if she lifted her arms toward him.

Angry with his own thoughts, he mixed a few dried milk balls in a portion of the good water and offered it to her. She grimaced as she drank.

"It's sour."

He threw her half of a dried apricot to relieve the taste.

"Mi'kal, do you think they have found him yet?"

"Maybe not."

"I know who will find him. Zamir."

"The blacksmith's little girl?"

"I promised to teach her to dance. She said she would come this morning just as soon as the cocks crowed."

"Maybe she will oversleep," Mi'kal said, but he wasted no time rolling up the sleeping mats.

Zamir did not oversleep. She was up before the roosters crowed and was the first to go through the unlaced flap of the small tent. She stumbled over the body and ran out screaming.

Gutne reached the tent first, followed by Raaschid. Slaves carried Sa'ad from the tent, and then they found the old woman. She was buried without ceremony.

A search began for the silver-haired girl. Slaves, sent to give the horses their morning rations, came back distressed. Both El Gamar and Centaurus were gone.

Then a search began for Mi'kal. Quintira refused to say anything about either her son or the girl. Raaschid left her tent furious and frustrated.

She had placed herself in mortal jeopardy. He would be forced to condemn her.

Duag and Kwa were ordered to find Mi'kal and Leyla and bring them back alive. As the slaves left camp, Raaschid stood with his arms folded and his fingers clenched. He tried to shut out the sound of the wailing. Like Job, he was bereft of children.

But crushing his heart, as though it were grain under a grinding stone, was the knowledge he must punish the woman he loved. Grief and anger locked horns as though they were rams fighting for a female.

Kwa knew that the young prince was no fool. The boy would instinctively follow the Roman supply wagon. He found the tracks easily enough, one set of horse hooves overlaying another. He pointed them out to Duag and watched the Egyptian's yellow eyes brighten.

They rode rapidly in silence. Duag had chosen a red camel named Jusuf, a large, raking beast with a long stride. A sand-colored shepherd's cloak floated about him like the wings of a carnivorous bird. He rode with his feet crossed before him on the neck of the mount.

Kwa selected a fawn-colored female with a high-swung belly and delicate legs. Maha had just dropped a calf, and her udder swung heavy with milk. Kwa wore a gazelle-skin vest that hung open over his chest. The tribal marks glowed with sweat.

He felt no elation over the hunt. To snare game or enemies was one thing. To net children was something else. He was not convinced of their guilt. He wanted to examine the area about the girl's tent and outside the edge of camp before they left, but the prince took no time to listen or understand. He ordered them to go immediately.

Kwa had noticed something else. Something Raaschid hadn't mentioned. Sa'ad's necklace was gone. He had been wearing it the last time Kwa saw him as he went into his tent with a flagon of wine shortly after the Romans left. Kwa could not believe Mi'kal would stab a man in the back and steal his necklace.

Over the years he had grown fond of the Jewess and her son. Quintira had doctored him more than once for hornet stings and poison thorns and a scorpion's sting. Once she had used hot garlic juice, and Gutne complained that the black slave stunk.

Kwa hoped he and Duag would fail in their quest. He had cause to be grateful to the desert chief, even as the Egyptian had, but he also had good reason to hate him. Bitterness lay in the back of Kwa's throat as he thought of the day Raaschid had bargained for him from the slave trader. Freya, the black mare, had circled him as the rider appraised his height and his strength. When the price was agreed upon—a little less than was asked because of his bowed legs—Raaschid ordered him to stand before him.

"What do they call you?"

"Kwa."

"What does it mean?"

"Nothing."

"Are you fond of women?"

"Yes."

Then Raaschid called for Duag, who was already in his service. At Raaschid's command, Duag and four warriors dragged Kwa out of sight. They held him down and emasculated him, sealing the wounds with boiling oil. He could still feel the pain and hear his own screams. He closed his eyes to shut out the memory and opened them to a bright glare.

They were entering a plain of shining flint mixed with fine sand. A brisk wind was blowing, and Kwa studied the ground carefully. He saw, as Duag did, where Mi'kal had lost the wagon trail.

"Where are they going now?" the Egyptian asked.

Kwa shrugged. "They won't catch up with the Romans this way, but they will hit the toll highway."

"We'll get them first?"

"Probably." He spoke without zeal.

Duag studied him sharply with narrowed eyes.

Less than an hour later, they entered the oasis where Mi'kal and Leyla had spent the night. Kwa could recite the whole story: the place of the sleeping mats, one with two persons for a time. (Had Quintira's son taken his first woman?) The grass matted as if someone had danced. Small, fresh mounds behind the bushes where bodies had relieved themselves. They had dug for water.

Kwa did some digging with the toe of his sandal, and while the camels drank from the pool, milk dripped from Maha's udder. The men drank.

As they hunched back, waiting for the camels to finish drinking, Duag said, "You have no taste for this hunt?"

Kwa mounted Maha. He stared down at Duag, scorn on his face. "Are we hunters who brag of catching crippled hares?"

"If we bring in the prey, we will be rewarded."

"I desire freedom more than gold."

"I am free compared to what I would be in the Phoenician warehouses. They work you like mules and feed you like pigs. I, for one, appreciate our master's charity." The Egyptian brought his red camel to its feet. "Now let us bring them in."

"They are not guilty. I saw signs to the contrary."

Duag spit. "You have sympathy for the Jew's whelp? Just because she has poulticed you with stinking salves?"

The black man tightened his grip on his camel rope. "Leave her out of this. She had nothing to do with Sa'ad's death."

"She'll answer for it nevertheless."

"Sa'ad was drunk."

"Do you think it takes wine to put fire in a man's veins? Perhaps you have forgotten?"

The fawn camel came to a halt. Kwa laid a hand on his knife. "I have not forgotten there is a debt long overdue."

"What I took from you that day was not of my choosing." Duag spoke with sincerity.

"If you feel regret for that deed, you will be doubly sorry if we carry innocent children back to be executed."

"Are you suggesting we fail in the chase?"

"They didn't do it!"

Duag gave his camel a touch of his stick, and the bigger beast lumbered beside the other. "Slave, take heed. Forget what you think you know, and do what you've been told to do."

CHAPTER FOURTEEN

I
n early morning, Mi'kal and Leyla were traveling an ancient river bed. Pebbles, rounded by years of rushing water, covered the floor of the water course. At times the horses stumbled.

Mi'kal realized when he found no signs of recent occupancy in the grove that he had lost the trail. Shifting sand and a declining moon were partly to blame. He was beginning to worry about fresh water. The water skins were getting flabby.

The silver stallion still moved with undiminished ease, but there was something wrong with Centaurus. He was limping. The horse's front right hock was swelling. Mi'kal wondered if he should use the last of the dried milk balls with a little of the water to make a poultice.

The sides of the water course narrowed and grew higher. Leyla turned El Gamar's head and clung to his neck as he scrambled to the top of the ridge. Mi'kal followed.

The air on the plain was fresher than in the river bed, but the heat was intense. Not a blade of saw grass moved. Thorn bushes were quiet as etchings on the sides of the jar-shaped hills. Mi'kal found a shaded hollow where the dune seemed to be held together by the twisting roots of the tamarisk trees.

Leyla was thirsty, and he handed her the goat skin. He scooped a shallow bowl in the sand and stretched one of the saddle skins over it to hold a little water for the horses.

Mi'kal searched a saddlebag for some of the baked cakes his mother had packed. They were hard, and the raisins fell out like dried seeds.

Leyla had not mentioned their random course but now she said, "We're lost, aren't we?"

"Yes. Quintillius mentioned black cliffs, but we missed them."

"Are we heading in the right direction?"

"I think so."

"When we get to Damascus will you stay with me for a few days?"

"No. I want to get to Quintillius and Aurans before they leave for Galilee. I want to travel with them."

"But why go to Galilee? Damascus has lots of things for you to see and do."

"I've told you. I promised my mother to find a Galilean called Jesus—to see if he is the Messiah. All of my mother's people have been waiting for the Messiah for centuries."

"Why? What is he supposed to do?"

"He will come from God to bring peace and love to everyone. He will reign over all the earth, and there will be no more war or envy among the nations of the world. And people who have lived according to Moses' Law will be resurrected to live forever. That's what my mother says."

"What will you do if you find him?"

The question caused him to think. "I don't know. If he is the Messiah, I won't have anything to worry about because he will bring peace to all of us. Even in the tents."

"I don't believe any of it, but I'm not going to argue with you." She turned away and scrambled to the top of the small sand dune. She stood up and looked out across the plain. The wind lifted her hair. She gave a little yelp and came sliding down.

"Mi'kal, I saw a fox. Isn't that a bad omen on the desert? A girl told me once—"

"Only if you see his tail end."

"But I did."

Mi'kal wanted to laugh. But as long as he could remember, men in camp were convinced that ill fortune came to those who saw a fox running away from them.

"I've heard it. But I don't think I ever believed it."

"But what if it's true?"

"We'll hope for the best."

"I know who can help us," she said. She ran to her saddlebag and drew out a wicker box. Mi'kal thought of his mother's citron-wood casket. Did all women have small boxes full of secrets?

She opened the box and took out a cloth bundle. Unwrapping it, she held up a small straw doll. The eyes were black beads, and the mouth was shaped from scarlet wool. She set the box on end on a flat boulder and knelt before it. Mi'kal felt cold along his spine. This was one of the heathen gods his mother abhorred. He had seen similar gods sitting on stone or wooden altars in the Bedouin tents.

Leyla's lips moved with an incantation that was as the murmur of bees. The sound was disturbing rather than soothing. Mi'kal felt a force of evil. He went to her swiftly and pulled the doll from her hands.

"God hates things like this," he said and threw it down. The straw loosened; the black beads rolled. The doll's red lips smiled up from the sand.

Leyla scrambled to gather up the pieces. Her words rushed. "Mi'kal, you must do something quickly to appease her. She will curse us."

"Appease a filthy idol?"

She faced him with worried eyes. "You must give her something you love. You must!"

Mi'kal saw her fear and felt remorse. What did she know of God and his hatred for idols?

"Mi'kal! What do you have that you love the most?"

His hand went to his waist.

"The scarf?" she said. "Then you must burn it! Build a fire right now and burn it." Tears flooded her eyes. "If you don't you will lose your second most precious thing before the day is over."

The thought that a heathen god would demand his mother's scarf made him angry. He grabbed the straw out of her hand and let the wind lift it. The red lips fell to the ground again and his foot ground the bit of wool into the sand. Leyla fell to her knees, trying to retrieve the scrap of cloth. Mi'kal kept his foot on it.

"Leyla, if I allow you to bring your hearth idol with us, *my* God will be angry. Then we *will* be in trouble."

Leyla's distress was real as she stood. "O Mi'kal, we are doubly cursed. First the fox and now this."

"No. Not if we trust my God. My mother calls him our strength and shield."

He brushed her hair back and noticed her sunburned face. Her eyelashes were dark with tears. She was as a child who needed comforting. "Trust me, Leyla. Please trust me. I'm sorry I've made you angry."

Her lips were parched, but he could not resist them. They were warm under his own.

"Am I forgiven?" he asked gently.

She pushed away from him. "No!"

"Please."

"Maybe." The anger was fading. "But your God better be able to do everything you think he can."

"He won't forsake us. I promise."

He looked up at the sky wishing he felt as confident as he sounded. No clouds floated, as ragged mantles, to shut off the face of the sun. It was folly to continue in the increasing heat, but they must. He helped her mount. She was still thirsty. He searched in his saddlebag and brought out the last of the dates. "Suck on a stone. It helps keep the mouth moist."

They rode without talking, dulled by the heat and the blaze of the plain. He was finding it hard to concentrate on anything but the torturous ride when an outcropping of clay and sand, edging a sharp ravine, gave way under Centaurus.

Leyla screamed as Mi'kal fell with the stallion. He rolled clear as they hit the bottom of the gully. The whinny of pain brought him to his feet. Centaurus tried to rise, and his brown eyes rolled as if to apologize for falling.

Mi'kal saw the broken bone in the leg that had swollen. Leyla saw it, too. She slid down the slope and stood beside him.

"What are you going to do?"

"You know what I have to do." His voice was thick with agony. He fell to his knees and gathered Centaurus's head into his lap. He leaned over and kissed the long nose. His hand ran down the soft cheeks and touched the velvety lips. Then, motioning for Leyla to go away, he laid his dagger to the horse's jugular vein.

Blood hit him in the chest. Centaurus kicked once. A shudder ran through the powerful body. Mi'kal stretched himself across his gallant friend and sobbed. Leyla searched through his things and found him a clean tunic.

They left the horse and saddle in the ravine. Vultures were already flying overhead. She mounted behind him on the white stallion and asked softly, "Now do you believe me? Was he not your second most precious thing?"

Mi'kal was too choked with grief to reply.

For hours Kwa and Duag swayed with the rhythm of the plodding camels through a plain that shimmered with heat. Kwa's ivory necklace lay like a pattern of black and white on his shiny skin. Duag, wrapped in his tan cloak, rode beside him, his face lost in the folds of the burnoose.

Maha was light-footed in the gravel, but the bigger camel was in trouble. Earlier they had crossed a field of lava spurs and Jusuf's pads were bleeding. Every step brought groans of rage and pain. The camel finally refused to move, and Duag killed it.

He would have to ride with Kwa, though both men knew the small camel would be overloaded.

By midmorning, Mi'kal and Leyla were crossing a valley of hard clay overlaid with shallow sand. Leyla had wrapped her grandmother's cloak about both of them, but their lips were blistered and dust lay thick on their cheeks.

A low rumbling could be heard in the distance. El Gamar pranced uneasily. Mi'kal reined in and looked toward the south where a saffron-colored cloud rolled toward them. "Leyla, there's a sandstorm coming."

"What are we going to do?"

"I don't know." His eyes searched the plain for shelter, but he saw nothing but low dunes. The rumbling grew louder. Mi'kal's panic rose with the rising sound. The first of the blowing sand hit them cutting like tiny knives. The dust burned in their throats and choked them. In a few minutes they would be unable to see anything.

She clutched at him. "Do something. It's going to swallow us!"

El Gamar quivered, jerked at the bridle, and bolted. His hooves cast up heavy sand. Leyla screamed and clutched tighter at Mi'kal, but her screaming was lost in the shrieking of the storm. Inwardly Mi'kal was screaming too. *Help us, O God!*

The blasts pushed at them as if to unseat them. All they could do was hang on. The cloud was closing in on them. They tried to protect themselves with the burnoose, but the wind was too strong. Mi'kal tried to see ahead. El Gamar was racing toward what looked like a dark sand dune, but a shift in the blowing sand showed a heap of fallen stones and burnt timbers.

Mi'kal yelled. "Leyla, we're saved! Look!"

Ahead of them, scarcely discernible through the sand, were ruins of what might have been an old outpost.

El Gamar lengthened his stride and jumped over a wooden barricade. Mi'kal leaped down and pulled Leyla into a corner of the collapsed wall. He yanked off the saddle roll and tossed her a blanket. "Cover up and hang on." He covered himself and rolled close to her. The stallion turned his back to the wind and faced a wall.

Light disappeared in the mustard-colored cloud. Heat came with the sand in blistering assaults. The rumbling became a growl as if the desert was angry at losing them. Wind whistled like arrows over their heads and gusts of sand battered the old timbers. Mi'kal tried to shut his ears to the terrifying sounds.

During a brief lull, Leyla yelled into his ear. "How long will it last?"

"Nobody knows. Days. Minutes."

After what seemed hours, they became aware of the decreasing heat. The pressure of the wind eased, and they pushed back the blankets heavy with sand and struggled up.

They stripped to their undergarments and shook out the sand. Even the purple scarf about Mi'kal's waist was weighted with sand. El Gamar shivered, and sand cascaded from his mane and tail like glistening water.

They were brushing the sand out of their hair with their hands when the cold came. Mi'kal knew freezing air often followed such storms, but he was not prepared for it. They were shivering before they got their blankets around them. Mi'kal coaxed El Gamar to lie down, and they huddled close to his belly.

The chilling wind went as quickly as it came. Horse and riders scrambled to their feet. The stallion stretched, shuddered, and then relieved himself in the sand. The sound and the smell eased the tension. They laughed in nervous relief.

Still laughing, Mi'kal climbed the highest portion of the wall to see if he could figure out which direction they should go. Many hours of travel still remained. His eyes studied the landscape. He knew north from south and east from west because of the ginger-colored sun.

His eyes fastened on something a distance away and then he shouted, "Leyla, come up. See if you see what I see."

He pointed it out to her. A gray line that ran like a thin ribbon across the plain. The roaring wind had swept an old road clear of sand. Perhaps this was the ancient road they had missed—the one the Romans had taken. Leyla threw her arms about Mi'kal and bounced with joy.

His heart rejoiced. His God had saved them.

A precipitous line of black basalt cliffs rising abruptly from the rolling floor of the desert saved Duag and Kwa from the fury of the sandstorm. They watched as the rolling yellow cloud obliterated everything in its path. When it was gone, they too saw the ribbon of ancient road, although they saw it from the east rather than the west.

Duag chafed with the slow progress of the over-loaded camel. For the last mile he had been riding behind Kwa with his hand on his dagger. The chance of a bonus or even a commendation from his lord was fading with every hour.

If he could get rid of Kwa, there was a good possibility he could reach the guilty pair before they joined with the Romans. He must sacrifice part of his reward, for he would be able to take only one of them back. Even if they had their horses and he could truss them like birds, he could not handle two of them. Besides, they would not be standing still waiting to be tied.

No. But one was better than none. Which one? Raaschid would not be happy if he brought in the prince and let the more likely killer go free. There was no doubt of the girl's guilt. The bloody scissors were evidence enough.

After he had her, then what? He did not have Kwa's ability to find his way in the desert, but he was confident he could retrace the way they had come.

Maha helped him make his move against the black slave. She grunted and slowed her swaying. He put his knife to Kwa's throat and ordered him to slide off. On foot, Kwa looked up at him. "Why are you doing this?"

"With two of us on this beast we will fail. I do not intend to fail. I am going to collect at least part of what's coming to me."

Kwa nodded. There was smoldering anger in his voice. "That you will surely do."

"If you want one last drink from the udder, drink!" Duag swung his legs up and pulled the hood of the burnoose over his bald head.

Kwa squatted by the camel and thought of trying to unseat his enemy, but he had respect for the Egyptian's skill with the knife. He could slice the legs of the camel with his own knife while he drank, but would he gain anything by injuring the gentle Maha? His thirst quenched, he stepped aside and watched as Duag disappeared into the shallow dips of the plain with his brown cloak flapping.

Kwa remembered they had filled the water bag and let the camel drink at a small spring that flowed from a ledge of a sandstone ridge that morning. The pool was rimmed with thick bushes. Duag was not a desert man. He would try to retrace their route. He would certainly come past the spring.

Kwa's filed teeth gleamed. He would be waiting.

CHAPTER FIFTEEN

Raaschid donned his headpiece. There was no need to call the council to confirm his judgment. The elders would be of one mind. The mother was as guilty as the son.

Why then the uneasiness within him? The fight must have been over Zalah's slave girl. He had not missed Sa'ad's jealousy and impatience as Mi'kal and the girl walked away toward the place of the boulders. Sa'ad and Mi'kal must have met at the girl's tent and quarreled.

The girl had evidently struck Sa'ad from the front. But the wound in the back had killed him. It seemed unlikely that Mi'kal would strike a coward's blow.

Memory stirred. A few years before there had been an angry fight between the brothers over a pet ostrich. Mi'kal had screamed that someday he would kill Sa'ad. Raaschid knew hatred against brother could linger and grow, as it had with his own brother, Muktar.

But no matter who was at fault, Sa'ad's blood called from the ground. Raaschid straightened his shoulders and stepped from the tent. The slaves he had sent to fetch Quintira had accomplished their mission.

Quintira had known that by refusing to answer Raaschid's questions about Mi'kal and the girl she would be judged equally guilty. When Raaschid sent orders to appear on his porch, she dressed carefully, choosing a white robe. She took particular care with her hair. When it was arranged to her satisfaction, she covered it with a purple mantle.

So when Selim and Nufud came to get her, she was ready. They grasped her arms, but she shook off their hands and walked with her shoulders back. She had willed herself to numbness, but when the falcon beat its wings against the perch on Raaschid's pavilion, she trembled in spite of herself.

The camp had gathered. The women whispered. The men were serious and silent, the children wide-eyed.

Raaschid saw the purple headpiece and closed his eyes. He remembered a girl in a white shift tying a purple scarf about the arm of a dead boy. The vision filled him with anger and longing. He threw the longing from him as if it were a fouled blanket, but the anger remained.

With her silence Quintira had made herself an accessory to the murder of his son. As he had taken what was his by right of conquest that day, so must he do what was required of him now as leader of men.

The camp grew silent as Raaschid spoke. "I have found this woman guilty of aiding the flight of those who murdered my son. Therefore shall I sentence her."

A murmur, almost as quiet as sunlight, crossed the camp.

"She is to be taken a half-day's journey into the desert and left with no sandals and no cloak. She will be given one small skin of water."

The murmur gave birth to consternation. Quintira held her voice steady. "Will you do unto me as our father Abraham did unto your mother, Hagar? If God saved her, will he not also save me?"

A nerve jumped in Raaschid's cheek. "Uncover her head," he ordered. Nufud yanked the scarf from her hair.

"Thistles!" Gutne screamed. "Lace her hair with thistles! As the mother of the slain prince, I demand it."

No one moved. All eyes were on Raaschid. He glanced at Quintira. Her face was pale, but there was no sign of pleading.

"So be it," he said and turned his back.

Gutne ran forward tearing at the dark braid, pulling at the white wings over Quintira's ears. The children seemed reluctant to gather thistles from the fire brush until Gutne goaded them.

One by one the burrs were twisted into the dark locks. Quintira could not hold back her tears. She could hear her father saying, as he peeked though the thickness of her mother's hair, "Is she not beautiful?"

Selim and Nufud couched a camel for her and she mounted. The two slaves rode together on a second camel. They carried a small water-skin and a saddlebag that held stakes and rope.

As they left camp, Raaschid dropped his curtain and sank to his couch. If only she had begged. If only... He had hoped she would fall at his feet, but she had given him no reason to lighten the punishment.

Only once did Quintira look back at the camp. Her eyes lingered for a moment on the green of the oasis. Gutne's final scream reached her. "May you still be alive when the birds peck out your eyes."

As they passed the Old One's tent, she saw him and her eyes filled with pleading. His gaze followed her. Astarte brayed as if sharing their grief.

When the last of the tents were behind them, Quintira put her hand over her mouth. Already her tongue was dry. Terror threatened to overwhelm her. Phrases from David's song rose from her heart. "The Lord is my shepherd.... Even though I walk through the valley of the shadow of death, I will fear no evil, for you are with me."

Then from Job, the man who had suffered the loss of all things, she whispered the words of his marvelous faith. "Though he slay me, yet will I hope in him."

Distances in the desert were often deceptive, as Mi'kal knew. But even so, the ride across the plain to the ancient highway took longer than he expected.

So far he had seen no signs of pursuit, but Kwa would not come down upon them screaming like an eagle. Rather, he would come as an owl upon a scurrying mouse.

Even if he got Leyla to the Damascus highway, there was no guarantee she would be safe. The closer they came to the traveled thoroughfare, the more danger there might be for her. The Old One had told him of desert raiders who worked the roads, taking women and girls to be used or sold as slaves or harlots.

He was disturbed at the possibility of Leyla in the hands of evil men. Even if he got her safely back to Rekha, there was no assurance she would not be sold again to the wrong person.

Or perhaps she could be tempted by silver and gold. In some ways she seemed very young. The Old One had told him about such a girl. At some time, in some place, he had fallen in love. He had lost his love to a rich man. On the day the Old One told Mi'kal the story, he spoke as if in pain.

"I saw her again years later, ignored and abandoned. She wanted to come with me, but I had no place to take her. My habitation was wherever I spread my sleeping mat. I gave her what coins I had with me, but I could not give her more, for my love had long since died."

He was still thinking of the Old One when Leyla shouted. "Mi'kal, look! There's the road!"

As the stallion stepped from the gravel and sand onto the hardened surface of a roadway older than the Roman conquest, Mi'kal and Leyla burst into excited shouts. There was no doubt this was the road Quintillius had taken to reach the main highway. Feathers and droppings marked the path of the wagon like the wet track of a snail.

Mi'kal dismounted and lifted Leyla down. "I feel like kissing the ground," she said.

"I wouldn't advise it." He grinned and pointed; she had stepped in a pile of drying mule dung. "We will rest the stallion a little before we go on. I think we are very close to the big highway, so I want you to change clothes." His tone was brotherly.

"Why?"

"It will be better if you look like a boy." She was busy cleaning her sandals on a clump of grass. He handed her one of his plain tunics.

She didn't argue. She stepped to the other side of the stallion and changed. While she was out of sight, he untied the purple scarf from his waist. When she appeared, he nodded. The garment fell almost to her ankles. No one could tell she was a girl.

"They will think I have no legs."

"Good. Now cover your hair." He handed her the piece of scarf. "I want it back. Take care of it. If anyone asks, you are my brother Nari."

"Nari?"

"It's a good boy's name. We'll walk a little and stretch our legs."

He smiled as she walked beside him, the long tunic flapping at her heels. He kept the reins in his hand as El Gamar followed them, making happy snorting sounds.

"My mother would have a story for this," Mi'kal said. "She has one for everything. She told me about Abraham, who took his beautiful wife, Sarah, into Egypt. He was afraid the king would desire her and kill him, so Abraham told everyone that she was his sister, and they didn't kill him."

"Did Sarah fare as well?"

"I asked my mother the same thing. The king took Sarah into his own house, but he gave her back when he found out she was married. He scolded Abraham, and I have always thought the father of the Jews must have felt awfully foolish."

"I know the real reason the king didn't want her." She looked up at him with a grin. Even with her dirty face and her hair covered, she was beautiful.

"Why?"

"She wasn't a virgin." Her laughter bubbled as the flush rose on Mi'kal's cheeks. The purple turban bounced on her head.

How like the desert children she was, he thought. Children of the black tents delighted in any little piece of beauty: a rag of color, a tinkling bell, a bright feather.

Mi'kal remembered the day he stood on his father's pavilion with Raaschid's curved scabbard dragging about his knees. He was surrounded with a host of little friends who bowed and knelt and called him "Lord." Quintira scolded him for his arrogance, but Raaschid laughed and lifted him into his arms. As he thought of them, the worry that had lain like a sleeping dog at the back of his mind for hours woke and howled.

What was happening to his mother? Was she being punished for helping them escape? Would Raaschid, for love of her, forget the law of the desert, "an eye for an eye"? Even if he wanted to, could he, and still retain the respect of his men?

Selim and Nufud came back at midnight. They hobbled their camels and refreshed themselves before approaching Raaschid's sleeping quarters. He was waiting for them.

"Is it done?" His face remained in shadow, as if by design.

"It is done." They backed away. Outside, where the moon made the world a platter of silver, they looked at one another. They were not pleased with what they had done. But tying her down was better than letting her run in circles, going mad and tearing at her own flesh. And it was plain to see the deed was a mess of worms in their lord's belly.

Inside, Raaschid picked up the purple headpiece he had kicked aside during the judgment. Now it lay in his hands, soft and pliant under his fingers, as Quintira had never been.

Slowly he rose and held the cloth over the flame of the oil lamp. It flamed, and the tent filled with acrid smoke. He dropped the flaming headpiece to the stones of his hearth and stamped on it. Later, he gathered the ashes into his hands and let the rising wind whisk them away.

Quintira's quarters were dark. There was no light. There were no shadows. How often he had called for her at night when he saw her outlined against the curtains, her arms raised, brushing her hair. Never again.

He shut his mind to the vision of her. He must forget. What better way than to take another wife? A young one who could give him sons. A strong one physically, but with no beauty to inflame him.

Tomorrow he would begin to look at the eligible girls. Perhaps the one with the tambourine. She was strong and plain enough, and she was definitely willing. What was her name? Ne'ma. Ah, yes. The daughter of the concubine his brother had cast out.

Raaschid stretched. He was getting old. He had desired no more women after Quintira. "Curse her," he groaned softly.

The next problem would be to make peace with his brother and appease the fury of the disappointed Zalah. He would as soon bathe in boiling oil.

He dropped the curtain and stumbled to his bed.

Quintira's tent was not the only one empty that night. The Old One was gone, too.

In early afternoon he had begun to choose the things he would need. He straddled Astarte and rode about camp calling to all. "Firewood. Who needs firewood? I am going for firewood."

When he left camp in early evening, he was leading two pack animals—old racing camels that shuffled along in a slack, hang-kneed pace which could go on forever. The camels carried an ax and some ropes. Camel bags and water skins hung low under both bellies. In one bag he had placed his store of fancy belts. Lumpy pouches on Astarte's rump were too familiar to be noticed. Not even the dogs barked as he left.

The sun dropped, and the Old One was in open, sandy desert. The night was going to be cloudless. The early moon hung over the eastern edge of the horizon like a crock of creamless milk. The air was still, and he prayed that it would remain so. Following Selim and Nufud's trail would not be difficult if the wind did not rise. But he must be sure to stay out of sight when they passed him on their return to camp.

Many years before, an Arab from the Sahara had taught him to track. "Come, Prince," he would say. "Let us find ourselves a gazelle or a lion or an antelope." He smiled as he remembered. Not all of his young years had been bad.

But he also remembered the march through Rome under the triumphal arches. Sometimes, even yet, his ankles hurt with the weight of the shackles. Sometimes in the night he awakened to the sobs of his sister and his younger brother.

Now he would see how much he had learned on his many flights to freedom. Perhaps it would be wise to ask the help of the gods, especially Quintira's God, for he was reputed to be full of wisdom and mercy.

CHAPTER SIXTEEN

A lthough the journey with the livestock had been without incident, except for the tattered end of a sandstorm, Quintillius breathed easier when they reached the main Damascus road.

He and his companions had rested little during the night. They passed the black lava ridge before dawn. At midday they ate and rested in the shade of sandstone cliffs while the animals grazed.

The trip had been pleasant. The camel boy sang. And once in awhile, he jumped off and walked, his broad brown feet ignoring stones and creeping vines. He delighted in finding patches of special foliage for his camels. He called it *ghada*. The shrub had long, milk-white stems the camels munched with ecstatic groans and gruntings.

By afternoon they were all tired, and when the wagon wheels began to turn on the paved road, the boy shouted with joy. Quintillius relaxed.

He was pleased with the visit to the Bedouin camp. He had enjoyed the bargaining. There was much to remember: the magnificent woman with the yellow garment; her "Alexandrian" son; the audacious dance of the cross-eyed girl. He was forced to admire the Bedouin prince, although he was as much a scavenger as the jackal that flew on his banner.

Aurans broke into his reverie. "Sir, when we leave the garrison, what are your plans?"

"We'll go straightway to Capernaum. You've been assigned to the Antonia, and I'll sit on the porch of my villa and watch the fishing boats."

"Dolmicius will be happy to see you."

"And I him. It is not granted to many men, or women either, to have a very close friend of the same sex. A friendship and love that is pure."

Aurans nodded. He had spent little time in Rome, but he was already aware of the other kind of affection. Several times he had been forced to repulse comrades whose words or hands offended him.

Quintillius started to speak again, but he stopped abruptly and held up a hand. The wagon crunched to a halt behind him. Aurans watched as the centurion lifted his head and studied the pass ahead of them.

The road was hewn through a high ridge of soft, yellow sandstone. The walls of the cliffs reared high on either side and were covered with thick shrubs. Ditches on either side of the road were overgrown with thick grass and tall reeds.

Quintillius dropped his hand to his sword. Years of skirmishes had honed his sense of danger.

"What is it?" Aurans whispered.

"I'm not sure. Stay alert."

Behind them, the mule driver sensed the centurion's wariness and began his own perusal of the ditches. He looked up at the bushes on the face of the cliff. It was thick enough for men to hide behind, but he saw nothing. Nevertheless he braced his feet, ready to jump. The camel boy dropped to the ground, prepared to dive into the concealing grass.

Quintillius could feel an ominous silence, and then shrill yells reverberated against the cliff. A half-dozen armed men sprang from the bushes and the grass-filled ditches. The horses reared.

"Zealots!" Quintillius shouted. "Protect what is Caesar's."

The mule driver dove into the ditch, and the boy followed. Both disappeared as if they were sand grouse.

The mule bolted across the ditch and the wagon tipped. Squawking fowl ran free. Goats blatted, and the young camels bawled.

The fight was fierce for a few minutes. Aurans saw rather than felt the slash of the sword across his thigh. He saw Quintillius lay open the brains of one of the ambushers and then sway and fall with an arrow in his neck. He felt his own warm blood gushing as rough hands yanked him from his horse. A red haze rose to meet him.

Overhead, the carrion birds began to gather.

Mi'kal and Leyla, mounted on the rested horse, finally reached the Damascus highway. It stretched out on either side of them in undulating waves of ever-increasing heat. They turned east to follow the trail the wagon was leaving. The one milestone they had seen was unreadable, but both were confident that over each hill or around each encroaching cliff they would catch sight of the Romans. The waste from the animals was not completely dry on the road.

"You think we are safe now?" Leyla asked.

"We will be when we get to the tollhouse. I don't know if Damascus is east or west, but wherever it is, they'll help you get there."

"I won't have to sleep with any more crawly things?"

"No."

"You don't believe I heard crawly things, do you?"

"Sure, I do."

"You can be sure I won't be bothering you anymore after I get to Rekha."

"You weren't any bother."

Leyla's hand joined Mi'kal's on the reins. El Gamar lifted his hooves high and sniffed the wind.

"Remember, if we meet anyone except the Romans, you are a boy."

She leaned over his shoulder and pulled his head back. He turned his face and her lips landed on his nose. He growled, "If you want a kiss, I'll give you a kiss." He turned his head until they were facing one another and then he kissed her. They pulled back, stared at one another in wonder, and then kissed again.

El Gamar turned toward them, his ears flicking. Then he lifted his head and snorted.

Leyla pulled back from Mi'kal and leaned sideways peering ahead. "Mi'kal, I heard something."

"Probably my heart."

"Be serious. Listen."

When the thumping in his chest settled down, he heard the distant clash of iron against iron, shouts of anger, and sounds of bedlam from chickens and camels, wild fowl and men. He pulled El Gamar to a halt. The sounds terrified him. They meant only one thing. Ambush!

Slowly the dreadful noise faded. Leyla had her hands over her mouth, and her eyes were tragic. The stallion moved forward snorting and prancing, smelling blood before Mi'kal saw the carnage.

The wagon was tipped halfway into the ditch. Broken crates littered the roadway. The two Romans sprawled motionless among the debris. Blood lay in drying puddles. Vultures were landing, and he screamed at them. They rose in a dark cloud of wings.

He told Leyla to cover her eyes, but she saw and went white.

Mi'kal knelt by the dead centurion. The blood had quit flowing. He turned to Aurans and saw a flicker of life. He yelled at Leyla. "Give me something to staunch the blood."

Leyla lifted her tunic and tore at her shift. Mi'kal grabbed a handful of a weed growing by the wagon. The weed had sharp leaves and reddish flowers. He crushed the leaves and the flowers between stones and handed the pulp to Leyla.

"It's a healing plant," he said. "My mother used it. Tie it on the wound."

Leyla did as he ordered. He brought two slats from the chicken crates, and she tied them over the poultice with more strips from her shift.

"Mi'kal, he needs a doctor. Could we get him to the garrison? They usually have a doctor."

Mi'kal examined the wagon. The axles and wheels were intact. He used a broken plank for leverage, and finally the wagon was out of the ditch and upright on the road. They piled El Gamar's gear into it and laid out the blankets and the mats for the men. They lifted Quintillius and covered him. They tried to keep Aurans's wound from bleeding as they laid his head and shoulders against the saddle.

The stallion shied and grew stubborn as Mi'kal attempted to back him between the wagon shafts. In frustration, Mi'kal struck him with a stick. The stallion reared, pawed the air, and vaulted across the ditch. He disappeared in a flash of flying hooves behind the hummocks. Mi'kal felt as if he had been kicked in the stomach.

"Did you think he was going to work like a common mule?" Leyla asked quietly from the bed of the wagon. She was trying to loosen her skirt from a splintered floorboard.

"Could you have done any better?" He was instantly sorry for his angry response, but Leyla was not listening. She was staring over his head while still struggling with the tunic. "Look!"

A camel rider crested another of the hummocks and careened toward them. A tan cloak streamed behind him.

"It's Duag! Get out of there! Hide in the bushes!"

From the top of the rocky rise, Duag had not been sure the smaller figure standing on the wagon bed was the girl until he heard Mi'kal yelling. Then he headed straight for the wagon. The camel cleared the sand and gravel and reached the highway.

Mi'kal grabbed up a heavy wooden slat and threw it. The slat hit Maha's rump. She slowed slightly and squalled. He grabbed at the bridle, but Duag knocked him down with his foot.

Leyla pulled loose with a ripping jerk from the broken board and was poised to jump when Duag reached the wagon. He leaned to the side and swept her up. She screamed and struggled as he hauled her face down across the camel's shoulders. Her legs kicked at the wind, and she screamed as Duag turned back into the desert. Her frantic cries, "Mi'kal! Mi'kal!" continued until she was out of sight behind the covering hillocks.

Mi'kal beat his hands against the side of the wagon in frustration and grief. The sting of failure burned in his eyes and throat.

CHAPTER SEVENTEEN

From a barrier of tangled shrubs, halfway up the cliff, the red-headed girl had seen the robbery and murder. She had not been able to warn the approaching wagon train without putting herself in jeopardy. An arrow could pick her off the shelf, and men who robbed and murdered were known to rape.

By the time the thieves gathered up everything, including swords and helmets from the Romans, she caught sight of the boys on the white horse. A fair distance behind them she saw the camel rider with his cloak blowing like a leaf in the wind.

She wondered if the boys were being pursued and were unaware of their approaching enemy.

Because of her apprehension, she stayed hidden as the two of them struggled with the wagon. She had not realized one of them was a girl until she heard him call her name, and her high screams for "Mi'kal!"

The watcher on the cliff grabbed her backpack and started down as the camel disappeared with the screaming girl and the boy collapsed by the wagon in despair. The pack was cumbersome among the bushes, but she never went without it. Wrapped with the mat were her blanket, a spoon and small copper pot, a shovel, and a flint for fire.

In addition, she carried a bronze-handled knife in the Roman belt that bound her waist over a leather vest. Her garment was heavy brown hop cloth. The skirt was usually pulled up between her legs and tucked into the belt.

She came upon the boy quietly, for she had learned to walk as the young lions walk. Mi'kal jumped when she touched him.

"I've come to help," she said swiftly as his hand moved to his knife. "I saw everything from up there." She pointed to the cliff.

121

Mi'kal stared at her. The hair was a mop of uncombed red. Her cheeks were broad and her mouth wide.

She suffered his appraisal and then snapped, "When you've finished gaping, we'll try to get these men to the garrison."

"I'm sorry. How far is it?"

"Less than the distance between two mile posts. You pull. I'll push."

Mi'kal stepped between the shafts, and the wagon began to move. The shafts were rough. He knew it wouldn't be long before his hands blistered.

"Who was the girl? Your sister?"

"No."

"Why did that man take her?"

"He was from my Bedouin camp. He was sent to bring her back. They think she killed my half-brother. He was trying to rape her, and she used her scissors."

"Good for her. I suppose she was beautiful?"

"Yes."

"Are you in love with her?"

Only the squeaking wheels broke the silence. Then she said, "I'm never going to fall in love."

"Why not? I thought every girl wanted to fall in love."

"Not me. Your happiness always depends on someone else. I'm never going to be dependent on anybody." The words were emphasized by a hard shove. The shafts lurched in Mi'kal's hands. He heard a groan from the wagon.

"How's Aurans doing?" he asked.

"Still bleeding some. You know him?" She sounded surprised.

Mi'kal told her briefly of the Romans' visit to the camp.

"You mean you're the son of a desert chief?"

"Yes and no," Mi'kal replied. "I mean he's my stepfather. He killed my father and kidnapped my mother."

"That's terrible. Was your father handsome like you?"

"My mother says I look like him."

"I don't look like anyone in my family. My sister is pretty. By the way, my name is Zeus."

"That's a boy's name."

"So what?" The girl stopped pushing. "Let's rest for a minute. I'm winded."

Mi'kal was glad to oblige. His muscles were cramping and his hands were getting sore. Zeus went on talking. "My mother named me something awful, so I prefer Zeus."

"I'm Mi'kal."

"I know. I heard the girl calling for you. I thought she was a boy at first."

"I tried to make her look like one for her own protection."

They fell into silence. Mi'kal took up the shafts again, and Zeus resumed her pushing. Sandals slipped on the cobblestones. Perspiration dripped from their chins.

Zeus was thinking she must remember to tell Captain Gaius at the garrison that it was not Zealots who ambushed the wagon. She was friends with many of the hill rebels. They were blamed for many things they never did and were not suspected of a lot they did do.

"You want to rest again?" Mi'kal called.

"No, we'd better keep going. I'm fine."

Indeed she was. She was congratulating herself. She hadn't expected much when the day started, but look what had happened! She had seen an ambush; she was helping save a wounded man; and she had also met a curly haired hero. Valiant men were heroes, even if they failed.

She had seen a kidnapping, too, and heard of the attempted rape and murder. The girl must be beautiful. Mi'kal's mother must be beautiful, too, if two men fought over her.

Yes, this was surely one of her very best days.

Kwa's belly was rolling with hunger. The camel's milk failed to satisfy him. Now he searched for an ostrich nest. He had seen fresh two-toed prints and droppings. Finally, he found three eggs in a shallow nest of stones and sand, with one egg left outside to serve as food for the newborn chicks.

Kwa poked a hole in the end of one egg and began to suck, keeping watch for the adult birds. He had no desire to be attacked by an angry parent. He had seen both dogs and horses disemboweled with one kick of an ostrich's powerful claw.

Although his stomach threatened to rebel, he drained the egg. Then he started back to the spring. He stood for a moment on a pinnacle overlooking the plain. The sun gleamed on his chest. The initiation marks stood out like an inscription on a black obelisk. An elixir of joy stirred within him, and he lifted his arms to the breeze that stirred the stubbly grasses in the valley. He was free!

He had been left to die, but the egg and the spring would save him. He would wait under the bluff where the waters came secretly from the underside of the ridge that hung like heavy eyebrows on the face of the cliff. He would bathe and eat wild onions and grapes and wait. Duag would die. He and the children would go free.

He began a slow bounce from one bowed leg to the other. A long forgotten chant rose to his lips. The chanting and the dancing prepared his people for the lion hunt.

His chanting complete, Kwa began to descend the hill, jumping from boulder to boulder. The wine of freedom bubbled within him. The sun was hot, but the anticipation of his revenge was as a shade of palm leaves over him.

Leyla rode belly down across Duag's legs. He had spread part of his cloak to protect her from the sun, but the sun was now declining. At last, because every muscle of her body ached, she promised to behave if he allowed her to sit behind him.

She found a position that was fairly comfortable. She leaned and put her head against his back and braced her knees into the hip bones of the camel.

They halted briefly to drink. Duag drew milk for her from Maha's udder, but she refused to drink from his hand. She knelt and caught the squirting stream in her mouth.

They mounted and rode again. She was never sure how long they traveled. Her throat cried out for water, and she poked Duag in the back and complained.

"We will have water before long."

He sounded sure of himself, and she wondered where he would find it. She and Mi'kal had found none except in the muddy pool at the wadi. But then they had not come this way, where the line of black cliffs straggled in what seemed an endless caravan across the rounded hills.

Leyla closed her eyes and tried to forget her thirst and her fear. What would happen to her when Duag dropped her at Raaschid's tent? Maybe none of it had happened. Maybe she was dreaming. Maybe Duag wasn't real. Maybe Kwa... What about Kwa? Where was he? Once she asked. Duag shrugged and said nothing. When she asked again, he muttered something about "disloyalty."

Leyla finally realized the sun was gone. Lingering light showed on the golden strata of the lava cliff. Duag was trying to make the tired camel run. He spoke of a spring under an outcropping of sandstone where vines grew from the face of the cliff like curtains in a tent. They would stay there until dawn. He wouldn't tie her down if she promised not to run.

Mist began to creep about them. "We are almost there," Duag said. Maha lifted her long neck and bellowed. They dismounted in the deepening shadows. Leyla was almost too stiff and sore to walk.

Duag was stiff, too. Together they moved slowly toward the sound of running water. No light remained at the spring; the moon had not yet cleared the cliff. An owl hooted in a tree whose roots were anchored in the wall, halfway up the precipice. Frogs croaked around the pool. A bird swooped low and uttered a sharp protest.

Leyla could see the iridescent sheen as the water splashed into the pool below. She knelt and reached her hands to the small stream. Water ran down her arms and off her elbows. How good it felt. She began to bathe her face.

Duag, too, stooped a little beyond her. She was spared the sight of his death. All she heard was a sharp gasp and a crack, as if a dried branch had broken.

She looked up and screamed. A large shadow loomed. It dropped the limp Duag to the ground. His head was strangely twisted. Legs and arms jerked. Leyla had seen chickens die like that. She screamed again as the shadow came toward her. She struggled to rise, but fell backward into the shallow water. A black hand reached out to lift her. She pushed it away. "No! No! Don't hurt me!"

The fingers gripped hers and brought her to her feet. She looked into Kwa's face. Something about the grasp of his hand told her she had nothing to fear. Later, as he shared wild onions and grapes and a tuber he had dug and peeled, Kwa told her how Duag had betrayed him and left him to die.

"Did you have to kill him?"

"I have thought about killing him for years. Now I have to decide what to do with you because I am not going back."

"You could help me find Mi'kal." She told him then about the ambush and the death of Quintillius. "I don't know where Mi'kal is right now, but I do know he is going into Galilee to find a man called Jesus."

"I cannot spend time looking for anyone. Is there somewhere I can leave you this side of Jordan?"

"Damascus. I belonged to an entertainment troupe there. Rekha, the owner, will take me back. I was never intended to be a slave. Sa'ad promised that I would be as the bride's sister. A companion, never a slave."

Kwa nodded. "I will be no man's slave from henceforth." He rose to his feet. "We will sleep here. I will take him out of the way."

Leyla closed her eyes, but she could hear the body being moved. She hugged her knees and thought of Mi'kal. Someday he would love her, for she intended to ask every god she could think of to bring them back together.

Later, she listened to the night sounds. She heard snarling and knew that hyenas or jackals were tearing at Duag's body.

She shivered and called to Kwa. He awoke instantly. "I am here. If you wish, I will build a fire."

She watched his silhouette against the flames and felt contentment. "Kwa, have you ever loved a woman?" She had no idea why she asked, but her thoughts of Mi'kal were wrapping her like a blanket.

His voice was hoarse. "Not for many years."

Something in his voice told her to ask no more questions.

CHAPTER EIGHTEEN

One of the sentries posted at the tollgate was the first to see the camp wagon. He squinted and then yelled for the man in the custom house.

"Quartus, get out here. Something has happened. The redhead is bringing in the centurion's wagon."

"Ambush," they muttered as they ran. One looked into the wagon and swore. "By the gods, it's the captain and the lieutenant." They laid their hands to the cart. Both were shouting for the physician.

Mi'kal and Zeus dropped back as they cleared the gate of the garrison. They were breathing hard and their faces were streaked with dust.

"They knew you, didn't they?" Mi'kal said.

"Everybody knows me." Her eyes were laughing at him. He could not decide if they were blue or gray.

A young officer came running, fastening the sides of his linked breastplate as he ran. An older man came behind him. Zeus introduced them as Gaius, the commander of the garrison, and Beldu the physician.

Inside the court, Zeus and Mi'kal dropped to a bench. He watched as a brown bird with a speckled breast came down to sit on her knee. She stroked its neck and held it out to him, but when he reached for it, the bird lifted in a short flight.

Gaius stood in the doorway, shaking his head. "Our surgeon is not sure he can save the lieutenant. He has lost much blood. The doctor says he would have been dead by now had it not been for your tight poultice." He pressed his heavy boot against the opposite door jamb. "Curse the Zealots. Curse them!"

Zeus stopped him. "They weren't Zealots. Just ordinary brigands."

"How do you know?"

"I saw everything. There were no yells of 'For Israel and the temple!'" She began to tell Gaius about her day. Mi'kal tried to stop her when she spoke of him and Leyla, but she went on. "He wants to try to rescue her, so you must let him have a horse and saddle."

"You can have anything you need," Gaius said, turning to Mi'kal. "But first, both of you should eat. In the meantime I will send a courier to warn several small companies of my men about brigands. They will be returning from field practice on that road."

Mi'kal watched as the courier rode out of the gate. He was on a pitiful mount and dressed to match. Gaius explained.

"On these highways, the more a man's horse looks like vulture bait the better. One person often goes unnoticed, but several seem to indicate that there is something to protect."

After the courier left, Mi'kal and Leyla ate. The men had already had their supper. There was a bowl of mutton and gravy, a pitcher of diluted wine that was not much better than Aurans had described it, and a loaf of dark bread. A small boy brought in a bowl of onions and radishes, bragging he had raised them himself.

Mi'kal watched Zeus eat. She used both hands. Large chunks of bread wiped up the gravy. She chomped happily on the vegetables. But even though she ate lustily, she seemed to savor each bite, as if it would have to suffice for a long time. Now and then she dropped an onion or a radish into her copper pot which sat beside her.

She saw him watching and she grinned. "They will never miss it."

"But wouldn't they give you anything you want?"

"It's more fun this way."

"I don't understand you."

Zeus smiled, and then she grew serious. "That reminds me. There is someone I don't understand. Have you ever heard of Jesus of Nazareth?"

Mi'kal laid his knife aside and forgot the honey for his bread. He stared at her. "Do you know him?"

"Yes. I've seen him lots of times."

"Do you know where I can find him?" He could feel the increase in his pulse.

"I'm not sure where he is now. But he spends a lot of time in a village called Ephraim. It's a safe distance from Jerusalem where the priests want to arrest him."

"Arrest him? Why?"

"They are jealous. The people pay more attention to him than they do to the priests. He says he can forgive sins just for the asking, but the priests want everyone to buy pigeons and lambs to sacrifice."

"Have you ever heard that he can raise people from the dead?" Mi'kal realized he was holding his breath.

"Yes. I saw him do it once. A boy."

Mi'kal dropped his knife. "You saw him?"

She grinned as the jewel flecks ignited in his eyes. "I saw the whole thing."

"Tell me about it. Aurans told me Jesus raised a little girl from the dead in Capernaum, but he didn't see him do it."

"We were in Nain, a city near the great plain of Jezreel. The funeral was at night. The torches were lit, and they were on the way to the cemetery."

"Did he do anything strange? Say anything? You know, like magicians do?"

"No. He just told the boy's mother—his name was Nathan—if she really believed he could do a miracle, he would. She said she believed. Then he took the napkin off Nathan's face and said, 'Rise, Nathan.' And Nathan sat up. The whole city had a party, all night long."

"That's all? He didn't say or do anything that made him sound—you know—like a god?"

"You mean shaking the mountains or making the stars fall?" Her gray eyes were laughing at him. Then they sobered. "He doesn't have to sound like a god. He says he is God."

"Are you sure he didn't say a god? From what Aurans told me about him, I think he might be the Phoenix come to life."

"The Phoenix?" Zeus stood up. She was angry. "That's the worst thing anybody ever said about him! He isn't a silly bird."

"An old friend of mine in the camp told me the gods often came down from Mount Olympus in human form. So why couldn't the Phoenix?"

"Jesus didn't come from Olympus! He came from heaven. He says so!" Zeus dumped the rest of the radishes into the pot with a clatter that matched her angry disgust.

Outside, a drum sounded. The argument was forgotten. The men were moving slowly past the wagon where Quintillius lay covered with a Roman banner. There was never any delay in burying the dead. The soldiers were not in full armor, but each man held his sword before his face as he stood for a moment at attention before the body.

Mi'kal felt a surge of the old anger. Death had won again. Surely this was not the way God wanted it to be. If Jesus came from God, perhaps he could explain it.

Maybe he should give up his stupid attempt to rescue Leyla and go on to Galilee.

Gaius was speaking to him. "Everything is ready, but it might be best to wait until morning. We gave you another saddle. Yours was badly stained with blood."

The small boy brought the horse. Gaius fastened an army belt and a sword about Mi'kal, in spite of the boy's protests. Men gathered about as Mi'kal mounted. One shouted a good-natured jest. "Take care, Perseus. Your Andromeda is waiting for you."

Mi'kal smiled, glad that the Old One had told him the story of the lovely girl tied to the rock to be devoured by a sea monster—unless she was rescued by the heroic Perseus.

As he left the fort, no one could have felt less heroic. Zeus followed him to the gate. Her hair was still uncombed, but her face was clean. Her eyes were really gray.

She put a hand on his foot. "Do you think we will ever meet again?"

"I hope so."

"Maybe I'll see you in Galilee."

"I'll watch for you."

"I live in a little village called Papyron, near Jericho. Right on the river."

"I'll remember."

"If you find Jesus, tell him I send greetings."

"Will he remember you?"

She grinned. "Everyone remembers me."

His eyes held hers. "I surely will."

Zeus's hand slapped the horse's rump. As it broke into a canter, the sunset sky changed from pink to apricot, then flared into red. Mi'kal's gloomy thoughts shut out the beauty. What hope had he of catching up with Duag? Even if he did, how did he intend to outwit him?

He was riding through a phalanx of colors when a small line of Roman infantry passed him. The men staggered from weariness. One man brushed against him, and Mi'kal moved his foot in an unconscious effort to get rid of the weight. The man, tired and surly, interpreted the action as belligerence and grabbed at Mi'kal's saddle.

Mi'kal tried to move on, but the soldier held to his leg and yelled. "Captain, this fellow has a garrison horse."

The officer turned his mount and came back. "Come on, Annius, get back in line."

"I tell you, this fellow has our property."

Mi'kal shook his head. "Captain Gaius at the garrison loaned me this horse."

Annius shook a fist. "An accursed Zealot! That's what he is. Probably one of them that ambushed the wagon. Remember what the courier said."

"I'm not a Zealot!" Mi'kal's voice rose. "I haven't stolen anything. And I'm in a hurry."

The captain looked more closely at the saddle.

"Get down," he ordered.

Mi'kal shook his head.

"Look," another man yelled. "He has one of our swords, too."

"Why the thieving little—"

Mi'kal would have given them the sword, but the order to dismount and the expletive made him angry. His heels dug into the mare. He tried to swing wide. A soldier grabbed for him, but Mi'kal kicked him off. Another just missed snagging the bridle.

The mounted soldier swerved his horse into Mi'kal's and threw himself against Mi'kal's back. They rolled to the ground. Mi'kal tried to get up, but a gauntleted fist hit him.

Boots smashed into his ribs. He covered his head with his hands and tried to crawl away. The boots kept coming. He screamed in pain and rolled head first into the ditch. He tried to keep his eyes open, but the pain pressed down. The rays of the setting sun faded as his eyes closed.

While the sun was fading on Mi'kal in the ditch, Quintira was working desperately at the thongs about her wrists and ankles. No amount of effort could loosen the stakes to which she was spread-eagled. Selim and Nufud had gone one step further than Raaschid had ordered. A touch of mercy. Death would be less painful this way than dementia in the desert as she wandered, blinded by the sun.

Darkness always came suddenly in the desert, and already a paralyzing cold wind was blowing. She tried to remember the warm times. Her mother's lap. Her father's arms. "Uncle" Jacob's house with its glowing braziers. "Aunt" Huldah's kitchen with the smell of baking bread. The water at the pool, with Myndus holding her tight.

Still, the cold made her teeth chatter. A jackal snarled, and she closed her mind against the horrors she could imagine. She would prefer carnivores to the carrion birds. The birds almost always started with the eyes.

Quintira felt the sand stirring about her, and she thought of snakes seeking her warmth for the night. She bit her lips and repeated fragments of impassioned pleas. David in dire distress. "O Lord, do not forsake me; be not far from me, O my God. Come quickly to help me, O Lord my Savior."

The whispering sands became an army of creeping scorpions. Above her, strange, gray mists swirled. She began to think of them as angels. "The angel of the Lord encamps around those who fear him, and he delivers them."

Quintira had no idea how long she lay, hopelessly resigned to her fate. The stars faded under the tears in her eyes She was stiff from cold. A shadow moved above her. She saw the glint of a knife and screamed. The angel of mercy had changed into the angel of death.

CHAPTER NINETEEN

A s Mi'kal returned to full consciousness, he realized he was riding belly-down on the rump of a mule. Where was he? He lifted his head to ask.

The rider in the saddle quit whistling and yanked on the reins. "Hold up, Moses." The voice was pleasantly deep.

Mi'kal slid off as the mule came to a jolting halt. The world spun for a few seconds and then settled down.

"You all right?" his companion asked as he dismounted.

Mi'kal nodded. "I think so." His ribs ached and his arms felt numb, but he was safe from hobnailed boots. "Where are we?" He looked around in confusion. "Who are you?"

"Call me Oreb. It's not my real name, but it'll do."

Brown eyes twinkled at Mi'kal, but something in their depths warned him that this man should not be taken lightly. Black locks stuck out from under a leather helmet old enough to have been left by Antony's army. A heavy Roman sword swung low on narrow hips. Somehow the outfit was ridiculous, but Mi'kal did not laugh.

"I'm Mi'kal. How long have I been riding with you?"

"Since yesterday evening when we found you spraddled over a ditch. What happened?"

"I was jumped by foot soldiers who thought I was a thief."

"Are you?"

"No! Have I been unconscious all this time?"

"You were at first, and then you fell asleep. You must have been tired out."

"I was." He paused. "It's a long story." As Mi'kal moved about easing

133

the cramps in his arms and legs, he explained as much as he thought necessary. "As you can see, I failed in everything."

"Not everything." The deep voice was reassuring. "You mentioned your desire to get to Galilee. That's where we're headed. Not exactly as the crow flies, but we'll get there. Sometimes it takes a pillar of fire to keep Moses moving."

"Is that why you call him Moses?" Mi'kal found himself grinning as his hand rubbed at his itching whiskers.

"That, and the fact that all he hears from me is 'mutterings and murmurings.'"

Mi'kal laughed. He said his mother thought only the cooks had a right to complain about the lack of onions and cucumbers, leeks and garlic on the flight from Egypt. His friend chuckled.

"And only those who like to walk should swear at a balky mule, eh Moses?" He brushed his hand over one of the mule's long ears.

The two of them mounted again, and the mule plodded onward. The shape of the land changed. Valleys cut deeper, and green embroidered the shoulders of the hills. Vineyards and olive groves laced the slopes of the hills one to another.

Oreb did not mind going through most of the scattered villages, but he avoided other places, especially the Roman stations or tollposts. Seeing one in the distance, he would turn Moses into the fields or up a creek bed or old trail.

Mi'kal noticed something else too. Oreb never missed a thing. The slightest movement of grass or tree caught his attention. He was constantly alert, and Mi'kal began to wonder why.

Once, as they passed a plowed field lying fallow, Oreb dismounted. "Let Moses graze. I am going to find us some food." He bounded away and came back with a handful of quail eggs.

After they sucked the eggs, Oreb asked, "You have some particular reason for coming to Galilee?"

"Yes. I'm looking for a man called Jesus."

"So are a lot of people. Especially the authorities in Jerusalem. Why do you want him?"

"You'll laugh at me."

"No, I won't."

"I think he knows the secret of living forever." Mi'kal felt the red coming into his cheeks. The idea was beginning to sound stupid.

"And you want to live forever?" Oreb crushed the last of his eggshells and dropped the pieces beside the tree where they were sitting.

"Don't you?"

"I don't think about the future. I'm busy keeping myself alive day by day."

Mi'kal looked at him. The eyes were sober and secrets seemed to be moving in their depths. He felt compelled to go on.

"My mother says our souls live forever, whether in Hades or Paradise, depending upon whether we have pleased or displeased God. But I want to live as I have always lived right here. Walking and talking and—"

"I suppose she has taught you the commandments of Moses?"

"Of course."

Oreb spoke slowly, his eyes closed. "If killing sends a man to hell, Mi'kal, I'm doomed."

"I don't think I could ever kill, but there are other ways to displease God."

"Killing gets easier as it goes along," Oreb said. "No man is immune. Let him love enough, hate enough, fear enough, and he can kill."

"No." Mi'kal shook his head. "I don't think I could." He thought of Duag. "Not unless I was protecting somebody."

Oreb sat up, his eyes resting steady on Mi'kal's face, but a twinkle beginning. "You are an uncommonly handsome boy. What if some Roman noble took you for use as he would a woman?"

"That's a stupid question!" Mi'kal could feel the heat in his cheeks.

Oreb persisted in painting the picture. "He would curl your hair and put perfume on you and give you silken loin cloths."

Mi'kal grinned suddenly and the tension went. "I have always worn silken *futahs*."

"Good. I will pass the word." They laughed together and mounted.

Sunset came with streams of color that ran from horizon to horizon.

135

Mi'kal and Oreb slept on a pile of barley chaff near a threshing floor and woke to a dawn of the same colors, as if there had been no night.

Workers came into the fields, and Oreb was not above asking for a portion of their bread and cheese. A few of the men seemed to know him. Mi'kal stood aside as they conversed secretly. He caught snatches of their conversation.

"Plowshares made into swords…" "Hoes sharp as chopping axes…" . Something about their voices and their gestures made him wonder if they were part of a secret brotherhood. Was Oreb a rebel? Were these men helpers, as his grandfather, Ithamar, had been? Mi'kal wanted to know, but he was reluctant to ask. Perhaps it was better for him not to know.

By noon they were entering a marsh. Cool air rose from the swamp grass. The uneven roadway was a mixture of unpeeled logs, stones, and piled dirt. Plumes of grass waved over their heads. Herons with arrogant strides moved stiffly through the papyrus. Beetles raced across small dark ponds, leaving sparkling wakes. Oreb explained that they were going through part of the swamps surrounding Lake Huleh, the first of three lakes. To the south there were two others, the Sea of Galilee and the Salt Sea.

"We must thank God for every mud hole. If it were not for the springs that make the marsh, there would be no Jordan River. The snows from Hermon provide water for the springs. Without the snows and the river there would probably be no Galilee."

Mi'kal was fascinated with the life of the swamp: butterflies and iridescent insects; birds of all colors; turtles and water snakes.

The first time he noticed a swimming snake, the memory came, terrifying and sickening. He saw again the glare of the viper's eyes and the smell of the glutinous remains.

A large golden butterfly with "eyes" of bright blue on each quivering wing poised for a moment on the very tip of the mule's ear. The ear twitched; the butterfly rose in time to be caught by a swooping shrike and carried away to be impaled on a thorn for later feasting. Mi'kal shivered.

As they climbed out of the marsh, the air became brisk and smelled of warm grasses, ripening fruits, full blossoms, and harvested fields.

At the top of the rise, Oreb guided Moses toward the edge of a precipice overlooking a wide valley. He pulled on the rein, but Moses kept on plodding. Oreb yanked and yelled, "Stop, you son of Satan! Stop!"

The gray ears twitched, but the legs went on. Mi'kal was sure all three of them would catapult down the slope. He rolled off and Oreb followed him.

Oreb leaped up cursing. His invectives were enough to ignite the dry grass. Moses stood with his front legs braced on the very edge of the drop-off. He lifted his long nose. His lips curled in a grin as he turned his head and glared at Oreb with one bulbous eye.

Oreb shook his fist. "You brother of Beelzebub! You had no intention of killing yourself."

Mi'kal wrapped his arms about his knees and laughed. Oreb growled and dragged him to his feet. "Come. Look." Below them Mi'kal saw the green and gold of grass and grain. Tiny flat-topped, whitewashed houses rimmed the fields. Pomegranate and almond trees flourished. Date palms swayed. Women and children moved about the courtyards. Men worked in the gardens.

"There!" Oreb pointed. "There is an edge of your Galilee. Breathe deep. Close your eyes and taste the winds. Are they not sweeter than a woman's lips."

Mi'kal pulled away. Oreb threw up his hands. "Don't tell me you have never held a girl tight enough to grow dizzy with her perfumes?"

"It's none of your business if I have or not."

"All right. You know something? I talk a lot about things I don't know much about."

Mi'kal looked doubtful.

"No, by all that's holy, I speak the truth. I know no more about women than you do. I have spent my youth with other things."

Mi'kal looked at him. Oreb was shorter than he, but much wider of shoulder and heavier with muscle. He might look young when he was shaved, but with the growth of beard he seemed much older than Mi'kal. But even with his uneven beard and his ridiculous helmet and drooping sword, Mi'kal was sure any woman would find Oreb attractive.

Oreb walked to the edge of the slope and lifted his arms to the breeze. Mi'kal followed him. His gaze went beyond the valley. Far away, among the hills, he thought he caught the sheen of water.

This was Galilee! The land his mother loved. Someday, if Raaschid had spared her, he would bring her here.

Clouds passed overhead, making shadows on the valley floor. Mi'kal looked up. Some of them might have floated over the black tents. He flinched with worry and longing for his mother.

As Oreb and he stood together on the bluff, an eagle soared. Below, the narrow road curved behind a hill. Two Romans rode abreast, past the houses and the gardens.

Oreb gripped Mi'kal's elbow.

"Breathe again, friend. Smell the stench of Rome!"

The soldiers disappeared. Oreb lifted his sword and held the blade high with both hands. His cry went out as shrill as the scream of the eagle.

"For Israel and the temple!" He brandished the sword. Sun glinted on it. Men in the fields below lifted their rakes and hoes. Mi'kal heard the answering cries. "For our God and his kingdom."

A quick jubilation swept through him. He raised his arms and shouted, "For Galilee!"

Oreb replaced his sword and gripped Mi'kal about the waist. They whirled. Below them the men continued to shout defiance. Above them the eagle shrilled his own cry of freedom.

"Do you think we will ever be free again?" Mi'kal asked.

Oreb's reply held the determination of countless generations of Jacob's people. "We will never give up."

As they left the bluff, Mi'kal knew he had grown older. Inside, in some way, the ground of his soul had been plowed and seeded. He also knew he had no need to ask his question. Oreb was indeed a Zealot.

CHAPTER TWENTY

M i'kal sat with his arms wrapped about his knees, feeling out of control. What was he doing in a cave full of Zealots listening to a wild-eyed man declaring it was time for a Messianic revolution?

Why had he allowed Oreb to persuade him to stop at the Hornet's Nest? Was it because he was afraid to search for Jesus on his own? Or was he reluctant to leave his whistling friend?

After they left the bluff where they had both cried their defiance to Rome, Oreb made no secret of the fact he was a Zealot. He gave Mi'kal a short history of the national fighters who would never let Rome rest.

He told of Ezekias, reputed to be the founder of the resistance army of Palestine during the reign of Julius Caesar. Ezekias began with a group of men who plundered the Roman ports on the Phoenician coast. Herod the Great of Palestine, working for Caesar and Marc Antony of Rome, subdued him. Ezekias and hundreds of his rebels died.

Rome was pleased with Herod, who was a young man, and Marc Antony persuaded the Roman Senate to make his friend ruler over Palestine. He was given the title of king, but his authority was limited to what Rome wanted. When he died, one of his sons, Archelaus, was given the title of ethnarch and command over one-half of Herod's kingdom. The other half was divided between his other sons, Antipas and Philip.

Judas of Galilee, a son of Ezekias, renewed the struggle for freedom during the reign of Archelaus. With the help of a Syrian commander, Archelaus destroyed Judas and hundreds of his followers. Three thousand rebels were hung on crosses along the Galilean roads.

But Archelaus's reprehensible actions caused him to fall into disfavor in Rome, and his brother, Antipas, was given rule over a portion of his kingdom: Galilee and Perea. He was given the title of tetrarch.

Philip, his brother, ruled over several small provinces at the foot of the Lebanon mountains. These provinces included Batanea, Trachonitis, and Gaulanitis, and together were called Iturea.

Judea and Samaria were put under a non-Herod procurator, Pontius Pilate.

"Judas of Galilee had three sons," Oreb said. "One of them was my father. All of them saw my grandfather crucified. They pledged themselves to die for Israel. They have."

Mi'kal stared at him. No wonder the brown eyes carried painful memories.

"Some of the other men you will meet in our cave are the second and third generation of rebels. Grandfathers and fathers have paid with their lives for defying Rome."

"But what will the men say about me? I am not a Zealot."

"Someday you will be."

"No." His rebuttal was quick and definite.

"If you love Galilee enough."

"I could not kill. Not even for Galilee."

"All Zealots are not fighters. They help in other ways."

Mi'kal thought again of his grandparents, Hiram and Deborah, who had died because they helped. And the farmers who were helping the Zealots now were probably equally doomed.

Oreb began to explain. "I was on a mission for Neophron when I found you in the ditch. A friend had sent word that there was a large shipment of freight in a warehouse at Palmyra, to be brought to the enemy at Caesarea. I went to the warehouses to check the manifests. Now we know which caravans to stop and which to let go on. We have many such friends who keep us informed."

"But how do you get in to see the records?"

"Coming out is the hard part. Sometimes I get stopped. Then I pretend to be witless."

"You?"

"I posture and slobber and grin like a witless child. They find me laughable but not dangerous."

"But someday it might not work."

Oreb shrugged. "If it was good enough for David at Gath, it's good enough for me."

Then Oreb told Mi'kal of the time he had been given the old helmet.

"They caught me in the armory, and I began to make faces and drool. I postured with the helmets and swung the swords, and the soldiers laughed. They gave me this helmet, moldy and cracked, and a broken bow and some crooked arrows."

He turned the helmet over in his hands and brushed sweat from the head band.

"I fixed the bow and straightened the arrows and caught one of their own fellows between the shoulders on the next raid."

There was no apology or regret in his voice. He started to whistle. Mi'kal wondered if his friend whistled in order to forget.

At the end of the day, Moses was picking his way under craggy cliffs and through scrub oak ravines. Mi'kal noticed that Oreb no longer whistled aimless tunes. He began a communication with "birds." Answering cries and whistles of jay and wood thrush were not from feathered throats.

At the base of a high hill they began to climb. They left Moses in a makeshift corral of boulders and brush where there was a cache of water and grain. Evidently there were many such stables in the hills.

Mi'kal's legs ached and his stomach was growling before they reached the cave. They passed a couple of sentries, skirted a large boulder, and then Oreb guided Mi'kal down a well-worn incline.

They came out into a wide sandstone room. The cave was full of men's voices and the smell of roasting fowl. Sunlight poured through wind-carved "windows" at the rear of the cave. Beyond the fire pit the smoke curled outward through the windows to dissipate among the oaks on the mountainside. For a moment, Mi'kal thought of the fires burning by the black tents.

The conversations stopped for a few minutes as the men greeted Oreb with shouts of affection.

Mi'kal was introduced to a large man tending the long spit of roasting pigeons. He was Neophron, the Vulture, leader of the men in the Hornet's Nest. Oreb had told Mi'kal that Neophron's reputation among the Romans was equal to that of Barabbas who led the Judean rebels. Mi'kal felt a flash of fear as the leader gave him a sharp look.

The men waited to see what Neophron would do about the stranger. When they saw he was accepted, they relaxed and turned back to their discussion.

One man stood apart from the others. He was remarkable for his difference. Dark locks fell on either side of a thin face. His chin beard was black, oiled, and trained into two pointed sections. He wore a tunic of fine gray wool. A green jewel glowed in the ring on his right forefinger.

A man sitting beside Oreb whispered a quick explanation. Judas of Kerioth had come representing a group of men who were disciples of the notorious Jesus of Nazareth. They believed Jesus was the Messiah. Neophron had allowed Judas to visit with them on the request of Simon of Cana, a former member of the band who was now a disciple of the Nazarene.

Judas was urging them to join an uprising to put Jesus on the throne of Israel. The coup would come at Passover, which was drawing near. The men had been arguing among themselves as to the wisdom of such a revolution.

At the mention of Jesus, Mi'kal unwrapped his arms from his legs and put his full attention on the speaker. Judas had evidently been exhorting the men, for his eyes held a wild light.

"I tell you Jesus of Nazareth is the Messiah. He must be forced to declare himself. Thousands believe in him and are ready to give him a triumphal entry. If he doesn't do it soon, it will be too late. He is angering the authorities."

The man seated near Mi'kal spoke. "And who is going to fight with us? Will he call down Elisha's horses and chariots of fire?"

Mi'kal noted the two knives stuck in pockets on the heavy boots. One time the Old One had mentioned the Sicarii, the most feared of the Zealots. They were men skilled in the art of assassination by dagger. Was this man one of them?

Mi'kal felt a repulsive chill and forced his thoughts back to Judas.

"Jesus could call down ten thousand chariots to help us if he wanted to. We must make him want to. He speaks much of meekness, but if we put him to the test, he will have to use his might." He swung a slender hand outward and the ring flashed. "Why are you not willing to act, as your brothers in Judea are willing? I have talked to them."

Neophron dropped the fire poker and rubbed at a spot where the flying embers had burned him.

"You have talked with Barabbas and his men?"

"Yes. He is anxious to strike. Why are your men doubtful it should be done?" Judas sounded contemptuous, and then his tone changed. "Most of you sucked in hatred for the Romans with your mother's milk. Did she not tell you God set you apart in her womb to lift the weight of dominion from your brother's back?"

An assenting murmur answered him.

"Some of you had fathers and grandfathers who gave their lives for Israel and the temple. What would they say to your reluctance to put the Messiah on the throne? Why would God send his Anointed One if he was not sent to reign? He is one of you, I swear it. He speaks often of his kingdom."

"Are you certain about Barabbas?" Neophron asked.

"Yes. He has plans to take the temple and the Antonia. After Passover, he says the heads of Herod Antipas and Pontius Pilate will be eaten by the dogs."

Neophron nodded. "I will send someone to confer with him." His eyes roamed over his men and lingered on Oreb. Mi'kal's heart leaped. If Oreb went to Judea, he would go, too. He would be happy to endure the embarrassing teasing and the "mutterings and murmurings."

Oreb lifted his hand. Neophron nodded. "Prepare to leave at daybreak. What about your friend? Is he staying with us?"

"He will come with me. Later he may join us, for he loves Galilee as much as any of us." He stuck his helmet over the red-gold hair. "Is it not so, friend?" His eyes signaled.

Mi'kal responded with a raised arm. "Israel for Israel!" he said. A friendly cheer went up.

When it was time to sleep, Judas joined Mi'kal on the mat Oreb had given them. Lamps in recesses along the walls were extinguished. Judas began to snore. Mi'kal found it hard to fall asleep. Everything that had been happening seemed unreal.

He rose carefully and went outside. A sentry spoke to him. A cradle moon swung low over what must be the plains of Jezreel, far below them. Mi'kal caught the faint odor of a stable.

Somewhere in the hills the wild asses answered the bray of a donkey—probably the one Judas had hired in the village of Ephraim, near Jerusalem. He had told Mi'kal about it as they ate the roasted birds with hunks of Roman bread.

The stable owner's boy had come with him to care for the beast. The boy was called Aziz. A Zealot guide had met him and brought him to the cave blindfolded. Mi'kal wondered why Oreb hadn't blindfolded him? He smiled at his thoughts. Oreb wasn't stupid. He knew full well that Mi'kal had no idea where he was.

Again the lonesome cry of the wild asses came, and a similar cry rose in Mi'kal's throat. He had left all that he loved in the black tents. Quintira remembered Galilee as if it were Paradise, but Mi'kal was seeing a darker side. Every piece of equipment, every stool and crate in the cave, had probably cost a man's life. Soon the whole nation would be prodded into violence if Judas had his way.

Was this what a Messiah King meant to Israel? Quintira had said he would bring peace. How he longed to talk these things over with her. By some miracle, he was safe in Galilee. Now he must find a way to earn his bread and prepare to rescue her from Raaschid's tent. If all else failed, he could appeal to his grandfather, Aretas, King of Petra.

And what about Leyla?

She was no doubt dead, even though he persisted in thinking she was alive. Her straw god would be no protection against the justice of the black tents.

The wild asses brayed again. It sounded like mocking laughter.

CHAPTER TWENTY-ONE

The descent from the cave was without incident. Judas was led blind-folded until Moses was taken from the corral. Aziz and the donkey were waiting. When Mi'kal saw Aziz his heart constricted. The dark, long-legged child was much like Kaleb.

As they traveled south, Mi'kal noticed again that though Oreb whistled, his eyes were unusually alert, and his hand often rested on the hilt of his sword.

The day was beautiful. Jerusalem lay ahead. Mi'kal nodded and spoke to many who passed. Oreb and Aziz were impressed that he knew the customary salutations for Greek or Roman or Jew.

Aziz always lifted his donkey switch and shook it in merry greeting. A soldier in a red cape passed on a white stallion, and Mi'kal thought of El Gamar. Was he racing through the hills mating with the mares, or had someone captured him?

He thought of Centaurus. The red stallion had died in vain if there was no Green Bird. He must hold on to his faith. If the emperor of Rome could believe in the Phoenix, surely a simple Bedouin could believe also.

Gods and goddesses were strange things. Everyone seemed to trust a different one. He had noticed many of them in the roadside shrines and on the gateposts of the villas. Most of them were forbidding and lewd.

His mother called all idols abominable. He could close his eyes and hear her quoting Moses, who had written on instructions from God, "You shall not bow down to them or worship them."

At noon they entered the gates of Chorazin, a city of greenery, clinging like hyssop to the black basalt cliffs that loomed over the northern shore of the Sea of Galilee.

As they drank from the well, a young girl drawing water told them that Jesus had done many wonderful miracles in Chorazin.

"Some of those who saw the miracles went away growling. They always argue, no matter what he does. My father says he could move Mount Hermon into the sea and it wouldn't stop them. Everyone thinks less of him because he comes from Nazareth."

"What's wrong with Nazareth?" Mi'kal asked.

"That's where everybody is who isn't anybody," the girl said seriously.

Even Judas laughed.

From Chorazin they descended to Capernaum on the lakeshore. Mi'kal asked if he might have time to find Quintillius's villa and tell Dolmicius, the old servant, about the death of the centurion. Oreb expressed no sympathy for the Roman but did agree to visit the villa. "But we must get through the Valley of Doves before dark."

The residence of Quintillius was not hard to find. The villa nestled on the shore of the lake, between two small villages. An old woman met them at the gate and then called her master, an elderly Macedonian in flowing white robe. There was an aura of peace about Dolmicius. Wisdom shone in his eyes. He was bald, but his voice was youthful and vigorous.

Judas seemed the proper one to state their mission. Dolmicius gripped Mi'kal's arm and led them through the covered atrium to the garden peristyle beyond. He listened soberly as Mi'kal told him of Quintillius's visit to the camp, the signs of massacre, and the military burial in the garrison grounds.

"I was informed of his death, but to hear from someone who was with him during his last hours is a gift from God"

"You meant a lot to him, sir," Mi'kal said. "His lieutenant told us about your healing."

"Ah yes. I gained two things that day from the Nazarene. Health and faith. Now tell me about the young Briton. How badly was he hurt?"

"He lost a lot of blood from the slash on his thigh, but the surgeon said there was no bone damage."

"Quintillius was very fond of him," Dolmicius said. "I, too, liked him very much the few days he was here. Since I have no one else, and it would please my master, he will probably get this place when I am gone."

Mi'kal looked around the colonnaded garden court. It was impossible to see all the beauty. Aziz was fascinated with the small golden monkey swinging on the perch. Oreb whistled at the birds in the aviarium and the birds answered him. Judas admired the wall hangings and the mosaic pictures on ceiling and floors as well as the statuary. Mi'kal walked among the flowers. Lavender blooms of the leeks in the herb garden reminded him of his mother.

Later, as they ascended from the lake through the depressing ugliness of the dung valley, Mi'kal tried to hold to the beauty and fragrance of the villa.

When they reached the plateau, they took turns riding the mule and donkey. Before they lost sight of the lake, Aziz pointed out the brilliant sails of the boats on the water and the new city on the southern point of the lake.

"Rich people live in Tiberias."

Judas growled. "That city is not fit to enter. Jesus has never set foot in it. It is unclean. Herod Antipas has built it over the bones of dead men."

Oreb agreed. "It is fit only for Roman pigs."

While Oreb and Aziz rode, Judas walked beside Mi'kal, explaining many things concerning Jesus and the villages they were passing. He pointed westward toward twin peaks.

"Jesus gave us one of his longest sermons from there. And beyond is the city of Nain where he performed his first miracle with death."

"Were you there?"

"No. Andrew and Philip were. Why?"

"I was wondering how he does it."

"Through divine power. He is the Messiah."

"But doesn't he say or do something different?"

"If you mean does he act like a sorcerer, no. Sometimes he just says the word and they are healed. Sometimes he lays his hand on them and they receive the blessing. But at all times he has direct communication with God."

Oreb leaned from the back of Moses. "Mi'kal thinks Jesus is going to tell him how to raise the dead, and then he expects to raise everybody."

"No such thing!" Mi'kal denied. "I just don't think everybody should have to die because somebody did something wrong a long time ago. It isn't fair."

Judas lifted his hand and his ring flashed. "I understand you. Everyone hates Death. Jesus speaks much about living forever, but none of us are sure how it is to be done. When he talks about being the Son of God and having a kingdom, I think I understand. But much that he says is not clear to us."

"When he talks about living forever, does he mean we will live down here on earth?" Mi'kal asked. "I don't want to float around like a cloud doing nothing."

Judas gave one of his rare smiles. "I, too, am more anxious about the present and the familiar."

"But if he only wants twelve of you to serve him, what about the rest of us?"

"He says that whoever the Father sends to him, he will receive into his kingdom." He stroked the double points of his beard. "But there is a price to pay. We must forsake all things—houses, land, and family."

"None of you have really done it, have you?" Oreb spoke with an edge to his voice. Mi'kal knew he was thinking of the Zealots who had given up everything for freedom.

"No. Not yet."

In late afternoon, Oreb walked beside Mi'kal who was straddling the donkey. "We cannot make Jerusalem today. We will stay with a friend of mine near Scythopolis."

He explained that Scythopolis was the ancient Beth-Shan, which had been a Philistine stronghold when King Saul reigned. He pointed out the mound of Gilboa where Saul and three of his sons, including Jonathan the friend of David, were slain.

"The Philistines took their heads to offer to their idols, and the bodies were hung on the city walls."

Mi'kal shuddered. One thing he was beginning to believe—men had to change before they deserved to live forever.

At dusk they stopped near a newly plowed field. Oreb jumped the thorn hedge and spoke quietly to the worker with the plow. They were invited to spend the night in the garden lodge. Mi'kal noticed a supply of blankets and a bin of hoes and rakes. He fell asleep wondering if the farmer was another one of the many friends who helped the Zealots but never killed.

However, if the entire nation was aroused to insurrection, even the sun-browned farmers would have to kill.

CHAPTER TWENTY TWO

They awoke, stiff and dirty. Judas was irritable. "We can't go on like this. We will stop at the springs of Salim and bathe. I will pay."

Aziz jumped for joy. Judas explained to Mi'kal that Salim was a place of warm springs near a ford where John the Baptist had often preached and baptized. They would find booths for food, too. Oreb added that the ford was a popular way to cross into Perea, but the eastern trail on the other side of the Jordan was often uncomfortably hot.

"You will enjoy the baths. They will give you soap and towels, and an old woman will scrape you down."

"I'll do my own scrubbing."

Oreb grinned.

An hour later Aziz began to shout. He pointed ahead to the river. Mi'kal saw a huddle of low, whitewashed buildings, striped awnings, and umbrellas. Carts and wagons stood side by side with chariots and litters.

The river beyond the buildings ran wide and shallow. Here and there, foam splashed against a few large boulders that had fallen from the cliffs on the other side. Tropical growth covered the far shore.

As they tethered the animals, Mi'kal's ears rang with the chatter at the outside tables and the noise of children playing in the river.

Aziz didn't wait. He ran into the water and dove under. Mi'kal remembered Kaleb's ten "thirsty camels." He closed his eyes and expected to hear a crow laughing.

Judas touched him and motioned for him to follow. Mi'kal felt completely ignorant as he entered the bathhouse built around the springs. His first reaction was panic. So many naked men. Bathers stepped from room to room, from pool to pool. He was horrified to find old women walking among them, offering towels and oils.

Mi'kal followed Oreb and deposited his clothes in a stone bin. He hesitated to take off his loin-cloth until he saw Oreb's mocking grin. He shed it quickly, glad to be rid of it. He kept the belt that held the scrip.

Oreb motioned to one of the old women and she came and picked up the garments.

"What is she doing?" Mi'kal asked.

"She will wash them for us. They will be damp but clean. You can trust her with your purse, too."

Mi'kal followed him into the first pool, which was moderately warm. He was thankful for the waist-high water. He wished his body hair was black like Oreb's. He watched as Oreb used a scraper, a short broad-bladed instrument that looked like a broken trowel.

He used one and his flesh tingled and burned, but it felt good. A man with a paunch stopped on the rim of the basin. "How are you doing, Golden Boy? Need any help?"

Mi'kal looked up. Admiration was plain on the lax-muscled face. Mi'kal bit his lips and turned his back.

Oreb laughed and punched him. "See? I told you."

"If he looks at me again like that I'll hold his head under."

Oreb pursed his lips and let out a small whistle.

They went from bath to bath, from hot to cold. The old woman came with the damp clothes. A little more than damp, but Mi'kal offered her one of his lesser coins and she took it as she kissed his hand.

He lingered for a moment, watching two muscled men pushing a heavy felt-covered roller over the floors to take up the water.

Outside he blinked against the sun. Aziz and Judas were already eating from a basket of fish and bread. A serving maid came with a platter of olives, radishes, and small cucumbers.

Mi'kal ate slowly as he watched the serving girls moving among the tables. Some were dark-eyed Jewesses. A few were black like Kwa. Some were warm ivory, like Leyla.

The thought of Leyla made him ache. Would he ever forget her? He could still see her dancing, telling the story of his mother's love for his

Nabatean father. Given a few more days with her, might he have fallen in love? Maybe he was in love. Certainly her dancing had brought a response from him.

Without intention, he became aware of the conversation at the table nearest them. Several men were conversing in Greek. He turned his head to concentrate. Yes, they were discussing Jesus of Nazareth!

Mi'kal excused himself to his friends. "I want to speak to those men."

"They're Greeks," Oreb said.

"I know."

Oreb watched with surprised and envious eyes as Mi'kal engaged the men in conversation. One of them patted the bench beside him, and Mi'kal sat down.

He came back with his face shining. "They say Jesus crossed here early yesterday. He had four disciples with him. They think he was heading for a city called Gerasa."

Judas nodded. "Very likely. A few weeks ago he sent out about seventy of his friends to see which village or city would welcome him. Gerasa has mostly Gentiles, especially Greeks. And Greeks are not afraid of new ideas or philosophies."

"Is it far?"

"Two days or more on foot for a stranger," Judas replied.

"If you want to be sure of finding him," Oreb said, "come to Jerusalem with me and wait for him there."

Judas agreed. "He will not miss the Passover."

Mi'kal considered it, then shook his head. "I am going to find him on my own."

"If you do," Judas said, "stay with him and come to Ephraim. We have a nice place there with the widow Susanna. A house with many rooms."

"If you come," Aziz said, his brown eyes shining, "I will get my father to loan you a donkey."

"I hope it is a gray one. I knew such a one a long time ago." Indeed it did seem a lifetime, although it had been but a handful of days. Homesickness swept over him. He was still sorry he had not been able to see the Old One before he and Leyla left.

Judas was trying to persuade Oreb to stay overnight with him at the widow's house.

"If she has a house with many rooms, she probably has a houseful of crying babies," Oreb said. "Besides I have to get to Jerusalem. Neophron will expect a quick report."

Mi'kal saw a rare twinkle in the black eyes. "I promise you, you will sleep very well at Susanna's."

"She must be a remarkable woman to take care of all of you," Mi'kal said. "Is she rich?"

"Only in gratitude and hospitality."

Aziz had been scratching through some lunch baskets on the tables, looking for crumbs to feed the birds. "Susanna used to be sick and Jesus healed her. That's why she's good to him and his friends." He looked up at Mi'kal and added quickly, "I wish you weren't leaving us."

Oreb began to explain to Mi'kal about the river trail that would lead up through the cliffs to the main road.

"You will find part of it hard going and hot. Generations ago, all of this valley was a jungle. There were even elephants. This side has been cleared out somewhat, but over there you expect to see hippopotamuses, crocodiles, and lions."

Judas smiled. "None of them are left, but be careful of the bridge over the whirlpool. It crosses a deep ravine where a small tributary comes down over a falls and rushes toward the Jabbok. You will hear the water."

"It can be meaner than a hyena with whelps," Oreb added. "If you change your mind and decide to come to Judea first, follow the river and cross at Jericho. You will go up to Bethany and then down to Jerusalem."

"I'll be careful. And I will see all of you again someday. I promise."

His friends yelled, "Go with God!" As he stepped into the river, Aziz came splashing and handed him a small cucumber.

"I saved it for you," he said.

Mi'kal tucked it into his girdle. How much like Kaleb Aziz was. He hugged him and turned away. He didn't dare look back. The sounds and smells of the bathhouses faded. Willows closed about him. Vines shut out the sight of the water. Cliffs came down in forbidding closeness. The air changed as the sunlight was lost.

He fought a rushing panic. He was on his own. On a quest that seemed incredibly childish. His mother had said he was stubborn and obsessed with the idea of thwarting death.

Perhaps she was right.

CHAPTER TWENTY-THREE

Raaschid placed the camp in the care of Mazir, the wisest of his elders, as he prepared for the visit to his brother's camp. He ordered Freya to be saddled and chose two warriors to accompany him.

As they left camp, Gutne watched him. Raaschid adjusted the hood of his white burnoose and offered her no farewell. He knew her thoughts. She had presumed, since Quintira was gone, that he would call for her. His plans were distinctly different. He rode close to Ne'ma's tent. She stood in the doorway, her eyes lifted in adoration. She was hugging herself. Ah, yes. She was ready and willing.

The day's ride was tortuous and tiresome. His thoughts were gloomy. Muktar would take Sa'ad's death as a personal insult—an attempt to leave Zalah without a husband and the Boar clan without a suitable future ruler.

From the time the twins were born, Zalah had been promised to Sa'ad. They were betrothed when she was twelve.

As Zalah matured, Raaschid grew uneasy and slightly sorry for his son. He couldn't deny her beauty, but beneath the beauty lay a quick temper and belligerent pride. Nevertheless, the eventual bringing of the clans together again would have been a good thing.

The sun was casting the last of its yellow light over the gray hills when Raaschid arrived at the Boar camp. Muktar came out of the tent to greet him with exclamations of surprise. They embraced lightly, and Raaschid's lips touched the rope binding of his brother's headpiece in the centuries old sign of respect.

Zalah came running. Light from the oil lamps struck rays from her silver earrings.

"Where is he? Where is my beloved?"

Raaschid shook his head and her full lips gathered in a pout. His explanation was interrupted by Muktar's invitation to eat. "Come, revive your spirits."

Zalah retired to the women's quarters, and Raaschid sighed with relief.

Muktar patted the cushion beside him, and Raaschid sat, ready to defer to his older brother in all things. He knew the question that respect for a guest's privacy prevented Muktar from asking. Why the unannounced visit?

Raaschid missed Zauf at the meal of roasted grouse and inquired for him. Muktar smiled fondly. "He may be here later. He has been gone for a few days to test a new mare and look for a proper stallion."

Raaschid said, "Ah, yes, the eaters of the wind, our mares. What would we do without them? None are more noble than yours, my brother."

The compliment was sincere.

"Zauf deserves whatever credit is given. He is not satisfied with less than the best."

Muktar leaned forward. Light fell on his face. His cheeks were thinner than Raaschid's, his nose smaller. Wrinkles ran from the outer edges of his eyes to the corners of his mouth, like old scars.

"I am glad to see renewed life in my son. Lately he has been moody. Angry without reason. If I did not know better, I would think he is sick with love." He took a piece of incense from the binding of his headpiece and threw it into the fire bowl.

"Perhaps it is so."

"No. He shows no desire for any of the girls in camp."

The platters were removed to the kitchen, where the women and children would eat, and a wizened slave poured the final cup of wine. The fragrance of the incense filled the tent.

Muktar sat his cup down and leaned back. "I did not expect to see you before the wedding."

"Brother, I have heavy news for you. There can be no wedding."

For a moment it seemed even the fragrance of the incense ceased.

"No wedding?" The exclamation was a mixture of disbelief and anger.

"Kaleb is dead. Sa'ad is dead. My tent is a barren womb." Then he told of the deaths.

Muktar laid a hand on Raaschid's knee. "My soul weeps for you, my brother, but surely you have exacted vengeance."

"Yes. For the first, the son of the Jewess was flogged with thorns."

Muktar's hand went to his lips. "An excellent judgment."

"When the guilty ones are brought back by my slaves, they will be executed. The Jewess has been banished for aiding the two of them to flee."

"Your judgments are fair." Muktar rose. "My Zalah must be told."

He called, and she came running. "Sa'ad has come?"

"No. Joy of my heart, your uncle has brought an evil report."

As kindly as he could, Raaschid told her of Sa'ad's death, of the stabbings with scissors and dagger. He watched her face as the storm brewed. All of it was there. The scream of the wind, the shaking sobs of thunder, the torrents of rain. As the gusts lessened, the anger came. Raaschid had tried to lighten the facts concerning the girl, but Zalah clutched at them.

"Who was she, this seducer of my love?"

"A dancer…a slave. He bought her as a wedding gift for you. A 'virgin for a virgin,' he told us."

"Was she beautiful?"

"Compared to you she was nothing…nothing. She had no color, no flesh."

"Did she entice him? Did she seduce him with a love potion?" Zalah's dark eyes narrowed. "I think not! He was forcing her. That is why she used the scissors. Is it not so?"

She turned to him, her arms raised, her fingers curved. "I am glad he is dead. I could feel no more shame had she been a harlot calling to him from the stalls of Damascus." Her voice rose. "If I had found them I would have ripped her eyes from her body and flung them to the dogs."

Her bracelets jangled as she clutched at her father. Muktar smoothed her hair. "Justice is being done, my lovely. The Jewess has been cast out and—"

Zalah stared at her uncle. "Cast out?"

"Yes, it was my judgment." His words trembled.

"Oh, Uncle," she laid her head against his chest, "you must know the emptiness I will forever feel."

Raaschid's arm closed about her as her brother limped into the tent. Zauf was tired and dusty. Under the light of the oil lamps, white fire glowed from the crystal in the brass necklace around his neck. Raaschid tensed.

Zalah stiffened. Her eyes, too, were on the necklace. Zauf felt the silence and the stares. His hand moved to the brass ball. Consternation crossed his face.

Zalah released herself from her uncle's arm. "Where did you get that?"

"I bought it. Today. From a trader."

"No. I would know that necklace anywhere." She touched the chain. "Sa'ad promised me he would never be without it."

"He never was," Raaschid said.

He appealed to Muktar. "Brother, if your son is innocent of murder and theft, let him convince us. My son died sometime after midnight, two nights ago. There was no necklace. I had not considered it until now. Where was your son two nights ago?"

"Here—" Zauf began, but Zalah interrupted.

"No. You had gone to see about the horses."

Muktar nodded. "Your sister speaks the truth."

"Father!" There was infinite plea in Zauf's voice.

"If you are guilty of your cousin's death and the theft of the ornament, tell us why, so I may deliver judgment."

Zauf pulled off the necklace. "Why did I kill him?" He turned on his father. "You preferred him to me. You were going to make him chieftain over the Boars. What is wrong with me except a shortened leg? Should I not rule my own people? And this!"

He shook the necklace in Zalah's face. "This too should have been mine. You bought it for me on our birthday, and then when he came, you gave it to him. Yes, I hated him. I hated him thrice."

Zauf was out of control, yelling at his sister. "Have you not known that I love you? Love you as any man loves a woman. O sister, my beloved, how could you not know?"

Zalah gasped. Muktar shouted. "You would defile your own sister? You would commit the sin of Amnon in my tent?"

His hand closed on his son's throat. Zauf struggled. "I loved her. I have always loved her." He grabbed for Raaschid. "You can understand. She was to me as your Jewess is to you. The wedding was coming near. I could not bear to think of his hands upon her."

Raaschid pushed his brother aside and swung the sword. The blade cut through flesh and bone. Zauf swayed for a moment, his eyes wide, and then he dropped.

Zalah fell to her knees beside him.

Muktar cried, "Brother!" He lifted his hand. "Could you not trust my judgment? Now his blood is crying from the ground."

Raaschid waited.

"I will have blood for blood," Muktar decreed, his voice low but determined.

Raaschid bowed. "So be it." His worse fears were coming true. He lifted the tent curtain and went quietly. Again, it would be brother against brother, as it had been from the days of Isaac and Ishmael, Jacob and Esau.

Muktar knelt and touched Zauf's cheeks, and his heart picked up a burden it would never lose.

Raaschid returned to his camp, exhausted and downcast. He had blundered. He was no longer sure of himself. He called for the council. He explained the truth of Sa'ad's murder.

They sat with their hands hidden in the sleeves of their abas and said nothing. This would be their leader's own private torment.

Upon hearing the declaration of "blood for blood," they chewed their lips and silently accepted what the stars ordained.

CHAPTER TWENTY FOUR

Mi'kal walked for what seemed like hours without seeing anything that looked like a pass leading upward. The river channel changed. The boundaries ran full. The main stream was muddy, but closer inshore, a few pools eddied with translucent colors.

He was tired and hot. He dropped his sandals on shore and crawled up on the crooked bole of a tree that had fallen into the river. He dipped his feet into the water. Ripples nibbled at his toes.

He closed his eyes and let the wonder sweep over him. His feet were in the Jordan River!

Joshua had crossed it to take the city of Jericho, the last stronghold to be defeated before the Israelites could claim their promised land. Moses had not lived long enough to enter. God had punished him for an act of impatient anger.

He tried to imagine that the water splashing against his ankles was water from the rock Moses had smitten.

It wasn't, of course, but it was the water over which Elijah had ascended into heaven in a fiery chariot. It was where Elijah had dropped his mantle of prophecy and power to his disciple Elisha. And it was the river in which Naaman, the Syrian commander, had bathed in order to be healed of his leprosy.

David, the shepherd king, had fled across it to escape his treacherous son Absalom. And more recently, the famous prophet John had preached and baptized at the river's fords.

Mi'kal bent and lifted a handful of water. He let it trickle back. "For you, Mother. A touch of the Jordan just for you." He stretched out on the fallen tree and ate the cucumber Aziz had given him.

Above him, a kingfisher plunged and came up with a struggling silver crescent. Dragonflies swooped low to admire themselves in the mirror of the pools.

He felt refreshed and hopeful as he tied his sandals and stepped back on the trail. Almost immediately, he saw the narrow cut that led up through the cliffs.

The passage was hard to climb; its stones were worn smooth. Rivulets of water stained the walls, and the air was damp and chilly. A low rumble reverberated from the walls.

Mi'kal began to think of others who had made this climb to the heights above. He could imagine the clanking armor and the slap of sandals as David's men fled from pursuing archers. He saw sparks from the iron heels of Medes and Persians, of Babylonians and Greeks and Romans. No doubt the Zealots still used this pass before and after raids. Did their zeal for Israel justify the robbery and murder?

God had commanded, "You shall not murder. You shall not steal."

The smell and sound of roaring waters brought Mi'kal to attention. The trail made a sudden right turn, and he came out almost on the bridge. The cold spray caught him in the face. Through the heavy mist, he could see the continuation of the trail to the road on the other side.

The bridge, made of palm trunks laced with rope, swung over a double falls. Water rushed down from twin channels and met in a growling whirlpool. Each cascade thrust itself deep into the maelstrom and came up again, as if to escape its fatal embrace.

A heavy chain stretched the length of the bridge. He clung to it as he started across. The wet logs heaved under him like waves. Spray blinded him as he stared down into the angry water.

He gripped the chain harder and closed his eyes. He was on a three-tiered galley riding a mighty storm! Where was he going? Cyprus, Corinth, Cairo?

The swaying caught his stomach unawares. He opened his eyes and his head spun. Sky and water converged as they must have mingled before God called forth the dry ground.

He loosened one hand to wipe the water from his face. The wind caught the corner of the bridge floor and upended it.

He screamed as he fell.

The waters sucked him under.

Down and around and then up. His arms flailed, his screams choked in his throat. He was rolled against the rocks and pulled under again. His shoulder and head slammed against a boulder. He went limp, and the whirlpool spewed him out in disgust.

Above him another kingfisher, poised to dive, uttered an angry protest.

A blue heron, walking in the shallows, lifted its long neck and gazed with interest at the strange thing floating past the willows.

INTERLUDE

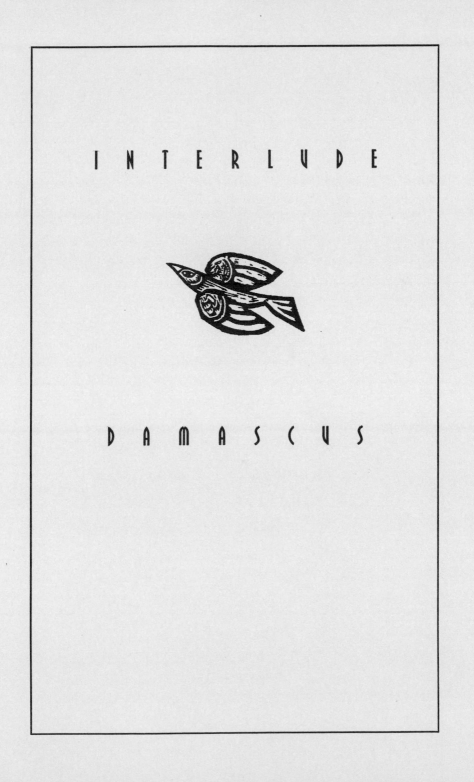

DAMASCUS

LEYLA

Kwa and Leyla left the spring at the first sign of dawn. Most of the time he walked while she rode the fawn-colored camel. During the morning, she made him a shirt from two strips of Duag's cloak and tied it with strings of cloth. She made the neckline high enough to cover his ivory necklace.

"You must put the gazelle skin vest away and cover yourself as much as possible, in case Raaschid sends someone to find you. There is not another man in Syria with a chest like yours."

At noon they rested in a ravine, thick with shrubs and tall grass, close to the Roman road. The milestone was encouraging. They were not far from Damascus. Kwa milked Maha, and while he drank, Leyla tried to convince him not to go into the city with her.

"I can find my way from here. It might be dangerous for you in Damascus. Raaschid may have sent men to look for me there."

"No. I will see you safely back with your friends. Then I will decide what I want to do." His white teeth gleamed. "I may go to Caesarea. As a boy I loved the sea."

He picked a stalk of small lavender flowers from a shrub near him and handed it to her. Suddenly she felt like a girl again. Her hand went to her head. She unwound the purple scarf and let the silver strands fall.

"Mi'kal insisted I should cover my hair and look like a boy."

"He was wise."

She held the scarf up by both hands and let it billow in the wind. Maha, contentedly munching on a thorn bush, turned at the sound of flapping. She belched and Leyla laughed. "I'm sorry you don't care for purple."

Without warning, Kwa reached for the camel's rope and ordered her to couch. Leyla crouched in a clump of high grass. "Listen," he said. She heard nothing as she wound up her hair and covered it with the scarf. The blue flowers were forgotten. A beetle ran over her ankle, and she brushed it away.

Then she began to hear it. The earth was responding to the tread of feet. She smelled rising dust and heard the garbled sound of voices.

"Soldiers?" she whispered. He shook his head and motioned for her to stay low and be quiet. Leyla watched as a long line of frightened and tired young boys passed, tied to one another. Most of them were black, some were ivory, some brown, a few were sunburned whites.

A few walked free. Several men with long whips herded them. A few of the guards wore quivers and carried bows.

Many of the shackled ones walked in silence. Those who were untied talked among themselves and threw stones at the grouse or white herons in the grass along the highway.

Leyla looked at Kwa and whispered, "Why don't they run away, those that are free?"

Kwa leaned close to her. "They fear the archers. The shackles are for the fighters. The others are the meek."

"Where are they going?"

"To be sold in the markets."

"Where do they come from?"

"Stolen from farms, cities, anywhere. All of them are meant for Rome. Those not pretty enough will work. The others will be offered to the nobles who prefer young boys to their own women."

Leyla gasped. "But that...that is awful!" She almost forgot to whisper. Kwa laid a hand across her lips.

Two of the slave dealers walked near them. "How much longer do we have to take care of this herd?"

"Tomorrow they will be sorted at Damascus. Have you seen one to your liking?"

"I'll stick with the wenches at the inn."

The column moved on slowly. Leyla rose and looked at Kwa. Her eyes were shining with a new idea.

"Why don't I go the rest of the way with them?" She pointed to some stragglers.

He shook his head vigorously.

"The guards will never know they have a girl. I'll be meek."

"No!" The word was final. But he could not grab her quickly enough. She was out of the gully and running. She joined the end of the line where several of the meek were walking.

One of the guards growled at her and grabbed her arm. "Where have you been?" She jerked loose and spoke with impudence. "Doing my business." He grunted and shoved her ahead. "See that you stay closer after this."

Only once did Leyla allow herself to look back. Kwa was watching. She hoped he knew she would be all right. She wasn't shackled, and she could run if she had to. In Damascus she would find Rekha and everything would be fine. It really would have been dangerous for both of them if Kwa was seen there.

And some day, if she could, she would go into Galilee and look for Mi'kal. All she would have to do is inquire for the whereabouts of Jesus of Nazareth, Mi'kal's Green Bird.

For now, she would have to remember not to go behind a bush with a boy.

ARETAS

Leyla and the convoy of slave boys entered the gates of Damascus that evening. She darted behind a vendor's stall, unwound the purple scarf, and let her hair fall.

Rekha was surprised, but glad to see her. As usual, the Lebanese director and owner of the dancing troupe was wearing a slim tunic over baggy trousers caught at the ankles.

She listened as Leyla explained about the attempted rape, the death of her grandmother, and her flight from camp. Rekha asked only one question. "Did he violate you?"

"No."

Rekha patted her shoulder. "Good." Leyla knew the approbation was as much for the director's good fortune as for hers.

Rekha prided herself on the quality of her merchandise. All of the girls were of good birth and became her property only through misfortune. She handled them with a firm hand. Obey her, work well, and all would be pleasant. Disobey, neglect practice, argue, or talk back, and she could rip the skin off with her tongue.

The girls were not chattel. They were free to leave, be bought, or marry, but none could stay after they had lain with a man.

The purity of her goods caused the rich to buy, but not for slaves. Rekha sold no girl for a slave. Her girls must be given a respectable place in the family. Only the royal could take them for concubines. Sometimes a close member of the girl's family was allowed to stay and work to help the troupe in many ways. Ammoni, Leyla's grandmother, had stayed.

When Leyla entered the dormitory, her friends screamed with delight. Newer girls felt a flash of jealousy.

Rekha put her on a strict regimen of bathing and oiling. Her hair was washed and brushed and then brushed again. Her skin, roughened and reddened by the sun, became lustrous again.

Leyla doubled her applications of oil and ointment when she learned they would soon be entertaining at the palace. Lysanias, the governor of Syria, had come from his capital in Abilene to his Damascus residence for an important meeting regarding a change in the administration of the city.

Rekha told them that the evening would be one of great importance because Lysanias was entertaining two other rulers: Herod Philip of Caesarea Philippi, who was the tetrarch of Batanea and Trachonitis; and King Aretas of Petra, ruler of Nabatea. At one time, Aretas's grandfather had ruled Damascus. And Rome, who was interested in keeping peace with the Nabateans, was thinking of putting Damascus back under Nabatean rule.

Leyla felt her heart leap at the mention of Aretas. She knew what she must do. Rekha might be willing to help her, and then again she might not. Better to do it on her own.

On the night Rekha's girls entertained, slaves with torches led the way. Musicians followed. The dancers were carried to the palace in ornamented litters. Silken curtains, embroidered with a motif of sylphs, concealed them. The entire city came out to see them. Crowds gathered, and Rekha did not object if the girls lifted the curtains and threw kisses or accepted flowers or candies.

Guards with long lances held back the public at the foot of the wide black and white marble steps. Flaring torches in heavy golden bases illuminated the entrance. The steps reminded Leyla of the zebra bench on Raaschid's porch.

Rekha led. Tonight she wore a silver sheath with a sheer red drape falling in a long train behind her. The girls were dressed in filmy, full-skirted costumes in varying shades of blue and green, lavender and purple, rose and scarlet. While the garments were similar, each seemed fashioned exclusively for the girl who wore it. The colors brought out the startling differences in their beauty.

Leyla wore lavender; a misty blue veil was fastened to her shoulders with silver brooches and tied to her wrists. When she lifted her arms she seemed to float. Her hair was in a knot on her head, with the silver strands streaming over her shoulders, much as she had worn it on her first day in Raaschid's camp. The knot was held by a scarf of purple.

As they left the steps, the hallway ahead was a mural of colors. The walls shook with welcoming applause. Women shimmered in silks and jewels and studied the girls' hairstyles. Men wore tunics and togas bordered with purple and gold.

Leyla drew a deep breath as she entered the banquet hall. Large lamps hung by chains from the beamed ceiling. Long tables held golden and silver platters and plates. Elaborate couches flanked the tables. Flowers were everywhere.

The dancers were led past three ornate chairs on the dais, each with its private table. Leyla knew Lysanias would have the middle position. He was rotund and bald and wore a circlet of golden leaves about his forehead.

The first man was thin, with a pale face and scanty beard. He would be Philip from Caesarea Philippi.

The third man must be King Aretas.

Leyla bowed slightly as she passed the first two chairs, but her eyes lifted to the face of Aretas. His chin beard was brown with a touch of red, but the hair close to his ears showed traces of gray. He wore a white turban with a large red jewel.

The girl behind pushed and Leyla went on, but she felt rather than saw Lysanias lean toward the King of Petra.

She could not hear, but the Governor of Abilene was saying, "There are always prizes in Rekha's girls. Look and take your pick. But not for dallying, mind you. Rekha would have your head—king or no king."

Aretas smiled. "I am too old for dallying and not young enough for a new wife. As I have told you, I lost my desire for women when my Mumtaza died. As for the girl, I was simply admiring her."

Lysanias shrugged. He, too, had admired the silver-haired girl, but she had definitely set her mind upon the Nabatean. And why not? He was a handsome figure in his embroidered *aba.*

Philip scarcely noticed the girls. His eyes were on the young woman reclining at a nearby table—Salome, his wife. Her dark eyes flashed him a gentle warning. "Look, if you wish, my husband; but remember, you belong to me."

Philip's face flushed with pleasure as she lifted her palm, kissed it, and blew him the kiss.

Leyla saw the exchange of tenderness and felt a pang of jealousy. Would she ever know such love? She had been attracted to Mi'kal, but his face was growing hazy. She had enjoyed tormenting and tempting him, but she was thankful he had not been enticed.

In spite of the back-end view of the fox and the destroyed straw god, she had been protected from her own foolishness. She remembered she had prayed for help as Duag, the Egyptian, carried her back to certain death. Her prayers had been to the Hebrew God, the God Quintira and Mi'kal loved.

Tonight, Leyla felt older. Older than Mi'kal. Maybe Salome felt the same way. Girls in the dormitory had told her about Salome's drunken dancing at a birthday party for her uncle, Herod Antipas, that resulted in the death of a popular preacher. Those who professed to know said Salome suffered much from her part in the murder and that she married the older Philip, her uncle, in order to get away from her mother and step-father.

But now, it was plain to see Salome truly loved Philip.

Leyla watched them. Maybe Salome needed the love of an older, kinder man. Passion was fine for someone like Ne'ma, who had professed love for Raaschid, her lord, but reverence and gentleness might be better for Salome.

While still thinking of Salome, Leyla took her place among the girls on large mounds of cushions, chosen by Rekha to enhance the beauty of each girl and the color of her garment.

Festivities began with a flourish of trumpets and drums. Jugglers cavorted and wrestlers strained and groaned. Girls and men in leopard skins swung on ropes overhead.

A brown bear and an African elephant were brought in to perform.

Lions jumped through fiery hoops held by black African natives. The roars of the big cats shook the chandeliers and brought screams from the women.

Leyla's head rang with the applause and the shouting.

A charioteer rode through the hall driving a zebra. He threw small but precious gems at the women who squealed with delight and were not above crawling on their knees to find the valuable favors.

As the food came and the wine was poured, Rekha gave her musicians the cue. First a few long drumbeats, and then the whistling flutes and pipes, followed by the singing lyres and lutes.

The girls began together, but as the dance continued, each was given a chance to perform alone. Some played instruments or sang. This was the time the bids were made, sometimes with hand signals and sometimes by whispering couriers.

As Rekha accepted or declined the offers, she remembered her sale of Leyla. She had taken the troupe into the bazaar for a morning of shopping and the desert prince stopped to ask the price of the silver-haired girl. He wanted a gift for his bride—a companion.

She had made a mistake with Sa'ad. She should have read the dark face more carefully. Tonight, if a bid was made for Leyla, the price would be doubled. She had not missed the whispered conversation between the two rulers.

When it was time for Leyla to perform by herself, she danced as she had danced for Mi'kal in the grove, a fantasy of tragic love.

She forgot the banquet room. She was back under the trees, and Mi'kal was watching from his sleeping mat. The passion came. The sigh of the flutes was as the awakening birds, adding beauty to her love; the rosy toes of dawn joined her in the dance. She felt her love running toward her…felt his arms, felt the consummated love and then the parting…felt the dying. Drums sobbed with her, and the stringed instruments wept.

As if Death had really taken her, she dropped to the first step of the dais. Her blue veil settled slowly, like the wings of a dying butterfly. She reached for the scarf and let her hair fall in a silver cloud.

Behind the screen of hair, her eyes sought the eyes of the king.

Applause shook the banquet hall. Her lips moved so only he could hear.

"Myndus!" she said. "Myndus! I can tell you something about your son's death. O my lord, take this. Take it!"

She thrust the piece of purple scarf into his hands. A strained look crossed his face. He rose and lifted her to her feet.

"Tomorrow," he said. "In my chambers here, at the second hour. You will come?"

"Oh, yes, my lord." She dropped to one knee as he touched her head. The guests were still applauding.

Rekha watched and congratulated herself. There would be a courier from the king tomorrow.

Lysanias misunderstood, too. "She is indeed a rare one."

Aretas frowned as he tucked the scarf into his girdle. "Your thinking is crooked."

"Don't apologize. Some like them young." He nodded toward Salome.

"If you will excuse me?" Aretas rose and walked slowly out of the hall. In his chambers he sat with the piece of scarf draped over his knees. He had seen the other half many years before. Scouts had found the body of his son and brought his clothes and the purple cloth to Petra. They said someone had been with Myndus in the hollows and the pool. Small footprints ran with the larger. Perhaps the woman's scarf had something to tell them.

Mumtaza held it to her face. Her eyes, green flecked with jewel light of gold and black, filled with tears. "My beloved, we must keep this. As the curtains of our room are fragrant with love, so is this." She folded it carefully.

Aretas found it in her box of precious things after she died.

THE OLD ONE

ays of travel through the flinty plains of Syria had been hard on Quintira and the Old One. She greeted the rose garden suburbs of Damascus with thankfulness.

While he took the donkey and the camels to a khan, she found a place to rest by a public fountain. She knew she looked like a beggar in the ragged hempen garment the Old One had brought from his tent for her. He had shaped a peaked hat out of soft saddle leather to protect her from the sun and to hide the tufts of hair where the thistles had been cut out.

She closed her eyes and ears to the confusion of the street traffic and remembered how she cried as the dark locks fell about her. Tears such as she had shed as Raaschid cut the braids from Mi'kal's head.

A small gourd of water was thrust into her hands, and she smiled up at the Old One in gratitude.

"Now, what shall we do with you?" he asked.

"I am too tired to think. Do we have any money?"

"Some. And I brought several of my leather belts to sell. We will have enough for rooms in an inn and food and clean clothing. Tomorrow we will inquire about Mi'kal and the girl."

"Couldn't we do it today? After I rest?"

"No. You have reached your limit."

"But I must know if he and Leyla reached Damascus safely. I keep thinking Kwa and Duag caught them and took them back."

"Where is your faith?"

She blushed at the gentle rebuke and followed him quietly. The inn was fairly clean. No one paid particular attention to them. Disreputable looking travelers were as common as storks on the rooftops.

As soon as Quintira entered her room, she fell across the narrow bed and was asleep before the Old One closed the shutters against the sun and noise.

On the great street called Straight he offered his belts to a few of the booth-keepers. Not satisfied with their offers, he decided to hawk them himself. The decision was a good one. Discriminating buyers appreciated the skillful work and the unusual leathers, everything from aurock hide to zebra skin.

The Old One's purse was heavy when he left the street of vendors to find a barber.

Then he began to shop for Quintira. He took his time and chose carefully. An olive green robe, full sleeves lined with delicate rose, with a cloak to match, caught his eye. He asked the price, shook his head, and walked away. The shopkeeper yelled at him to come back. After a few minutes of heated haggling, the price pleased both.

In another shop, a woman helped him with the undergarments and sandals. His last purchase was a small vial of rose perfume and an amber comb and brush. Later, she could choose her own cosmetics.

He found her bathed and wrapped in a blanket, a towel about her wet hair. The room smelled of honeysuckle. She laughed. "The soap smelled good and I used it all."

As he unfolded the new clothes, she tried to hold back her tears. "They are so lovely. And the perfume... O Grandfather, how kind you are."

"I promised it to you. Remember?"

"I remember." For a moment, all the pain and anger of that humiliating day returned.

"Dress," he commanded gently. "After we eat there is something I want to do."

"No gambling, Grandfather." She held up a forbidding finger.

He smiled. "No. No gambling."

When he came to escort her to supper, Quintira stared at him. He wore an ankle-length tunic of soft gray. Patrician sandals enclosed his feet.

She studied him with sober eyes.

The Old One of the tents was gone. This man was someone new, someone with nobility. How and when it had happened, she didn't know. Perhaps it came with the haircut and the shaped beard. His eyes twinkled as he saw her surprise and admiration.

As they ate thickly buttered slabs of bread and barley soup with slivers of onions and carrots, she caught a half-smile on his face. What was he planning? She felt as expectant as the children of the camp who could hardly wait to see what was in the bags on Astarte's back.

"I have something I want to tell you," he finally said. "It's a long story. Do you want to talk here or go out and find a quiet place? Maybe on a bench near the river?"

"Oh, yes."

They walked slowly past flower gardens and rose arbors, past small groves of pomegranate and almond trees, past villas with fancy gates and carved shutters, past taverns with singing and laughter.

They were enjoying the freshening breeze from the river even before they heard the sound of oars and faint slapping of sails and saw the swinging lanterns on the boats.

They sat on a bench, and the Old One began slowly. "You may not believe what I am going to tell you, but every word is true. First, I want to show you something." He laid a small golden object in her hand. "Hold it while I talk."

"What is it?"

"A *bulla*. Roman fathers gave them to their children on their purification day or when they were born. Boys wore them until they put on the toga. Girls sometimes kept them as jewelry."

"Then you *are* a Roman. Mi'kal and I always knew you were no ordinary camp follower. You are too wise. Too educated."

"You have heard of the men I want to talk about—Julius Caesar; Octavian, who became Augustus Caesar; and the two who were most important in my life: Marcus Aemilius Lepidus and Marcus Antonius. Marc Antony, my father."

Quintira gaped at him. "Your father?"

He smiled at her surprise. "I was born to Cleopatra and named Alexander Helios—for the sun. My twin sister was Cleopatra Selene—for the moon. We had a younger brother named Philadelphus, in honor of Cleopatra's brother, whom she conveniently murdered in order to secure the Egyptian throne for herself."

The tone of his voice—cold, hard, bitter—took some of the beauty from the night.

"My mother's throne was in danger, and she appealed to Julius Caesar. He helped to strengthen her kingdom and stayed several months. When he left for Rome she was pregnant with his son, Caesarion, my older half-brother.

"Then she met my father. He must have loved her, for she destroyed him. She ruined the friendship between him and Octavian. He made military conquests all across this country, and she maneuvered to get a large share of everything. My father forgot where his allegiance lay. The conquered lands belonged to Rome, and Octavian did not let him forget it.

"Herod the Great ruled in Palestine, and he hated my mother's influence on his friend, Antony. Herod had been promoted to his rule over the Jews after my father convinced Julius Caesar that Herod was fit for a kingship.

"Herod repulsed my mother's wiles, and so did the young Octavian when the tide turned against her and my father. Octavian's naval victory at Actium meant complete defeat for her.

"Within the year, my father committed suicide. Then, rather than face disgrace alone, she too took her own life. Some say with an asp, but I doubt it. Poison was more her style.

"Her enemies cleaned out Alexandria, where she reigned. We were carried away to Rome. Octavian marched us in his victory parades. We wore chains, my sister and I. Philadelphus was too small to march. They displayed him naked in a cage on the back of one of my mother's royal elephants. I watched as her army and naval generals were beheaded and her political counselors pierced by the archers.

"Octavian had further plans for us. We were to be sent to Numidia as slaves. My sister was promised to a Numidian prince. I do not know what happened to her or to my little brother.

"One night a hand was clapped over my mouth. I thought I was being taken out to be murdered, but it was Lepidus. He came to rescue me. Octavian had turned against him too. He was deprived of all lands and honors except part of Africa.

"Lepidus had always shown a fondness for me. We traveled the world until I was old enough to take care of myself. Then one day he was gone, and I was on my own. I heard that he lived and died quietly in a small villa on the western shore of Greece. I hope so. I will inquire about him when I get to Rome."

Quintira had not spoken until now. "Rome? How do you expect to get to Rome?"

"In style, as befitting my position." He thrust his right hand under his left arm as if wearing a toga and lifted his chin. His eyes smiled at her in the light of torches from a nearby gate.

She shook her head. "No, Grandfather, you must not go to Rome. No matter how many years have passed, you might not be safe."

"Octavian is gone. Tiberius has no reason to hate or fear me."

"But where would you get money for your ship passage?"

"Ah, here comes the important part. Herod Philip is still in Damascus. I was listening to the gossip in the barber shop."

"Don't you always?"

"I will appeal to him. He is a just man. He carries his *curule* chair and purple cushion with him and sets up court anywhere there is a problem. I will show him the *bulla,* and I will remind him that my father helped his father become ruler of most of Palestine, some of which he and his brother, Antipas, still rule."

Quintira was looking at him with awe. "My father always said Marc Antony was one of the world's greatest military men."

"He probably was. For that reason I believe any Roman official will show me respect. Rome loved my father. Off and on," he added with a touch of humor.

"But they hated your mother?"

"With just cause. She was a leech upon the land. Never satisfied.

Never, never satisfied." He gave a heavy sigh.

Quintira reached over and touched his hand. "Helios?" The name sounded strange. She looked at him, a question in her eyes.

"Now that I know your real name, what shall I call you?"

"I have grown used to Old One. And it warms my heart when you call me Grandfather." He lifted Quintira's hand. "I am going to ask you something, and you must not say no."

"I doubt if I could ever refuse anything you ask."

"In the morning I am going to try to get an audience with Herod Philip. If I succeed, I want you to come with me later and ask for an audience with King Aretas. He is still here."

"Oh, I couldn't. He would never, never believe me."

"Of course he will. Your eyes and voice speak truth."

"I can't."

"You must. You owe it to yourself and to him. And certainly to Mi'kal."

Quintira shook her head. "Let's forget about me. Is it safe to reveal your identity to anyone? Old political fires often flare up with a slight shift of wind."

"I won't do anything rash. I shall do as Augustus Caesar advised on his seal. *Festina lente*—'make haste slowly.' When I see Philip, I will explain that Lepidus assured me there is a trust fund in a bank of Rome and a villa waiting for me. I will not be a burden on their treasury."

"But would your inheritance still be there? After all these years?"

"Lepidus believed it was a perpetual trust—forever—unless someone could prove I was dead. I will claim it. Then you and Mi'kal must come and live with me. You can travel and see the world."

"Mi'kal would like that," Quintira said, as they left the bench. "Will you travel with us?"

"No. I will stay in Rome and indulge my favorite vice." They were passing a gaming house. He cast a wistful glance.

She took his elbow. "Not tonight, Grandfather."

He chuckled as they walked on together.

HEROD PHILIP

The next morning the golden *bulla* secured Helios an immediate audience with Herod Philip. The tetrarch was seated on his official chair with the purple cushion as he received Helios with respect. He spoke only enough to encourage Helios to verify his story by relating memories of his childhood.

Helios told of riding the royal galleys, of playing with the pet monkeys, of days of sunlight and laughter with his twin sister, Selene. He spoke quickly of the bad days—days when neither father or mother could be found in the echoing halls of the Alexandrian palace.

"If you can arrange passage for me to Rome, I have been assured there is a trust fund and a villa for me. My father did not forget about me before he took his own life. As for my mother—she had thoughts of no one but herself."

Philip nodded. "I am well aware of how the desire for power and wealth can consume a person's soul. I have tried to rule with fairness."

His voice grew gentle. "But there is little compassion in this world, little honesty and goodness. Except for my Salome." He closed his eyes for a moment. "When she came to me she had nightmares. She could not forgive herself for the death of an innocent prophet."

His eyes opened and a smile flashed. "She is no longer tormented. She has listened to a Nazarene rabbi from Galilee. He came to Caesarea Philippi. I, too, have heard him."

A light crossed the tetrarch's cheeks. The Old One knew that Death had marked this man, but the smile was warm and living.

"My Salome loves me. Can you understand? I don't, but it is true. She loves me."

Philip called in his secretary, Gryphus, who was instructed to write letters of credit and arrange for passage on a ship to Italy as soon as possible. Alexander Helios, son of Marc Antony, was to have everything necessary for a royal journey.

Philip laid the *bulla* in the Old One's hand. "Come back today at about the second hour. The papers will be ready for you."

"Thank you, my lord."

"Go in peace, and may good fortune attend you."

At his desk, Gryphus, liaison with Tiberius, emperor of Rome, frowned as he wrote. He liked the tetrarch, but the man lacked political sense. He failed to realize that Rome seethed with dissatisfaction toward the present emperor. All it would take would be one tiny spark of renewed loyalty to Marc Antony. His flamboyant exploits and charms were still remembered by the older citizens of Rome. The younger ones tended to clothe him in a hero's toga and speak of his deeds as "fabulous" during the time of an "invincible" Rome.

Gryphus chewed the tip of his pen. Without doubt he would be accountable if he did not inform Tiberius that Alexander Helios had appeared out of nowhere and was departing for Rome from Caesarea on the coast. He also knew Tiberius would never want Marc Antony's son to reach Italy.

QUINTIRA

Leyla was escorted into King Aretas's quarters the moment she arrived at the palace in early afternoon. He was waiting for her, seated behind a desk with ebony legs and an ivory top. He rose and came forward to greet her.

As she knelt she glanced at his eyes. They weren't green like Mi'kal's. They were almost black. His narrow beard followed the corners of his jawbones, and Leyla remembered Mi'kal's chin and jaw. Her cheeks grew warm. Aretas noticed. "Please sit down. Do not be embarrassed."

The piece of purple scarf lay on the desk beside him. His hand touched it. "You said you can tell me something about my son, Myndus. About his death?"

"Yes." Leyla began too quickly, almost stuttering in her haste. "Slower, please," Aretas urged. "Take your time."

Occasionally he would interrupt and ask her to repeat something. He often reiterated her words. "Quintira...Bathrya...Raaschid!"

As Leyla's own story of her stay in the camp became meshed with Quintira's story of murder and kidnapping, Aretas inquired, "Are you certain my grandson had nothing to do with the death of your attacker?"

"Nothing, my lord. He was not in my tent. I only am to blame."

"There is no blame."

"I wish his mother was here to tell you all of this. She is beautiful and wise. You would be proud of her."

"I am. If she has produced a son with red-gold hair and green eyes like my beloved Mumtaza, I know I would cherish her."

"He is handsome, my lord."

"When he is angry, do his eyes burn with black and yellow fires?"

"When he is very angry, it is so. He was angry at me once. He threw my straw god away. That's when all our troubles started. I saw the tail end of a fox, too."

"Ah, yes. Bad, very bad. Do you have any idea where we can find him?"

"He intended to go to Galilee to search for Jesus, the man from Nazareth who has been doing miracles."

"His fame is spreading."

"Mi'kal thinks he knows the secret of bringing people back to life. He hates Death more than anybody I ever saw."

"Everyone hates Death."

"Mi'kal thinks Jesus might be the Phoenix."

"The Green Bird of the black tents?"

"Do you know about it?"

"Yes, indeed. He may find the prophet, but he will find no Green Bird. But if he is in Galilee, we must locate him. I will send an escort to help you. Would you like to do this?"

"Oh, yes! But what about Rekha?"

"I will do what is necessary. I would go with you, but I must remain here for a few days. Later, perhaps I can join you. Then I will expect both of you to come to Petra with me."

He rang a bell, but before anyone came, Aretas said, "This desert chieftain who slew my son. His name again, and his clan?"

She told him and then wondered if she might be bringing trouble for Raaschid.

"Yes, my lord?" The man's voice from the doorway was deep and respectful.

"Leyla, this is Silvanus. He will be your escort into Galilee. You can have complete confidence in him."

Leyla turned to look up into a pair of eyes as brown and shiny as wet barley seeds. He was tall. His face was as Mi'kal's should have been—an oval of warm brown, a straight nose, and black curly hair. He was dressed in a short tunic, and a white silken skull cap embroidered with silver lay on his curls.

"Silvanus, prepare to leave for Galilee in the morning. I will assign you a covered wagon. Leyla, take as much baggage as you require."

"Thank you, my lord." She bowed. Suddenly nothing could have stopped her from going.

"Now, wait for us in the hall. I wish to speak to Silvanus for a moment."

The hall was almost as big as the banquet room. At either end, long winding stairways went from one floor to another. Persian rugs covered the mosaic floor and hung from the walls. There were numerous doorways, and benches were provided where people could wait for an audience with the official they came to see.

Leyla's glance passed over the people on the benches. Startled, she looked again. Surely she must be mistaken!

"Quintira!"

Quintira leaped to her feet, her arms wide. "Leyla!" The man with her stood up, surprise and pleasure in his face. For a moment Leyla did not recognize him.

"What are you doing here?" Both women spoke at the same time. "I thought you were dead!"

The explanations poured out, crowding and pushing against one another like sheep leaving the fold. Finally, each understood enough to take turns.

"You are waiting to get the Old One passage to Rome?"

"And Aretas believed you when you told him about Myndus and me and—"

"Yes! Quintira you must teach me how to properly thank your God."

Quintira smiled. God would be glad to hear praise from a new believer. She hugged Leyla again just as King Aretas and Silvanus came into the hallway.

Leyla loosened Quintira's arms and ran to the king.

"My lord, she is here! Mi'kal's mother is here. Right there!"

Aretas of Petra lifted his eyes and looked at a woman in olive green. A beautiful woman with a noble countenance and tears in her eyes. He held out his arms. "Welcome, my daughter."

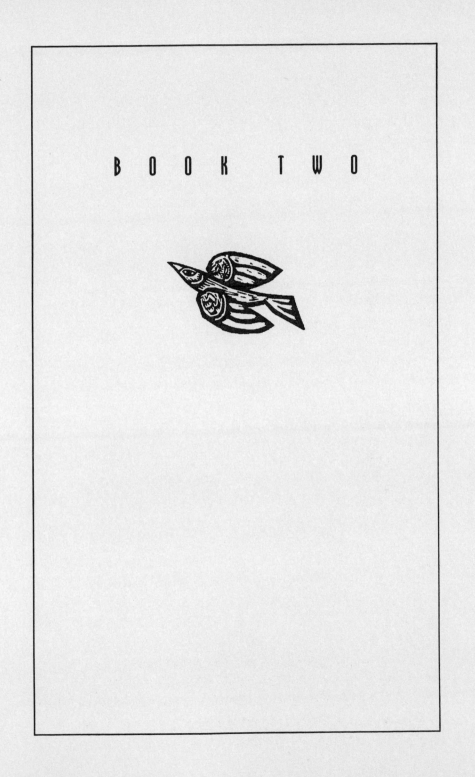

BOOK TWO

Another pair of eyes other than those of the blue heron saw Mi'kal floating in the Jabbok River after the angry waters of the whirlpool spewed him out. Strong, round arms pulled him to shore and pounded the water from his lungs.

He opened dazed eyes and tried to sit up. "Where...what?" He closed his eyes until the whirling in his brain stopped, and then he tried again. He was beginning to discern things—a mist of coppery-red above him and the fact that he hurt all over.

As his brain cleared, the mist changed to a mop of red hair. He blinked and groaned. His chest felt as if someone was sitting on it. Every breath brought a measure of pain.

The owner of the red hair bent closer. He tried to say her name and stumbled.

"Zeus?" The noises in his head and ears had stopped. He struggled to sit up. He was beginning to see: the blue sky, the clouds. And Zeus squatting beside him.

"Are you all right?"

"Almost. I'm trying to remember what happened."

"I found you floating in the river. I thought you were dead."

"I think...I remember falling into the whirlpool. But how did I get out?"

"From the looks of you, you were thrown out. You look like the remnants of Sisera's army."

"I remember." He tried to sit up. She put her arm under his shoulder and tried to help. "The wind flipped the bridge and—"

"You must be related to Jonah. Nobody escapes that whirlpool."

"I was warned."

He tried to stand and groaned. She steadied him. "Zeus, do you always appear out of nowhere? You did the same thing on the highway when I needed you."

"I wasn't expecting to see you either." She was smiling. "How did you get here and why?"

"It's a long story."

"Then you'd better sit down."

She helped him walk to a driftwood log. A mass of fiery abrasions burned his arms and legs. He had lost his sandals. His tunic was ripped from one shoulder and flapped wet against his legs.

His hand went to his waist. The small money bag was still securely tied. Silently he thanked God.

She sat on the ground in front of him as he told her about Oreb and Moses and the trip into Galilee. He did not mention the Zealot cave. He made his meeting with Judas sound casual and concentrated on his conversation with the Greeks at the warm springs.

"They said Jesus crossed the Jordan early yesterday to visit a city called Gerasa. I decided to come over and find him. The others went on to Judea. I will go to Jerusalem later."

"You caused quite a little trouble at the garrison. Captain Gaius sent men to look for you after the foot soldiers brought in the horse he had loaned you. They found the place where you fell into the ditch, but you were gone. We didn't know what happened to you."

"The ditch wasn't my idea. I didn't exactly fall into it."

She grinned. "Evidently you've given up trying to save your white-haired friend. What was her name?"

"Leyla. And her hair wasn't white." He cast what he hoped was a deprecating look at her shorn locks. "It was silver and hung clear down her back."

"Really? Well I hope she doesn't get hung up in it like Absalom."

There was a moment of uneasy silence and then Mi'kal relented. "I know I was foolish to think I could help her, but I didn't want my stepfather to execute her. Is there anything wrong in that?"

"Why would he punish her for protecting herself? He must be a cruel man."

"No. He tries to be just. He suffered a great loss. Sa'ad was his first-born and prince of the tribe. He would have been the next leader."

She considered what he said and nodded. "Israel has its way of being cruel, too. The Jews stone a woman for adultery or a man for blasphemy. They have a regular stoning ground in Jerusalem below the hill where the Romans do their crucifixions." Her eyes clouded. "Crucifixion is the cruelest of all." Her smile was gone.

He leaned forward and touched one of her red locks. "Thanks for saving me. Now let us talk no more of death. Tell me, why are you here?"

"For the same reason you are—I am searching for your Green Bird. Two of my good friends, Mary and Martha of Bethany, need him. Their young brother is very sick. The doctor says Lazarus is dying."

"So they sent you to find Jesus?"

"No. They sent a young man, the son of the miller."

"Then why are you—"

"Gideon was stupid. Like you falling off the bridge. He came down the Jericho road when the sun was too hot. He fainted right by the river in front of Dannah and me. We didn't know Lazarus was sick, so when he told us what he was trying to do, I told Dannah to take care of him. And I came to get Jesus."

"But you must have just got home from the garrison."

"I told you. Mary and Martha are my friends. I was glad to come. The hills are always calling me." She hesitated and looked at him with troubled eyes. "Do I sin when I leave my family so often and answer the call of the hills?"

"Zeus, I believe one must answer the call—whatever it is, wherever it leads."

She stood up and motioned toward the eastern mountains. "You think he is in Gerasa?"

"That's what the Greeks said."

"Martha said so, too, according to Gideon. It's a beautiful city and I like to go there, but there are many hills between." She sighed. "I've

189

wasted a lot of time with you."

"I'm sorry if I've delayed you." He stood up. He still hurt, but the weakness was gone. "Now we can go together."

"No. I should send you home and let Dannah doctor you up."

"I'm all right."

"You couldn't keep up with me. You don't have any sandals."

"I'm part Arab and the soles of my feet are my sandals."

"No!"

"Listen to me." His hand detained her. "I didn't ask you to save me, but since you did, you can't leave me here to starve to death."

She brushed his hand away. "All right, we'll eat. Can you fix a fire?"

"Yes, of course." Could he fix a fire? How did she think Bedouins cooked?

As he gathered dried brush, his irritation eased. He saw her filling the copper pot with water. He remembered how she had taken radishes and onions during their meal at the garrison because it was more exciting to "steal" than to accept what would have been given her. She thrived on action and excitement.

He laid the fire as he watched her unroll her pack and take out a head of cabbage and her flint.

Today the same brown garment was hitched up into her Roman belt. The same wide mouth laughed at him; the same gray eyes mocked him; the same red hair captured the sunlight. She was still the girl from the cliff who had appeared so unexpectedly on the day of the ambush. She had brushed away his inadequacies that day even as she was taking care of him now.

Perhaps she was a ministering angel. Quintira had told him of angels mingling with mortals on earth. Often they were unrecognized. The thought of Zeus as an angelic being brought laughter into his throat as he built a hearth of stones for the copper pot.

"Zeus, how old are you?"

"Sixteen, but I feel much older. My sister, Dannah, is fifteen. I am years older than she is. I am even older than my father. He isn't right in the head. He imagines things."

"What kind of things?"

"He thinks he belongs to the Essene community, but he only grows vegetables for them. He never worships with them at Qumran or bathes in their pools or eats silently at their tables. Do you know about the Essenes?"

"Yes. My mother has explained all the religious sects. The Essenes are the extra religious ones who have nothing to do with the temple worship."

"Right. They are very strict and, I think, equally stupid." She set the copper pot over the coals.

"My grandfather felt the same way," Mi'kal said. "At least my mother said so. He thought they were useless because their righteousness, if they had any, could never rub off on anyone else."

"He was right. The more they deny themselves, the more rewards they expect to get. They call themselves Brothers, but if one of them makes a mistake, he is cast out of the family. To me that is not love."

The fire crackled and the smell of the smoke was pleasant. The heat felt good on his cuts and bruises as he listened to her and watched the bubbles rising in the water.

She told him she often watched the Essenes from the heights of a goat hill over their settlement near the Salt Sea. The only thing she admired was their work in copying the holy Scriptures.

"Someday the copies might come in handy. As for the other stuff, someone told me they seek sanctification. I'm not sure what it means." She looked at him as if he did.

"Maybe it means extra closeness with God."

She shrugged. "Who can be closer to him than I am when I walk in freedom over his hills?"

"I have felt the same way during a Syrian sunrise," Mi'kal confessed and felt his heart constrict. Always when he thought of the black tents his anxiety for his mother and Leyla became sharp agony.

"Zeus, doesn't your mother worry about you when you're gone all the time?"

"She's dead. My sister takes care of everything. Dannah is happy at home. I am happy here."

The late afternoon sun made a golden haze over the water. Black birds with scarlet epaulets swung on the clumps of bulrushes. In the swaying tufts of papyrus reed, insects sang. The world was indeed a beautiful place.

He watched as she walked along the edge of the water, bending now and then to turn the stones.

"What are you looking for?"

"You'll see. Ho, there!" She made a grab for something and came up with a hideous squirming creature. The claws and tail resembled a scorpion.

"Drop it!" Mi'kal yelled

"Never! This is our supper." She held it up and watched it wiggle.

"Zeus, I can't eat that thing!"

"Well, I can." She tossed it to him and laughed as he jumped back. She threw him a second and a third.

The "water scorpions" scrambled to get back to the river. Zeus ordered him to use a leafy branch to constrain them. She ignored his protests as she dropped the struggling creatures into the boiling water.

She tossed him her knife. "Quarter the cabbage."

He felt a flash of anger. What made her think she could order him around like a common servant? What would she say if he told her he was a prince of Petra? The cabbage cracked and he chuckled. She wouldn't be impressed if he were the emperor of Rome.

"Won't you find all this freedom a little difficult after you get married?" He sprinkled salt on the cabbage as he talked.

She gave him a steady look. "I'll probably get married when the Red Sea parts again. No man is going to tell me what to do."

"But it's the natural things isn't it? I mean for a man and a woman to…"

"Oh, I might lie with a man someday, just to see what it's like. But I'll never marry him."

Mi'kal's face grew hot. "That would be fornication. Fornication is a sin in the eyes of the Lord."

"I just said I might."

She was giggling as she lifted one of the shellfish from the pot on a forked stick. "Lunch is ready."

She tore the crayfish apart and stuffed a small piece into his mouth. "Eat it and be happy. Jesus says it isn't what goes into a man's mouth that defiles him but what comes out of it."

He was too hungry to spit the meat out. He watched as she tore off the claws and head and sucked them out. He didn't hesitate to follow her example on his second one.

As she threw the shells away she said, "The Pharisees are always quoting the law. They accuse Jesus of breaking the law, but Jesus has his own ideas about the law. He says if we love God and our neighbors, the law will take care of itself."

"My mother always felt guilty because we couldn't fully observe the Sabbath as a day of rest."

"She shouldn't worry. Jesus feeds his men when they are hungry— even on the Sabbath—with grain he picks in the fields. He heals people on the Sabbath, too. Once he did it right in the synagogue. When people condemn him, he tells them they wouldn't hesitate to pull their donkey or their cow from a mudhole on the Sabbath. And men are more important than donkeys and cows!"

The hot stones sizzled as she poured the kettle water over them. She looked at him and grinned. "Well, how do you feel?"

"Defiled—but satisfied."

He washed the cooking vessel in the river while she rolled up her pack.

"Now that we've eaten, I must go on. But I will tell you how to find our house in Papyron. You can wait for Jesus and me there."

"I'm not going to Papyron," Mi'kal said.

"When you reach the Jericho ford, you will see where the old city of Papyron used to be. It was destroyed a hundred years ago in a battle between the Romans and the Nabateans. Most of it is hidden in the swamp. Our house sits by itself near the river."

"No!"

"Now and then my father turns up a skull in his garden, then buries it again and washes in the Jordan to rid himself of defilement. I've never understood how a dead man could defile anybody."

"Zeus, you might as well tether your tongue."

"Dannah is very pretty. You'll like her. She follows the rules, as you do."

"I am going with you." His tone was final.

She gave him a nasty look. "All right. But I should warn you. We will have lizard for supper tonight."

He held his silence.

She broke down and laughed. "I will have to steal you a pair of sandals."

"I've got money."

"There are no shops between here and Gerasa. Besides, stealing is cheaper and more exciting."

"So you've said. But I think stealing is a sin."

"You have more sins hopping around in your self-righteous little head than Pharaoh had frogs." She sounded disgusted. "Come on. When we pass a field or a vineyard, we'll get you some sandals. They won't even be missed for awhile."

"Why not?"

"Wait and see." She shot him a sassy, knowing look that made him blush. "Oh, come on, innocent. You don't know as much as they do." She pointed to a pair of dragon flies mating on the tip of a papyrus plume.

"Zeus!"

She laughed. "What a baby you are."

"There are some things that a man does not—"

"Don't worry. If you were like most of the boys I know, I wouldn't be foolish enough to take you with me."

CHAPTER TWENTY-SIX

After leaving the river and climbing to the top of the Jordan gorge, Mi'kal was feeling the strain in his chest and legs. All his efforts went into keeping up with Zeus.

She moved with long strides, skirting bushes and large boulders as if she traveled a marked path. Mi'kal could see no evidence that anyone had ever been there. But various types of animal excrement littered the ground. At first she stayed many lengths ahead of him. Now and then she waited with an aggrieved look on her face. But finally they walked together.

Ahead of them, as far as he could see, the land was a series of sharp dips and shrub-covered hills between the protecting battlements of higher mountains.

After the climbing eased, they began to talk. He wanted to know what she had done after he left the garrison on his disastrous rescue mission. She told him that she had started home the next morning with a wagonload of recruits being exchanged for others at the fortress in Jerusalem. At home she had grown restless after only a few hours of cleaning her father's vegetables and watching the worm-eaten cabbage leaves float down the Jordan.

"Like the round-bottomed boats on the Euphrates," she added. "I don't know why I can't stay home like my sister. But I can't."

When asked about the young lieutenant, she told him Auran's thigh had stopped bleeding, but the surgeon said the injury would take many weeks of convalescence.

In the middle of the morning, after an arduous climb to a plateau of wheat fields, Zeus stopped. She held up her hand. Mi'kal could hear soft whispers, male and female, behind a thick hedge that bordered the field.

Zeus stooped and pulled him down beside her. She pointed through the interlaced branches of thorns and tiny yellow flowers. On the other side there was a carelessly dropped robe and a pair of men's sandals.

Mi'kal watched as Zeus eased the footwear toward her with a stick. Carefully she wiggled them under the hedge. She thrust them into his hands as they fled. Then, in spite of his scruples, Mi'kal joined in her laughter.

The sandals were too large, but he pulled the laces tight and blessed her. His "Arab" soles were wearing thin. He reached for her hand, and she did not object.

"Now, Mi'kal, it's your turn to tell me about everything you've done. You've had more adventures than Solomon had wives." She sounded envious. "Tell me more about Oreb. He sounds exciting."

He described Oreb—his awkward sword belt, his old helmet, and his whistling. She laughed when she heard about Moses, the mule, who suffered "mutterings and murmurings."

He told her of Aziz, the stable master's son from Ephraim, who promised him a gray donkey.

He knew she would have considered his visit to the Hornet's Nest the most exciting story of all, but again he withheld any mention of the Zealots. He did tell her Judas was anxious to see Jesus on the throne. And how the disciple had paid for their baths at the hot springs near Salim.

Later, as they grew hot and the landscape became monotonous, Mi'kal began to tell her about his short visit in Capernaum. He described Quintillius's villa, the monkey with golden hair, and the bright birds swinging in the cages. She already knew about his servant's healing.

By noon, Mi'kal's legs were cramping from the unaccustomed climbing, and his sandal straps were rubbing. He was glad when Zeus decided to rest by a mountain brook with a young shepherdess and a small herd of black and white goats. The girl shared bread and milk with them. When they left, Mi'kal surprised her with one small coin from his purse.

Several hours later, the sun sank and dusk filled the hollows about them. Fog rose from the banks of the peaceful river in the valley below.

Mi'kal tried to remember what Quintira had told him about the Jabbok river and Jacob, the son of Isaac.

Somewhere in this land beyond the Jordan, Jacob and his twin brother, Esau, had been reconciled after a family quarrel. Here by the river, Jacob's name had been changed to Israel after he had wrestled with an angel in some kind of an argument with God. Later, God changed Esau's name to Edom and promised both Israel and Edom they would be the founders of two great nations as innumerable as the stars.

As Mi'kal thought of the promise, he looked upward. The air was chilling. Night was flowing into the valley below, making pools of darkness. One by one the stars appeared in a pallid sky.

Zeus broke the silence. "It's getting late. I know where we can sleep."

"Shouldn't we try to go on?"

"Would it profit anyone if we fell off a cliff?"

They climbed between spindly oaks and outcroppings of dark sandstone until she stopped at the mouth of a cave. Mi'kal thought of the Hornet's Nest. Surely Palestine and Perea had more caves than Syria had sand grouse.

She ordered him to wait outside. She came back with a small clay lamp and worked with her flint and a handful of brush until a spark lighted the wick.

Inside, Mi'kal missed the "windows" of the Zealot's cave. The smell of cool sandstone was the same.

"How did you know about this place?"

"Everybody who goes by here knows about it."

"Everybody? You mean murderers and thieves and—"

"And lonely shepherds trying to get out of the rain, and tired travelers, and runaway slaves and…"

Mi'kal held his tongue. There was no way he could win with her.

Zeus threw him the flint. "Wood and charcoal are in the corner. I'll get some water."

Mi'kal busied himself with the fire and was glad to see that the smoke drifted upward through unseen crevices.

Zeus was slow to return, and the cave filled with loneliness. When she came back with water, he was surprised at his feeling of relief. They drank, and then she set the copper pot on the coals. She rummaged in the shadows and brought out a red clay jar sealed with wax.

"Let's trust the weevils aren't in it."

"What is it?"

"Wheat and barley and millet, with raisins and salt. You stir while I pour."

The porridge sputtered and spat. They ate from the pot. Zeus used a spoon, but he ate as the Bedouin eat, rolling the cooked meal into small balls between his forefinger and thumb and tossing them into his mouth.

She laughed as she watched and then did as he did. They washed their fingers with sand. When he started out of the cave, she yelled at him. "Go to the left. The spring is at the right."

He bit his lips. The girl had no modesty. None at all.

When he returned, she had added more wood to the fire, and shadows leaped high on the sandstone walls. He felt a sense of safety and comfort as he looked at the mat she had spread for him and at the blanket for herself. He was amused at the generous distance between them.

Mi'kal couldn't fall asleep. Finally he raised himself and whispered her name. She responded.

"Do you think Jesus will go back with you?" he asked.

"Of course. He's very close to his Bethany friends. Closer than to his own family."

"How do you know?"

"Andrew told me. He's one of the disciples. He has lots of hair. I like him very much. He's always with his friend Philip." She hesitated. "Are you anxious to sleep?"

"No."

"Do you want to hear a little more about Jesus?"

"Yes. I told my mother I would find out all I could about him."

"Did you know he is called the Son of God because he didn't come from a husband? His mother wasn't married. God planted the seed in her womb. She was pregnant when she married Joseph, but she hadn't been unfaithful to him. An angel told her she was going to have God's Son. And she was to call him Jesus, for he would save us from our sins. She also called him Immanuel. Father told me that means 'God with us.'"

Mi'kal remembered his mother singing of a virgin and her baby. He closed his eyes and tried to remember. Suddenly she was there singing, her hands moving in cadence. "Therefore the Lord himself will give you a sign: The virgin will be with child and will give birth to a son, and will call him Immanuel."

The song faded and he knew Zeus had been talking. "Afterwards she had Joseph's children, but they never understood Jesus. Like a lot of people, they don't believe in him."

"What are they to believe?"

"Whatever he tells them."

Mi'kal turned on his mat. "My mother always believed a Messiah would come someday who would rule from the throne of David. When Aurans told us about Jesus of Nazareth and his miracles, she thought he could be the one."

"I think he is. But I'm not sure he wants to be a ruler right now. I think he has come down from his Father to do something important, but I don't know what it is. Unless maybe it's to forgive us of our sins and teach us how to love one another. That's important isn't it? Especially to have our sins forgiven."

He was silent.

"Well, isn't it?"

"I suppose so. If you are a terrible sinner. To me the most important thing is whether he really knows how to outwit Death."

"Death isn't always bad, Mi'kal. What about people who grow tired of living? Once I saw an old woman in a field. She shared her lunch with me, and I gave her some rock honey I had gathered to sell in the next market." The light of the fire did not reach her, but he knew her wide grin was mocking him. "Sometimes I have to break down and buy things."

"Since you take no joy in thievery," he murmured.

She laughed and it was like the sighing of wind through the tent ropes. A sound he had not fully appreciated until it was gone.

"The old woman dipped her bread and told me she was going blind.

She was anxious to die. She said she was not afraid because she knew it was not the end of anything."

Mi'kal remembered his argument with Aurans in the tent. If the grass renewed itself each spring, surely the souls of men would be renewed somewhere.

"We'd better get some sleep," she said. "We'll rise with the sun."

In the silence, Mi'kal thought he heard the rustling of a bat over his head. He turned on his back and put his hands over his head. He thought of Leyla and her "crawly" things. In the darkness, her face floated before him, an oval of ivory framed by silver hair. He tried to keep her vision with him, but he fell asleep.

He woke to an empty cave, and the loneliness came again. He scrambled to his feet and went outside. Zeus was perched on a narrow ledge above the cave. Her hair challenged the first rays of the sun.

Below them, the Jabbok valley rolled with gray mist, mystical in its ever-changing patterns even as the gray of Zeus's eyes changed with her shifting moods.

She motioned for him to join her. "Today we will find Jesus," she said with assurance.

"How do you know?"

"A little bird told me." She drew a crude diagram in the dust on the ledge. "Here is where we are, and here is Gerasa. Someday you will have to visit that city. There are no such fountains anywhere, except in Damascus."

"Aren't we going there now?"

"No. Jesus never stays long in one place. He will be moving on."

"But you can't be sure. Can you?" The thought of not seeing Gerasa was disappointing.

"Mi'kal, he gets so tired and discouraged in a day's time. All the crippled and sick people come. And the mothers bring their babies, and everybody wants a miracle. But nobody wants him." There was touching sadness in her voice.

"If he is leaving the city this morning, shouldn't we be going?" He jumped from the ledge and turned to help her down. She hesitated for a moment with her legs swinging over the edge.

"I think he will go that direction." She pointed to the southwest. "He may be on his way to Judea, though they are very angry with him there. He probably knows all about Lazarus. He wouldn't be God's Son if he didn't. He seems to know everything." She looked down at him. The light of faith in her face caught at his throat.

He held out a hand, but she ignored him and dropped as quietly as sunlight beside him.

"Zeus, do you know you are beautiful?"

She stared at him. "You're as crazy as the king who ate grass."

"You really are. Beautiful!"

"As beautiful as your Leyla?" He couldn't see her face, but he knew the impudent gleam in her eyes.

"Yes, but in a different way."

"I want to be different." She turned toward him, her face flushed. "I don't want to be put into a little box and labeled. I am never going to grow old. When I die I want to go like the eagle plummeting from the sky. I want the mountains to hear me fall, as though I were a cedar of Lebanon."

She lifted her arms to the breeze and seemed to drink in the wind. On impulse he drew her close and kissed her. For a moment she responded, then pushed him away.

"Don't ever do that again!"

His hands gripped her arms. "Why? Are you afraid to feel like a woman? Is that why you took a man's name?"

"It's none of your business, and I'll feel any way I like." She grabbed up her pack and stomped down the hill ahead of him.

CHAPTER TWENTY SEVEN

They stopped to rest on the summit of a low hill. The anger of the morning was forgotten. Beyond the valley and the busy highway below, the white walls of Gerasa and the suburbs of the city dominated the slopes. A small tributary, swollen by spring rains and melting mountain snow, flowed past the city and joined the Jabbok below.

Roads converged near the enormous gates, and traffic was heavy. Palm and eucalyptus trees lined the roadways. Pedestrians took their chances with chariots, oxen carts, horsemen, flocks of sheep, camels, and human baggage carriers.

Mi'kal felt his pulses jump. Here was his first opportunity to see a city such as the Old One had told him about—with libraries and gymnasiums and theaters, with bazaars selling things beyond his imagination. There would be beautiful women in curtained litters and men with great minds arguing in the forum. Here was a sample of all of Rome's glory.

Zeus read his rapture. "Yes, the city is very beautiful. The buildings have mosaics of griffins and dragons and Egypt's two-headed dog and—"

"Don't you think Jesus might still be there?" The thought of bypassing the city hurt.

"No. I know how he is. He's down there somewhere among all those people leaving the city. We'll have to get closer to pick them out. He usually wears brown." She jumped to her feet and gave him a yank. "Get up. We're wasting time."

Quickly he made his choice. He would stay with her until they found Jesus, and then he would visit Gerasa while she went back to Bethany with Jesus. He would find Jesus in Jerusalem, later. Judea was a small place, and Jerusalem was the center of everything, as a man's heart is the center of his being.

For a moment Mi'kal was lost in the possibility, and then Zeus pulled at him again. "Come on. I'll race you to the highway." And she was off, running like a gazelle.

He had offered several times to carry her pack, but she always refused. Now it was jumping up and down with the shovel and the copper pot banging away with a clangor that roused the nesting quail on the hill.

How contrary she was! And unpredictable. Leyla had been the same. Girls were nothing but trouble. They intruded on your thoughts and then you did stupid things, like trying to kiss them.

Solomon had much to say about women in his book of wisdom, and not much of it was good. But Solomon had truly loved the girl of the vineyard, dark and comely.

Quintira knew the story and sang it as the song it was supposed to be—a story of a satisfied husband and a loving wife. Some of the words made Mi'kal uncomfortable, and Quintira explained that it was pleasing to God for a husband and wife to love one another, passionately and poetically.

His legs were beginning to ache again and his feet were sore, but he had to laugh at his thoughts. He was looking at Zeus through the eyes of Solomon. Her breasts were as young roes, her teeth white as lambs, and her lips scarlet. But her hair was not black as the tents of Kedar.

But then neither was he the eager bridegroom who came leaping over mountains and skipping over hills. His feet hurt too much.

He was still laughing to himself when he dropped down beside her. She was sitting on a knoll, breathing hard, her face flushed with triumph. The pack lay at her feet. He wrapped his arms about his knees and said, "The only reason you won is because these stolen sandals have taken revenge on my feet."

She ignored his excuse as if it were unworthy of him. The sound of traffic reverberated from the hills.

"Look," she said. "I think that's them." She pointed to a group of five men walking single file close to the ditch to avoid the wagons and carts. "Jesus is the one in brown."

Mi'kal leaped up. His heart was pounding. *Jesus at last!* He wanted to jump and shout. The jubilance died in his throat as his eyes settled on the man in brown. He wasn't sure what he had expected, but surely the Messiah of Israel would not be an ordinary man plodding along, stepping over animal excrement. His mother had spoken of him as a conquering King, a righteous Prince wrapped in heavenly glory.

Zeus missed his consternation and puzzled disappointment. She was squinting against the early sun. "I'm trying to decide who is with him. Andrew? Yes. He is always running his fingers through his hair. And Philip is always with Andrew. I'm not sure of the other two. Maybe Matthew and Thomas. Matthew is heavy in the middle, and Thomas always looks angry. Usually there are twelve of them, but sometimes he sends them out to minister. They may have gone on to talk in the temple."

Mi'kal had been trying to swallow his disappointment. She turned to him and her gray eyes were probing. "You don't seem very excited with your Green Bird."

"I'll jump and shout later." He was remembering that Jesus did miracles, whether he looked ordinary or not. "We'd better get him to Bethany right away if you want your friend to live."

She rose and picked up her pack. There was a determined look on her face, and he knew he wasn't going to like what she was about to say.

"Mi'kal, I don't want you to argue with me. I have decided you will deliver Martha's message to Jesus. No! I said no argument!" He had lifted a hand to remonstrate. "I'm going to take a quick way over the hills and tell them he's coming, because all of Bethany will be worried to death."

He dropped the hand and stared at her. "Zeus, you can't! The disciples don't know me. Jesus would never believe me."

"Listen innocent, if you ever tried to lie it would be as plain on your face as the writing on Belshazzar's wall."

"Zeus, please. I can't do it alone." He knew he was pleading, and he hated himself for it.

"Sure you can. You're a prince of the black tents. Remember? Why should you be afraid to talk to anybody? You tell them about Lazarus and then stay with them. They will come over the Jordan ford close to our house. We have a large—"

"Zeus!"

"We have a large mulberry tree in the yard, with a wooden bench in front of it. And there's a big crooked willow tree on the bank of the river."

"Zeus!" The second cry stuck in his throat. He could tell the argument was over.

"You will be all right, won't you?" For a moment he felt her glance linger on him. There was a warmth in it that was comforting.

"Yes," he said, knowing he wasn't.

"This is really the right thing, Mi'kal." She planted a kiss on his cheek and ran.

He watched as she went from rock to rock like a mountain goat. At the top she turned and waved. Her words came faintly. "I'll be waiting for you."

He stood for a moment feeling empty and miserable. He faced the inevitable and squared his jaw. As he ran to reach the disciples, he was praying hard for confidence in himself—and for faith in the man called Jesus.

Philip was the first to realize the tall boy with the bright hair was running to catch up with them. He and Andrew waited.

Mi'kal lifted a hand in greeting as he struggled to catch his breath. He looked at Andrew with the mass of thick hair. "Are you Andrew?"

Andrew nodded. "Yes, and this is my friend Philip." The second disciple was slender and slightly stooped, with a pleasant smile.

"Can we help you?" Philip asked.

"I have to talk to Jesus."

"Do you have a need?"

"A need?" For a moment Mi'kal was puzzled. "No. I have a message from his friends in Bethany. Lazarus is dying."

They were instantly concerned. Philip yelled, "Master! Wait!"

The two disciples walking closer to Jesus halted first. One man was heavy through the middle, the other wore a scowl—just as Zeus had described them.

Philip introduced him to Jesus, and Mi'kal found himself trembling before him, even though he seemed so ordinary, because the Nazarene's eyes seemed to hold the mysteries of the ages.

"Master," Philip said. "He brings sad news from Bethany."

Mi'kal stumbled a little as he explained about Lazarus. "The doctor said he can do nothing more for him. Zeus has gone back to tell Martha that you will be there. She thought they would be worrying."

"Zeus?" Jesus turned to Philip.

"Master, you have seen her. The red-headed girl with the pack who has followed us since Nain."

"Ah, yes."

A shadow of sorrow or regret crossed his face as Jesus said. "It is not the hour for me to return to Bethany." He turned abruptly and walked away, Matthew and Thomas following him.

Andrew and Philip showed surprise at their Master's answer but accepted it without argument. Mi'kal felt the force of the refusal, almost a rebuke. He stood, uncertain of his next move.

"Don't be embarrassed." Andrew laid a hand on his arm. "He will act in God's good time."

"But there is something else," Mi'kal said. "I have come to find him and ask him if he is—"

"Go on," Andrew said gently.

"You won't think I am stupid?"

"Any man who comes to Jesus with a sincere need is not stupid." Philip's smile made Mi'kal feel at ease.

"I have come from the black tents of Syria."

"You're an Arab?" Andrew asked as if in doubt. "You must have come from Esau, for he was reputed to have such hair."

"But so did David, our shepherd king," Philip reminded his friend.

The light exchange of conversation put Mi'kal even more at ease. "My father was a Nabatean, my mother is a Jewess." He hesitated and then went on, confident that the disciples wanted to be his friends. "I have come from my mother's tent to find Jesus of Nazareth because she thinks he might be the Messiah. And I...I had hoped he might be the Green Bird."

He expected a puzzled reaction, but they waited for him to say more.

"In my lord's camp, we sing of a Green Bird that dies and is laid to rest in a bed of spices, then comes to life again. When I heard that Jesus had raised people from the dead, I thought he might be the Phoenix come in human form—or at least know the Green Bird's secret of conquering death."

Mi'kal waited. Had he insulted their Master? Would they become angry as Zeus had?

Philip answered quietly. "We have heard him called many things, including Elijah and Moses, but we have never heard anyone refer to him as the Phoenix. But in a way you are right. He does know the secret of everlasting life."

Andrew interrupted. "But he is no heathen god come to life. Rather he is the one true God come to dwell with us as a man upon the earth. He tells us that whoever has seen him has seen the Father."

Mi'kal looked at them again with the same serious pleading. "I grew up hating death. When I was very little and sang of the Green Bird, I believed in it. Call it hope rather than faith, if you will, but when I heard of Jesus—"

"We understand," Andrew said.

"But as I speak it aloud, it seems such a childish thing."

"No. No it is not." Philip spoke with conviction.

"Even if it is," Mi'kal said with a flare of stubbornness, "I will never believe God wants Death to win. There must be a way for men to win over the curse!"

"Jesus is the Way," Philip said quietly. "He has said over and over that if we believe in him, he will give us everlasting life."

Andrew spoke with more force. "He has told us he is the only way for a man to gain life everlasting."

"I would like to believe, but I do not understand. Zeus has tried to explain but—"

"Stay with us and learn for yourself."

For a moment Mi'kal was tempted. Then he thought of Zeus. He must let her know that Jesus was not coming to Bethany. At least not immediately. He explained it to Andrew and Philip, and they seemed to understand

"I will see you again someday, and you can explain things to me," he said. He was fighting disappointment again. He wanted to stay.

He returned to the hill, turning once to look back, but the disciples were lost to view. He climbed steadily, wishing he knew the hills as Zeus knew them. He did remember they had crossed a well-traveled road leading toward the Jordan valley earlier that morning. He would follow it.

Before he reached the road he was troubled with thoughts of Oreb and the Zealot uprising to put Jesus on the throne. That he had seen nothing extraordinary about Jesus, except the strange wisdom in his eyes, still troubled him. Were brave men risking their lives for a man who was, in spite of what his disciples believed, no more than a prophet?

Jesus had raised the son of a widow in Nain, but Elijah had done the same for the son of a widow in Zarephath. Where was the difference? Who was the greater?

i'kal was helped on his way to Papyron by a wagoneer going back to the Salt Sea for another load of bitumen. The smell of pitch turned Mi'kal's stomach, but he was willing to trade the blistering foot travel for the stinking two-mule wagon.

The driver seemed at odds with the world, so Mi'kal kept his tongue quiet and his mind active with pleasant thoughts of Leyla. His remembrance of her open affection for him was like a soothing balm compared to Zeus's aggravations and superiorities.

He tried to remember details of their arguments on the flight from camp and his reasons for being impatient with her, but he failed. He should have been more loving. He had kissed Zeus and been kissed in return—and the world had not come to an end.

When the pitch wagon's lanterns went dry during the dark hours, the driver stopped for a few hours of sleep. He threw Mi'kal an old blanket. The edges were stiff with tar.

At midafternoon, Mi'kal dismounted at the Jericho ford. He washed in the river to rid himself of the bitumen stench before crossing to the Judean side. As he soothed his sore feet in the water, he chewed on some stalks of young cattails to pacify his growling stomach.

He had no trouble finding Hosea's house. He passed a large willow by the river and caught the sound of voices and the smell of baking bread. The house was small and built of mud bricks. Wooden shutters covered the windows. Mi'kal guessed there were no more than three rooms.

The only traces of the city of Papyron that Zeus had mentioned were mounds of rubble and a fire-charred city gate slowly sinking into the marsh beyond the house. He wondered if some of his Nabatean ancestors were among the skulls Hosea had found.

A boy and a girl sat on the wooden bench beneath the mulberry tree. They were talking and shelling peas. The girl must be Zeus's sister. He tried to remember her name. Dannah.

She rose to greet him as if she knew all about him, as she probably did. At least everything Zeus knew. Her eyes were large and dark, her hair a lustrous brown. Zeus had said she was pretty, and she was. She blushed slightly as she introduced Gideon, the boy who had started out to find Jesus and fainted by the river.

Zeus came running from the house with a joyful welcome. She was dressed in a woman's garment and tripped on the long skirt. He grabbed her to keep her from falling. He lowered his head as if to kiss her, but she pulled back, her face slightly warming.

Then began the rush of questions and answers. What about Lazarus? He was dead and buried three days ago. Why hadn't Jesus come? He had said it wasn't the time to come. Mi'kal learned all of Bethany was full of mourning, and Martha was bitter and blamed Jesus for not being here.

"Mary thinks he didn't come because he does not want to cause trouble in the city so close to Passover," Gideon said. "She seems to understand Jesus more than anybody else, so maybe that's why."

Mi'kal shook his head. "All he said to me was it wasn't time for him to return to Bethany."

"I'm sure he knew Lazarus was already dead," Zeus said.

Her defense made him angry as he thought of his humiliation in front of the four disciples. "Then why didn't he say so?"

"Delphine," Dannah interrupted. "I think you should check on Father in the garden while I look at the bread and put these peas on to boil."

Mi'kal could not resist. He chuckled. "Delphine?"

Zeus gave his neck curls a jerk as she passed him. Delectable odors were coming from the kitchen. Zeus returned smiling. Everything was fine with her father. He was picking vegetables for the Brotherhood. "But before our meal he will bathe in the Jordan as though it were a purifying pool."

"Delphine—"

"Gideon, I've told you. If you want to be my friend, you will remember to call me Zeus. Please. No matter what my sister says."

"I'm sorry. She says you have known Jesus for a long time. Do you understand him?"

"No. I don't know anybody who does. Not completely."

Just then Hosea came from behind the house in a tattered white garment bearing a basket of young onions and carrots. He was very thin, with wispy gray hair and vague eyes. He smiled at Mi'kal. "Welcome to the commune, my son," he said and went into the house.

Dannah called from the kitchen. "Delphine, come set the table. Gideon, I need some water from the cistern."

"Can I help?" Mi'kal asked.

Zeus gave him a little shove. "You sit here and think about tomorrow. We're going to Jerusalem to get you some new clothes." Mi'kal closed his eyes and laid his head against the bole of the tree. Jerusalem!

The sounds and smells from the kitchen reminded him of his mother. He could see her beside the cooking hearth. Outside the tent, the bright pennants of dawn flew above the parapets of the white cliff. He could hear the blatting of goats and the grumblings of camels. A soft morning wind stirred the tent curtains.

"Mi'kal." Zeus stood beside him. "Were you sleeping?"

"No. I was thinking of my mother and—"

"The white-haired girl?"

He nodded. He hadn't really been thinking about Leyla at all but...

"Don't let me stop you." Zeus swished away. He heard pot lids rattling.

Dannah called him to the table, and he ate until he embarrassed himself. Hosea sat in a wet garment for he had indeed walked into the river in penitential prayer.

What the meal lacked in meat was compensated for by vegetables—cabbages no bigger than a large walnut cooked in olive oil; stalks of celery filled with nuts and cheese; a dish of withered green leaves cooked in butter with caraway seeds; cucumbers in sour cream; and platters of Dannah's warm bread.

After the meal, Hosea went to his room to pray and read his scrolls.

Mi'kal helped Zeus in the kitchen.

Dannah and Gideon walked into the river and chased each other from stone to stone in the shallow ford. Mi'kal and Zeus smiled as they heard them laughing. She told him that Gideon had gone home in a covered wagon on the day he fainted. The next day he had come back to tell Dannah that Lazarus had died and was buried in a tomb near the olive slopes. Evidently they had fallen in love. Tonight he was invited to share a sleeping mat with Mi'kal on the floor of the kitchen.

As Mi'kal dried dishes Zeus said, "I've been wanting to ask you. What did you think of Jesus?"

Mi'kal hesitated. He had delayed telling her his first reaction because he wasn't proud of it and she wouldn't understand.

"I was disappointed—right from the start when you pointed him out on the road. I'm sorry."

"Disappointed?" She almost dropped the bread platter. "What were you expecting? Green feathers and a tail?"

"Forget it. You asked me and I told you. He just didn't seem like anyone who could be a Messiah or a king. And when I told him about Lazarus, he didn't seem to care much."

"What did you want him to do? Order down a chariot and race to Bethany?" Her face was as fiery as her hair.

"Zeus! I just think there ought to be something...well, magnificent and awe inspiring about someone who is supposed to be the King of Israel!"

Zeus was cool toward him as she put the dishes in the cupboard. He joined Gideon and Dannah by the tree. He studied the younger girl. There was nothing of Zeus about her, but she was lovely in her own way. He tried to compare them.

How would Dannah respond to a violent storm? She would close the shutters and put her hands over her ears. Zeus would stand, holding to a tree trunk, laughing at the bursting heavens. Water would run down her cheeks and off her chin. Her eyes would close against the pounding rain, and she would rise on tiptoe to meet the thrashing wind.

She would fling her arms wide to embrace the rain and slide down the ravines to roll in the water of the mountain gutters. She would stand under a waterfall, letting the cold bring pimples, and then she would run in the sun to get warm.

He had never seen her do any of these things, but he knew she would. Dannah's thoughts seemed to pick up his own.

"Mi'kal, why can't my sister stay home with us and be happy?"

He pointed to a night-hawk settling on the topmost branch of a tree. It was beating its wings to hold steady against the sway of the wind.

"That is your sister," he said. "You are satisfied with the lower branches. You have a peace and contentment that your sister will never know. Someday you and Gideon will have a family, and you will leave this life as quietly and as beautifully as you have lived it."

She laid her head on Gideon's shoulder and his arm went about her.

Mi'kal rose, a sadness settling in him. He felt old. Would he ever find such love? For the first time in many days he thought of his mother's purple scarf and wondered what had happened to it after Leyla died.

Dannah pulled free from Gideon as her father came out with a tattered scroll. He began to read aloud, and Mi'kal asked him questions.

"You have good knowledge of our prophets, son," Hosea said.

"My mother was a rabbi's daughter. She loved to study with him. One thing I would like to know." Mi'kal knew he was asking as much to humor the gentle Hosea as he was to know the answer. "It is said that your Brotherhood does not worship at the temple. Can you explain why?"

Zeus came to sit beside him and their quarrel over Jesus seemed forgotten. "He thinks the worship at the temple has been corrupted."

Her father nodded. "It is unclean...and will be until the Messiah comes."

Hosea found the proper place and began to read from the writings of Isaiah: "Stop bringing meaningless offerings! Your incense is detestable to me. New Moons, Sabbaths and convocations—I cannot bear your evil assemblies.... They have become a burden to me.... When you spread out your hands in prayer, I will hide my eyes from you."

Before retiring, Hosea made his ritualistic trip to the river. His wet garment clung to his thin frame. His lips were blue, but he refused the blanket Dannah brought him.

"Father, why do you think you must punish your body in order to please God?" she asked sadly.

He shivered and made no reply. Zeus put her arm around him as if to warm him. "Father you should listen to us. I have heard Jesus say that the only work anyone can do to get into heaven is to believe in him because he has brought truth into the world."

"Even so," Gideon said quietly, "there has to be a blood sacrifice."

Hosea said with quivering lips, "He is right. It is written, 'For the life of a creature is in the blood, and I have given it to you to make atonement for yourselves on the altar; it is the blood that makes atonement for one's life.'"

"Then how can Jesus forgive sins?" Dannah asked.

Hosea lifted his hands. "Who can tell? The ways of the Lord are past finding out." Then his face lifted in prayer.

"To you, O Lord, I lift up my soul.... Good and upright is the Lord; therefore he instructs sinners in his ways.... All the ways of the Lord are loving and faithful for those who keep the demands of his covenant.... Let me not be put to shame, for I take refuge in you."

The four of them said, "Amen."

Later, as Dannah and Zeus settled on their beds, Dannah said, "Delphine."

"Don't make me angry, Dannah. I didn't object tonight, but—"

"I'm sorry. Zeus, do you think it is all right for me to feel good when Gideon touches me?"

"Of course."

"But I get thoughts and feelings. I mean am I supposed to get thoughts?"

"It is right for you to do so. You are in love. You will soon marry and have a baby and—"

"That's what I mean. I get to thinking how it will be. Zeus, are you afraid of love?"

"No." The answer came too quickly. "I just don't intend to get married and have to live in one place all the time. I have to be free."

"Aren't you just a little bit in love with Mi'kal? He is very handsome."

"He is just a good friend. I have never known anyone like him. He has seen many bad things in the black tents, and yet his heart is as pure as yours. He is strong, like a young god, and yet inside he is as gentle as you."

"Zeus, I wish I could be like you. You seem to live so much more than I do. I mean everything you do is so much more of whatever it is. I love the birds, the sky, and the water, but you seem to be a part of them."

"You are more beautiful than I will ever be. You are wise and gentle. That is all Gideon will ever want."

"Even though you are different, sister, I love you with all my heart."

"And I love you. But I have a spirit that is different. I think it would be a wonderful thing to be killed by a lightning bolt! You would rather die in bed."

"Don't talk of death. I am afraid to die. What if I have not done everything right? Maybe I don't pray enough."

Zeus threw off her blanket and jumped to her feet.

"Dannah, didn't you hear what I told Father tonight? All we have to do is *believe.*"

"But what are we to believe?"

"That he came from God. That he is God. That he came as our Messiah and Savior."

"Do you believe him?"

"Yes. From the first day I heard him."

"Then I am going to believe in him, too." Moonlight fell on her cheeks. Her dark hair splayed across the pillow. She lifted her arms and drew her sister close. "Today I wanted to hug Gideon but I didn't. You don't think that was wrong do you? We really aren't betrothed yet."

"No. I think it is wonderful that you love him so much."

Zeus lay awake watching the changing patterns of moonlight on the shutters. She would take Mi'kal to Jerusalem in the morning. They would find a ride before the sun made travel on the Jericho road impossible. He needed clothes, and he said he had money.

Thinking of him made her hug her pillow. She pushed it away and slept with her head on the hard mat.

Mi'kal left his pallet as everyone slept. He walked out to the bench. The moon, with a lop-sided fullness, dropped behind the Judean hills. Mist filled the valley, rising in dancing swirls about the willows. The fish splashed and frogs croaked in the marsh. Mi'kal closed his eyes and laid his head against the tree.

Halfway between sleeping and waking, he saw a man in camel skin step from the river. He raised his arm and pointed; his voice reverberated. "Behold the Lamb of God who takes away the sins of the world."

The man who came to be baptized was dressed in brown.

Mi'kal opened his eyes with a start. The river ran quiet and the willows barely moved. The mist had left the shallows and lay heavy in the middle of the stream.

CHAPTER TWENTY-NINE

Zeus and Mi'kal started for Jerusalem at sunrise and were soon picked up by the driver of a wagon loaded with barrel staves. Mi'kal was eager to get to the Holy City, but Zeus insisted they stop for a few minutes to visit with Mary and Martha. Dannah had fixed a basket of vegetables to give to them.

Zeus explained there might be mourners in the courtyard, for sometimes neighbors and even strangers were paid to continue the lamentations for several days.

She was right. They could hear them before the wagon stopped in front of the big house. Seen through the open gate, the mourner's black garments contradicted the bright sunshine. If the low wailing and moaning had not been there, the court would have been a happy place, with hanging baskets of yellow flowers and rosy-breasted song birds in wicker cages.

He noticed the wide, open staircase rising from the elaborately furnished courtyard to the second floor. Zeus told him that the large upstairs room was used as sleeping quarters for Jesus and the others when they needed it. At the edge of each step was a large brass pot of geraniums, their scarlet blooms emphasized by the white walls.

Martha and Mary came to greet them and embraced Zeus. They thanked her for the gift basket of cabbage, young onions, and cucumbers.

Mi'kal expressed his sympathy and noticed the differences between the two women. Mary, the younger, had beautiful dark eyes and delicate facial lines. She seemed reconciled to the loss of her brother. Martha's gray hair was covered loosely with a draped headpiece. Her eyelids were swollen.

Zeus talked to the sisters quietly while Mi'kal tried to shut out the sounds of the mourners and listen to the singing of the birds. He was glad when it was time to go.

The road to Jerusalem from Bethany curved high and wide above the land separating the Mount of Olives from the Jehoshaphat Valley. Silvery-green olive trees stretched from the edge of the village down the slopes almost to the Kidron. The narrow but often angry river ran through the valley on the eastern and southern courses of the walls. Beyond the river channel, the walls of Jerusalem shimmered in a golden haze. Many tombs, both common and ornate, hugged the eastern wall.

The sun struck fire from the golden roof of the holy temple. On the northern walls, the four towers of the Fortress Antonia loomed ominously over the Damascus gate.

As they passed over the bridge connecting the Bethany road to the eastern gate, Mi'kal looked down at the rugged channel of rocks and dark water beneath them. It was here that Asa, one of the ancient kings, had burned his mother's idols. And a wicked queen, named Athaliah, had been executed for murdering the rightful heirs and usurping the throne of David.

Near the walls, Mi'kal felt he could feel the heartbeat of Israel's history. Inside the gate, sights and sounds blended into one word. *Jerusalem!*

Zeus stopped before an array of posters lashed to a heavy doorpost.

"What are they advertising? I can't read them," she said.

"They are in Latin and Greek." He read them to her. The current per-formance in the theater; dates of the next coliseum events, with the names of the gladiators or wrestlers; an award offered for the apprehension of one robber and murderer called Barabbas.

As he interpreted, he saw Zeus looking at him with awed respect. He silently thanked the Old One who had kept his promise to teach a small boy Latin and Greek. He didn't let Zeus know the name of Barabbas was not new to him.

They were no sooner in the street of merchants than Zeus said, "The first thing is some decent clothes for you. Then we will go wherever you want to go."

"The temple. For my mother."

Zeus knew exactly which shop Mi'kal should visit. He selected a purple tunic and woven belt of dark green and black. She pretended mock modesty when he asked for a cotton loin cloth. They bought new sandals and small things he needed for the care of his hair and beard.

Zeus piled his old garments and sandals on a refuse barrel, and Mi'kal was startled as a dirty hand grabbed them away. So many poor! Beggars everywhere. Children who were hungry. Old people struggling with canes and crutches. So many!

If he were rich, he would give all of them clothes and food and medicine and a place to sleep. A thought struck him. He could do many of those things if he went to Petra and explained that he was indeed the king's grandson. But, no. He had no desire to be a prince.

Zeus shook his arm. "Mi'kal, what's bothering you? You look as lifeless and flat as a Passover cake."

He pointed to a girl dragging one crooked foot. "How can anyone be happy when there are so many who are in need?"

"One soft-hearted Bedouin can't solve the problems of the world. Come on, it's temple time. You won't believe half of what you see." She was right.

Mi'kal could never have imagined the blinding grandeur and size of the temple, not even from his mother's description. Dazzling granite, alabaster, and marble; beams of cedar! Mi'kal thought if the dwelling place of God in heaven came to earth, it could be no more beautiful than the holy temple.

They climbed the wide, white marble steps and stood before the great bronze doors. A beggar sat beside the gate, and Mi'kal dropped a coin into his bowl.

"He's been there for years," Zeus said. "He was born lame."

Mi'kal looked up at the splendor of marble and cedar.

"How can people come in here pretending to love God when they let people go hungry?"

She considered him soberly. "You really do have a good heart, but even the good have to sacrifice. Come on."

There was a golden altar and a very large golden basin. There were musicians with silver trumpets and golden psalteries. Priests in robes with blue fringe walked among the columns that stretched forever in every direction. Zeus laughed as he tried to count them.

"Are you sure you can count to two hundred or past?" She was teasing as usual.

There were other things in and around the temple less beautiful. Sounds and smells. Stomach turning incense and aromatic oils. Smoke and burning flesh from the altar. Ear splitting haggling over the price of pigeons and sparrows on the merchant's porches.

And somewhere, under it all, the hideous smell of blood and the last chirp or bleat of a sacrifice. And over and around and above it all, the sound and smell of humanity struggling for righteousness.

Zeus led him through the technicalities of the priestly services. Mi'kal bought wheat and oil for a meal offering, but he refused to offer anything alive.

He was somber as they left. "Why must the killing go on? When will it all end? All those innocent things dying for what?"

"Our sins. You heard the Scripture last night. Now what else is bothering you?"

"The money lenders! Why do people have to exchange their money?"

"The priests will not accept a coin that has an image on it, such as Caesar's face and others."

"But the poor are being cheated. I learned about money exchange from the caravans and the Old One."

"That's why Jesus chased all of them out of the temple one day. He whipped them with ropes."

"He should have used thorns."

"Mi'kal, in many ways he's just like everybody else. He gets angry and tired and very discouraged. One day I saw him cry. He was pleading with everyone in the temple. He told them he was the Light of the world, and if they followed him they would not walk in darkness. He said he was the Bread sent down from heaven. The Pharisees were growling. They wanted to stone him for blasphemy.

"He knows they want to kill him. He was challenging them, I think, when he said no man could take his life from him, he would lay it down himself. And if he wished, he could pick it up again."

She finally smiled, and the sadness lifted from her eyes. She grabbed his hand and told him she wanted him to see the Pool of Siloam and the ancient tunnel King Hezekiah had built to bring water into Jerusalem in case of a siege. They were going down to the old city when a man came bounding up the steps shouting his name. Mi'kal recognized him and shouted in return.

"Oreb!"

They greeted each other as though they had been separated for weeks rather than a few days.

Zeus looked Oreb over with an appraising eye. "So you are the fellow who pulled him out of the ditch." She thrust out a hand.

"And you are the redhead who helped him with the wagon. You just gave us one more Roman to get rid of." He smiled, but Mi'kal knew the darkness stirred in his eyes.

Zeus wasn't offended when Oreb asked to speak to Mi'kal alone. "Go on. I've got some shopping to do for my sister and for Mary of Bethany. I'll meet you in a few minutes at the Dolphin fountain in the square. The tunnel can wait for another day."

Oreb said little as he and Mi'kal climbed toward the southern porch of the temple and then into the colonnaded street. Oreb whistled now and then, fragments and rags of melodies. Mi'kal knew he was troubled.

"What is it, Oreb?"

"Mi'kal, the Zealots are going to need men. Are you willing to fight?"

"No. I have no heart for killing."

"But you do consider yourself an Israelite?"

"Yes. My mother is a Jew, therefore I am a Jew."

"Then why aren't you willing to fight for the temple and Israel?"

"I will not do Death's dirty work for him. Violence begets violence. My purpose in coming to Galilee is to find life everlasting, not death by the sword."

"Would you rather die in chains? If Jesus is the Messiah he will free us."

"Oreb, have you ever stopped to think that Judas could be wrong about Jesus? You may be fighting for a man who doesn't want to be king."

"Few men would turn down a chance to rule."

"That's not true. I—"

"I'm not anxious to die, either, Mi'kal. I have met the most beautiful woman in the world and I am going to marry her. Maybe this very night."

Mi'kal stared. "A few days ago you didn't know anything about loving a woman."

"I do now. Her name is Susanna."

Mi'kal stared at him. "The widow with the big house? What about all the babies!"

Oreb grinned. "Praise God, Judas convinced me I should stop. There are no babies. And she loves me, too. It was as if lightning struck both of us at the same time."

"Good!"

"Come with me now to Ephraim. Then join us when the call comes. You are an Israelite. Prove it!"

"No!"

Oreb started to give vent to his anger, but loud voices caused both of them to look toward the gate.

Beyond a corner of the square they heard the tread of boots and a rising hum of voices. Chains rattled.

Oreb put out a hand. "Stay back," he ordered. "Show ordinary interest, nothing more."

Some of Rome's weary mercenaries came into view. They were dragging and shoving a group of shackled men who had suffered sword cuts and heavy beatings.

Mi'kal noticed one young prisoner with hair the color of his own. The boy staggered and fell near a soldier with an ugly scar across his face. The soldier let out a roar and kicked the boy hard, then jerked him to his feet. The victim stumbled on, holding his ribs and groaning. Mi'kal heard Oreb mutter an oath and a name under his breath.

"Do you know him?" Mi'kal whispered.

"Yes. Neophron sent him out with several others to concentrate on the lone wagons and carts. Sometimes common farmers are anything but common."

Mi'kal remembered what Gaius had told him about one man and a poor horse drawing less attention than several men with good horses.

"Don't you ever get tired of killing?"

"I come from a long line of killers, but I kill only in the name of the Lord."

"And that makes the dead men feel better? Have you told your Susanna what you do?"

"No. Not yet. But she knows. She seems able to read my thoughts." He stopped and Mi'kal saw that his eyes were fixed on a soldier coming with a skin of wine. He was the one with the scarred face. They watched as he left the street and stepped into a narrow alley between two buildings facing the square.

"He's gone to defile the stones of Jerusalem," Oreb growled. He laid a hand to his sword and walked toward the alley. He slipped into the shadows, and Mi'kal refused to allow his imagination to picture what was happening between the walls.

Oreb came back whistling. "His captain will miss one man at muster tonight," he said calmly as if he had done no more than slice into a melon. He washed his bloody blade in the fountain. No one paid any attention. Mi'kal wondered if violence was so common in the street that one could kill or be killed without anyone caring.

Another procession was coming through the gate. Soldiers cleared the streets as bearers brought in wounded comrades on litters. A few were able to sit up.

"Where are they going?" Mi'kal asked.

"To the hospital. There is a part of the Antonia set aside for the wounded where they have the best physicians."

Mi'kal shook his head. "When is it going to end?"

"The minute the enemy moves out."

"No. The Jews have never lived in peace I know our history. Abraham and Lot, Isaac and Ishmael, Esau and Jacob, David and

Absalom—on and on and on. We are not a peaceful nation, no matter what we say."

There might have been more argument, but Mi'kal caught sight of a soldier with carrot-red hair on a passing litter.

"Aurans!" Mi'kal yelled and ran after the bearers. They stopped at a quick command from the injured man. Mi'kal's hand gripped the Briton's.

"How are you?"

"Not too good but I can't complain. I'm alive, thanks to you. The wound keeps draining, but they tell me we have good doctors here."

The litter bearers started to move, and Aurans ordered them to wait. "Mi'kal, have you heard about the raid?"

"What raid?" Somehow he knew even as he asked.

"At your father's camp. A blood feud between the brothers. I was sorry to hear it."

Mi'kal felt sick. He closed his eyes. Once, when he was little, Raaschid had taken him to an Arab camp after a feud. He could still smell the blood and the burning tents.

"Did you hear anything about my mother? Or the Old One?"

"Nothing. But we heard that Raaschid was badly wounded. We also heard he had taken a young wife. I thought it might be the girl who danced."

"Ne'ma? Never! Unless…" The thought was too dreadful to accept. He had hoped against hope. But now, with his stepfather taking another wife, he had to accept the fact that his mother was gone.

Zeus came up beside them. She was holding a small roll of cloth tied with a string. She recognized Aurans immediately. "Well, Lieutenant, I see you made it."

"Yes, thanks to both of you."

"Let's go," one of the bearers growled. They began to move. Aurans motioned for Mi'kal to walk alongside. "Stay out of Jerusalem until after Passover," he cautioned. "Something is brewing. I don't know what, but stay out."

Mi'kal watched until Aurans was carried out of sight. Then he turned to Zeus and lifted the bundle out of her arms. His voice was nervous and hurried. "Where did Oreb go? There is something I should tell him."

"He's gone. Said he was in a hurry to get back to Ephraim, and you'd understand."

Oreb was anxious to get back to Susanna, but his conference with Barabbas, leader of the southern Zealots, was fresh on his mind as he mounted Moses and rode past Golgotha, the place of crucifixions.

The sight of the hill always brought a churning to his stomach. When he was a child, he had seen his grandfather, Judas of Galilee, and dozens of his men hanging on crosses. If the coming revolt failed, many more fighters for the freedom of Israel would die.

During his conference with Barabbas at a small, unimportant inn, the older Zealot had leaned across the table as he laid out the plans for the coming revolt. The filtered sunlight through wooden shutters fell on his bearded face and shadowed the fanatical light in his eyes.

"Neophron and his Galilean men will take care of the northern walls. My men will take them from within the city."

"But can we surprise them?" Oreb had wanted to know. "They have spies among us. Even though we move as owls, they hear us. Judas Iscariot insists Jesus will take the throne. If he does, we will have help from the hosts of heaven. But if he does not, we will be fighting with scythes and bludgeons against pikes and swords, battering rams and ballistae."

Barabbas tried to reassure him. "Rome is already itching, as with a case of hives. We have been destroying storehouses and bridges consistently for months. Their caravans disappear every day. Those you said were coming from Palmyra have already been gutted."

"I wish I felt as confident," Oreb said. "So many times we have come out growling and slunk back whimpering. What if Pilate brings in his Syrian troops?"

Barabbas's hand hit the table. "I don't think he will. At least not in time. Where are your guts, boy? You came from the loins of Judas of Galilee, the greatest of our patriots. Where is your willingness to die?"

"Barabbas, I am not afraid to die for Israel. It is my destiny. I just don't want to die right now. I have found a woman I love. I want to give her a son."

As the mule plodded slower up a higher rise, Oreb remembered the sudden change on Barabbas's face. There was something of the leader Moses; something of the fighter Joshua; something of the rugged testimony of John the Baptist.

"I am going to tell you what I have revealed to no man. You say dying for Israel is your destiny. I too feel I have been chosen for a unique purpose. I do not know what part I am to have in God's plan for Israel, but I too have a destiny. I believe the time is near."

Oreb remembered there had been something that held him silent when the slatted sunlight fell like fingers of blessing on Barabbas's head.

Oreb heard the sound of cavalry and foot soldiers before he saw them. He was on a high rise overlooking a plain. Pilate's select Syrian troops, which Barabbas had thought might remain in the coastal capital, were strung out across the plain. Horsemen and foot soldiers, rank upon rank—one thousand, two thousand, and still coming.

The procurator and his wife, Procula, rode among the foremost chariots under streaming banners. The blinding glint of Roman armor and the arrogant challenge of Roman standards made Oreb's stomach churn. How he hated them!

And how he loved Israel! Where would it end? Certainly many good Zealots would die. He was as vulnerable as any of his brothers. For a moment he was tempted to forget the mission. But the blood of his father, Menahem, and the blood of his grandfather, Judas, coursed with renewed fervor through him.

He raised his sword and shouted, "For Israel and the temple." Then he shouted again, "For Susanna and the son we will have!"

The final shout died in his throat. Hopeless! He knew it was hopeless, but they had to try. Fighters for Israel had nipped at Rome's heels long enough. Now they must try for the throat.

i'kal was not anxious to stop at Martha's again on the way back to Papyron, but Zeus insisted. She had to deliver the embroidery thread she had bought for Mary.

The mourners who had come for the day were gone. Each had received a small loaf of bread, a drink of wine, and a small coin. When Zeus and Mi'kal came through the gate, the little rosy-breasted birds began to sing.

Mary was exclaiming over the thread Zeus had brought when they heard a man hailing them from outside the gate. He was shouting and pointing. "Some of the disciples are here. The Master must be coming. I will alert the village." He rushed away while they ran to the gate

Philip and Andrew came, and behind them Matthew and Thomas. They remembered Mi'kal and spoke to Zeus as to an old friend.

"Where is Jesus?" Martha asked. "Why is he not with you? If he had been here my brother wouldn't have died."

Philip answered her gently. "The Master is waiting to see you near the wine press in your neighbor's vineyard. He wishes to speak first to you and then to Mary."

"Why me? Lazarus was the one who needed him."

"Sister," Mary admonished, "you must not keep him waiting."

"I intend to speak my mind."

"Martha, remember you usually have to follow with an apology."

Martha shrugged, fastened her head covering under her chin, and went. As Martha left, Mary told the men to rest and she would wash their feet.

Thomas and Matthew dropped into chairs, and Andrew ran his fingers through his hair and dumped sand out of his sandals into a flower pot.

Philip began to talk to a small yellow bird in one of the cages.

Mi'kal watched as Zeus brought in the basin of water and Mary came with a towel. He had never seen this gesture of hospitality. In the black tents the guests might receive the eyes of the boiled sheep or prized organs of the carcass, but they would be expected to clean their own feet.

As Mary washed, Zeus brought in a jug of water wrapped in black felt to keep it cool. In their tent, Quintira had done the same thing.

Mi'kal's face flamed as Mary ordered him to sit while she stooped at his feet. His embarrassment brought a wide grin to Zeus's face. She had taken Philip's yellow bird out of its cage. Now, as it perched on her shoulder, she was trying to get it to sing by touching it softly on its throat.

Mary admired his new sandals and sympathized with the blisters from walking in untried leather. As she rose, she handed the basin of wash water to Zeus.

"Would you please empty this and then bring us the bowl of green grapes and salt?"

Mi'kal knew she would throw the water on the garden as Hosea would do at home. He listened and smiled. He was learning some things about her.

The conversation changed to other things between the men, and Mary went to the gate, evidently anxious for Martha's return.

Philip sat down on the bench by Mi'kal. "You were disappointed in Jesus, weren't you?"

Mi'kal hesitated. "Yes. A little." He didn't want another argument.

Zeus was offering them a platter of unripe grapes. "A little? You said he was a very ordinary man." She dumped a pinch of salt into his hand and filled it with green grapes.

"I know I did."

Philip smiled. "You expected clouds of glory?"

"No, not quite. But I did expect *something*. If he is to be our King Messiah, he should have at least as much glory as the angels."

Zeus laughed. "How many angels have you seen?"

"None. But my mother has told me about them."

Andrew joined them. "Perhaps you are like his brothers and sisters, children from Joseph. They do not believe either."

"So Zeus has told me."

Matthew scratched at his graying beard.

"They are fools. I believed in him the moment he stopped by my booth and called me to serve him. I knew in my heart that if I did, I would be changed."

"And you were," Thomas said as his heavy brows rose slightly over smiling eyes.

Mary asked Thomas about his twin sister, Lydia, who had stayed in Ephraim with Susanna while the disciples were with Jesus in Perea. He laid his hand on his stomach. "I think Matthew's son will be here before Passover." And then he laughed his extraordinary rolling laughter.

Matthew joined him first, and then all of them were laughing with him. It was well known that Thomas often knew from his own feelings how his twin was feeling. The laughter died as they heard the sound of running footsteps. Martha rushed in with a radiant transformation on her face. Mi'kal was reminded of a desert dawn.

"Mary! Jesus has told me a wonderful thing. And he will say the same to you. Hurry!"

Mary took flight, and Martha turned to those in the court.

"I am filled with joy. In exchange for my sorrow and bitterness, Jesus has given me gladness. I was bitter. I told him if he had been here Lazarus could have lived. And then he said that Lazarus would rise again. I thought he was talking about the resurrection that all righteous Jews will have, and I said I wanted Lazarus alive now. Today. Right here with us."

Mi'kal's pulses jumped. Martha felt as he felt. Not some misty living in the great beyond, but a breathing, walking, talking, eating life now.

She rushed on. "Then Jesus said a wonderful thing. I will never forget it. 'I am the resurrection and the life. He who believes in me will live, even though he dies; and whoever lives and believes in me will never die. Do you believe this?'"

Martha lifted her hands. "And I said, Yes, Lord, I believe. And I fell at his feet and worshipped him." She covered her radiant face with trembling hands.

Two words rang in Mi'kal's ears. *Never die!*

The little yellow bird was still on Zeus's shoulder but refused to sing. She opened its cage and sat it on its perch. There it lifted its throat in melody. Mi'kal laid his hand on her shoulder and said softly. "See. It is possible to be happy without being free."

She refused to look at him.

They heard Mary coming, accompanied by others who stayed outside the gate. Their voices were filled with excitement. Her face was as radiant as Martha's.

"Listen! All of you! Jesus wants us to come down to the sepulcher!"

They stumbled against one another in their rush for the gate. The courtyard swarmed with people greeting one another. On the road, Mi'kal ran with Zeus beside him. The crowd had increased, and she yelled that Peter and all the other disciples were now with them. They hurried over the slope that led to a ridge of limestone separating the burial cave from a grove of olive trees. Jesus was waiting for them there.

The sunset poured gold and crimson over the hill and gilded the city of Jerusalem far below them. The entire ridge of limestone took on a brazen glow. The crowd—men, women, and children—crowded together near the burial spot.

Rough, hewn steps led downward to the cave where a large stone covered the entrance. Jesus motioned for Peter and John. All on the hill could hear him as he said, "Roll the stone away!"

There was an audible inhaling of breath as the two disciples moved down the stone steps. Mi'kal heard Martha whisper. "Master, how can he come forth? He has been in the grave four days."

Jesus answered. "Did I not tell you in the vineyard that you would see glorious things?"

Jesus looked upward and raised his arms. "Father, I know you always hear me, but because of these who watch, I ask you to glorify yourself."

At the bottom of the steps, Peter put his shoulder to the stone, and John bent over him. They strained. The stone moved slowly, but not as slowly as the breathing of those who watched. Mi'kal forgot to breath at all.

The depths showed first as the sickle of a black moon, then grew until the entire circle of darkness could be seen. A rush of fetid air coursed upward.

Jesus stretched both arms toward the opened tomb. His voice was loud, and the words came back from the brazen stones of the grave, as if Death were repelling them.

"Lazarus, come forth!"

Mi'kal had wanted to see light about Jesus. Now he had to close his eyes against the brightness. Voices of praise and wonder shook the leaves of the olive trees and rebounded from the ridge.

"He's coming out!"

Martha and Mary ran to unwind the linen bindings from their brother. As the bindings fell, Lazarus could be seen, clothed in a white garment. He came up the steps ahead of his sisters and fell to his knees before Jesus. Jesus was crying. Lazarus lifted clasped hands. Jesus closed his hands over them and raised Lazarus to his feet.

Lazarus embraced his sisters. Some who had watched came forward to touch him. Others stayed back in fearsome awe. Words and feet tripped over one another as the crowd followed Jesus, Lazarus, and the others to the house.

There would be no sleep for anyone that night—and no rest for anyone for many days to come.

Mi'kal tarried within sight of the grave. He was in no mood for laughing and talking. Zeus was willing to sit with him, but he shook his head. "No. I want to be alone. You have seen miracles before. But for me, I must think about it."

This evening he had witnessed something he had dreamed of for as long as he could remember. Victory over Death! Could a man see such a thing and not spend the next hours in solitude as tribute to the mysteries of God?

He did not know until later that Zeus, feeling rejected, caught a ride to Papyron. She explained to her hostess that she wanted Dannah and Hosea to know the good news.

Mi'kal sat with his eyes fixed on the western horizon. The sun had gone, but the sky was ablaze with colors that were reluctant to fade. He looked from the open sepulcher, where the purple shadows were changing to black, to the vivid clouds over Jerusalem.

What did it all mean? What should he do with this Jesus of Nazareth?

Then he saw in the sunset green tail feathers spreading over Judea and Galilee, green wings hovering over the olive slopes. He could see the rosy breast speckled with delicate wisps of white, the golden beak lifted as if giving a high free cry, golden claws reached toward the earth as if to carry away all signs of death.

Jesus had promised Martha and all of them that whoever believed in him would *never die*. He would believe and teach others to believe.

If only Quintira could be here to rejoice with him in her Messiah. But she had believed that he would come, and some day, when the time came, she too would live again. He bowed his head to his knees and worshipped.

While Bethany rejoiced with Mary and Martha, the village of Ephraim was celebrating Susanna's marriage to Oreb. Never before had it happened just so, and it never would happen so again. There were no banns read, no arranged procession, no musicians hired, no extra-fine wine ordered. The rabbi, old and wise, had been cajoled, bribed, and coaxed to perform the ceremony immediately after Oreb's return from Jerusalem.

Susanna offered to buy several coveted scrolls for the synagogue. But it was the rabbi's secret knowledge of the impending uprising that convinced him of the emergency.

On the marriage certificate Oreb revealed his lineage. Eleazar, son of Menahem, grandson of Judas, son of Ezekias. Only then did Susanna know for sure what she already suspected. She was marrying a Zealot.

Aziz draped a cart with flowers and drove the bride and groom about the village, while those who had flutes and tambourines brought them out for dancing.

That night Susanna put her hands on her husband's cheeks and asked, "Have you killed many men?"

"Yes."

"Jesus will forgive you."

"I do not ask for forgiveness. I killed for Israel and the temple. I want you to understand. I will never change."

She closed his lips with her own.

CHAPTER THIRTY-ONE

N ews of the miracle at Bethany swept like a summer storm over the whole of Judea. It surged into every hovel and every palace. Even the Gentiles were swept along by the tide of wonder. Now the disciples understood why Jesus had waited. This was his greatest miracle.

The Sanhedrin was called into session by Caiaphas. He feared that a high priest greater than Melchizedek, King of Righteousness, had come to replace him. The council must find a way to get rid of the Nazarene rabble-rouser. Far better that one man should die than that the whole nation be destroyed.

The next day, Martha's flower beds and garden were trampled, the walls broken down, the gate knocked from its hinges. Crowds pushed, crawled, and fought to get a glimpse of Lazarus or Jesus. Lazarus no longer wore the dazzling white garment but was dressed instead in a soft, wheat-colored tunic with a scarlet belt.

The street and hillside filled with those who wanted their own miracles. They brought in the sick and the demon possessed. Some offered money for the resurrection of a loved one.

Cries echoed through the courtyard. "Why do you not call all the dead from the grave?"

Matthew tried to placate the screamers. "Did Elijah feed all the widows of Zarephath?"

But the shouts continued until Jesus stepped forth and silenced them with his words. "I tell you the truth, a time is coming and has now come when the dead will hear the voice of the Son of God and those who hear will live."

A roar of approval sounded. "Hasten the day, Lord. Bring them forth now!"

But the crowd grew silent as Jesus continued, a stern warning in his voice. "Do not be amazed at this, for a time is coming when all who are in their graves will hear his voice and come out—those who have done good will rise to live, and those who have done evil will rise to be condemned."

Consternation swept through them. How could one know if a loved one had done enough good or too much evil?

Mi'kal helped the disciples do all they could to protect Jesus, who grew weary during the day. They spent much time with him in the upper room, but Mi'kal was not invited. He had not talked much to any of the disciples except to an older man, Nathaniel, who was quiet and thoughtful and reminded Mi'kal of the Old One.

One time during a period of noisy unrest outside the house, Mary invited Mi'kal to talk to her alone. She unwrapped a small alabaster vial, and he thought of the perfume Raaschid had poured into the sand. As she opened the vial, he expected to smell roses. When she handed it to him, he did not recognize the odor.

"It is spikenard. I have saved it for his anointing."

"As Messiah?" Excitement glowed in his eyes.

Mary put the vial away. "No, Mi'kal. For his burial!"

"What are you talking about?"

Outside, the repetitious praises had begun again. "Hosanna to the Son of David. Blessed is he who comes in the name of the Lord. Blessed be the King of Israel."

Mi'kal motioned toward the street. "They believe he has come to reign forever on David's throne. He can't die!"

"They are as children calling for sweets. No, Mi'kal, Jesus has told all of us he is going to die. But like you, they do not want to believe him."

"No!" He pushed closed fists against his ears. "I won't listen." He turned and walked away.

She called after him. "Mi'kal, we aren't without hope. He has promised to rise again after three—" Her words were lost to him.

In the courtyard, Mi'kal tried to throw off the turmoil Mary's words had brought. He looked at Jesus. His cheeks were brown with health even though his face showed weariness. He wanted to ask Nathaniel what Jesus had said about dying, but all the disciples had gone into the upper room and Jesus was following them.

After supper Jesus told them he was going to leave Bethany the next morning, before dawn, and go to Ephraim. Mi'kal caught the eye of Judas. The disciple nodded, and Mi'kal knew Jesus was going to Susanna's and the house with many rooms. Oreb would be there, too.

Mi'kal, who had slept on a mat in the courtyard, begged Philip to inquire of Jesus if he could go with them. He watched and prayed as Philip approached Jesus. Under the flames of the lamps, Mi'kal felt the intensity of Jesus' gaze, and then he saw Jesus nod.

He saw Lazarus embrace Jesus and heard him ask when Jesus would return to Jerusalem.

"For Passover—for then my hour will come."

Mi'kal saw sudden tears in Mary's eyes. She and Martha knelt at his feet and kissed his hands. He saw Jesus give Mary a reassuring smile.

The group from Bethany reached Susanna's house an hour after early moon rise. The sun was still going down over the Great Sea. Susanna greeted Jesus and the others with jubilation. She was happy to know that Mi'kal was the Syrian prince Oreb had told her about. Matthew made haste to embrace Lydia, his wife, who was big with child.

Susanna apologized for Oreb's absence and explained that her new husband had gone on a business trip into Galilee. He had promised her he would hurry back. She blushed when she said it.

Mi'kal knew his friend had gone to report to Neophron on what had been said in the meeting with Barabbas in Jerusalem. He was sure Susanna had no idea how dangerous Oreb's business trip could be.

Supper was laid and wine glasses were filled. All the guests were invited to rejoice with Susanna in the happiness of her marriage. Mi'kal watched Susanna minister to her guests. She was dressed in a garment of pale yellow, and her hair, the color of rock honey, was caught back with amber combs. Mi'kal understood why Oreb had fallen in love so quickly.

Susanna was beautiful in all ways.

During the rush of talk that always accompanies the arrival of guests, no matter what the hour, Matthew picked Lydia up and sat with her in his lap. The others smiled as he put his hand on her swollen stomach and looked at her with pride. Now and then Lydia gave a loving pull on her husband's graying beard. Mi'kal soon understood that Matthew and Lydia had waited a long time to have this child.

Mi'kal noticed how much Thomas and his twin sister looked alike. Each seemed a little grim with heavy dark brows and somber faces—until they smiled. Now, as Lydia looked at her husband, her dark face lightened with love.

The disciples spent the later evening drinking apricot wine and eating from a bowl of pickled, boiled eggs. Mi'kal marveled at the disciples' relationship with Jesus. They were not afraid to ask questions or to touch him.

Ever since his quiet time on the slopes, Mi'kal had found it difficult to act as if Jesus was actual flesh and blood. His wonder at the great miracle and his unbelievable joy in the heavenly sign had made him awkward and uncertain. The others, although reverent, seemed able to talk and eat with him in ease.

Every disciple was different. He knew five of them, so he tried to remember the other names. Peter was Andrew's brother; Nathaniel was the oldest; John and James were brothers; another James, smaller than the first, and his brother, Thaddeus, were some sort of relatives to Jesus; then there was one identified as Simon the former Zealot; he and Judas usually were talking. They were the ones anxious to see Jesus take David's throne. At least Judas was.

Tonight, as he listened to all of them laughing and arguing, Mi'kal decided that where there was sincere love, there was sincere worship.

Someday Jesus of Nazareth would be the Messiah of Israel, the King upon David's throne. But until then, Mi'kal determined to think of him as a very good friend, as the others seemed to do. Even so, he would keep his heart bowed in worship. He had one continuing regret. His mother was not here to rejoice in her Messiah.

The evening was a time for Jesus to relax. There was no preaching, no teaching. They all sat in the court while the cooler breeze rose and the stars came out. Susanna brought Judas a lyre he could play. Matthew asked for a love song as he sat holding his wife's hand. Other disciples who were thinking of their own loved ones settled down to listen.

Mi'kal noticed Thaddeus, the youngest one. He seldom spoke unless spoken to. He sat with his eyes closed and his hands locked under his chin. Mi'kal wondered what girl he was dreaming about in Galilee.

Jesus sat on a bench under the large sycamore whose branches covered a large part of the courtyard. Vines of purple flowers ran around the top of the walls, and pots of yellow roses bloomed by the doorway.

When Judas touched the strings of the lyre, Jesus closed his eyes and stretched out his bare feet. Judas sang with a deep and touching voice:

> Ah, my beloved, how lovely your countenance;
>> how like the sweet pomegranate your lips under mine.
> Oh, my beloved, thy love is as honey,
>> your sweetness as grapes on the vine.
> Drop now thine eyelids, my pulses are reeling.
>> Thine eyes make me stagger as if drunken from wine.

The moon was lost behind the hills before the disciples began to leave for their rooms. Mi'kal was surprised that there were so many, but Philip explained that Susanna had been married to a man whose father had a large family. Room after room had been added. After the father died, his son had inherited the house. Susanna had never had any children, and when her husband died she had opened her home for the benefit of Jesus and his disciples.

Two by two the disciples retired. Mi'kal asked if he could sleep in the courtyard, as he had done at Martha's.

The lamps were extinguished, and the court became quiet except for the song of a night bird in the sycamore. Mi'kal knew he would never be able to settle down. He sat on the bench to think, and his hand fell to the lyre that Judas had left there. Without thinking, his fingers plucked a key.

The sound was no louder than the faint sounds of the night insects.

"Can you play?" Mi'kal looked up. Jesus was standing in the doorway. There was starlight enough to see him.

"No."

"Would you like to?"

"Yes." He felt enveloped in understanding and love. "There is a song I would like to sing because I think it is about you."

Jesus sat down beside him. "About me?"

"It is about a Green Bird who knows how to overcome death. I have sung it since I was a child. When I heard about your raising of the dead—" He stopped, remembering how horrified Zeus had been when he called Jesus the Phoenix.

Jesus was chuckling. "You thought I might be the Phoenix?"

"To me you are…only much, much more."

"I would like to hear this song. Why not try the lyre again." As Jesus laid his hands against the strings, they seemed to respond.

Mi'kal tried to see his face. Was he teasing him? Or was he testing him? But then with an assurance he actually felt, he plucked his hands softly over the strings and melody came. He began to sing as softly as the night birds.

"O Green Bird, who sees you rejoices, even your sister, Bough of Incense, laid you to rest in the box of spices and you came again to life. O Green Bird…"

Jesus listened with his eyes closed. As Mi'kal finished he said, "The song is about me. You have sung more truth than you know. Like the green bird I will die and be laid in a bed of spices by those I call my brothers. Incense will be burning in the holy temple as the veil is rent. And I will rise again."

Mi'kal laid the lyre aside, and when he looked up, Jesus was gone.

Early the next morning, after breaking the night's fast, Jesus and his disciples prepared to leave for Galilee. Matthew and Thomas planned to rent a small wagon and mule for Lydia's return to Capernaum before her baby was born.

239

Susanna asked her to stay. "I would be happy to see a baby in the house."

Lydia smiled and kissed her. "You will, before our son is a year old. But as I have told you, I want our first son to be born in Matthew's house. We have waited so long for him."

Mi'kal went with Matthew and Thomas to the stable where he was met by a small whirlwind of a boy. Mi'kal hugged Aziz and remembered the cucumber he had given him as he crossed the Jordan. Hiram, Aziz's father and owner of the stable, was a large man eager to please his customers.

Mi'kal watched as the disciples left Ephraim, with Matthew and Lydia on the driver's seat and several of the others on the bed of the wagon, their legs dangling. Mi'kal saw Thaddeus walking quietly with Jesus. He wished he was walking with them.

CHAPTER THIRTY-TWO

Oreb came in late morning. He clasped Mi'kal's hand hard and looked surprised and pleased. He smelled of sweaty mule, but as he flung his sword belt aside and lifted Susanna with a rousing yell, she didn't seem to notice it. Her face flamed and her arms held him tight.

Mi'kal felt like an intruder as Oreb carried his new bride out of sight. Last night, when everyone was together, he had felt comfortable in Susanna's house. Now he wasn't sure he should stay since he wasn't a disciple.

He saw Oreb's sword and began to smile. The weapon would be awkward, heavy, and frightening, but it might give him a small excuse for being here.

He waited until Oreb had bathed and they had eaten the noon meal before he mentioned the sword. "Oreb, would you teach me how to fight with a broadsword?"

Oreb showed his surprise. "You've decided to join us?"

"No. I just want to learn."

Susanna stood in the doorway beside a vine of yellow roses. "Jesus might not be pleased with you, Mi'kal. He does not encourage violence."

Oreb laughed and chucked her under her chin. "Maybe he doesn't cultivate it, my love, but it certainly springs up around him." Then he lifted her from the doorstep and deposited her on the bench. "Mi'kal, do you know that my Susanna is named for the most beautiful flowers of the field? The lilies."

"They should be jealous."

"They are. For they shall fade with the summer, but she will become more beautiful. She has told me she believes we are going to have a son!" She laughed and blushed as he untangled her arms from his neck and turned to Mi'kal.

"Have you never used a sword?"

"Not like yours. Our warriors use a lighter, curved blade, usually made from Damascus steel."

Oreb pulled the short, wide sword from its sheath and handed it to Mi'kal. "I don't know why I should waste my time, but..."

Mi'kal had known the iron weapon would be heavy, but even as he felt its unspoken challenge he grew excited about mastering it.

Susanna watched the first day's practice, sometimes a little amused at Mi'kal's ineptness. Oreb tried to cover some of the art of foot fighting. Thrust! Parry! Thrust! Move swiftly, but keep your balance. Thrust for the shoulder and the belly—especially the belly.

"Practice every day," Oreb advised. "Your wrist and arm will become strong in no time. When you're good enough, I'll give you a sword all your own."

A few days later, Oreb was preparing for another trip into Galilee. He would be taking one of Hiram's wagons with a false bottom to collect weapons from outlying villages and deliver them to secret depots. He had tried to minimize his danger, but Mi'kal knew Susanna was afraid. Her amber eyes were worried.

"I would appreciate it if you could stay here with Susanna while I am gone," Oreb said to him in private.

Mi'kal accepted the responsibility with joy. Now he was needed. He would wait for Jesus and his Twelve to return to Ephraim after Passover— unless Jesus decided to proclaim himself King of Israel and start his reign on the throne of David!

A few nights later, as Susanna lay with her head on his shoulder, Oreb told her, "I am leaving early in the morning. Mi'kal has agreed to stay with you while I am gone."

Tears choked her voice as she kissed him and said, "O my love, take care. I would not want to live without you—nor would your son growing in my womb."

Early the next morning, before Aziz came with Moses and the wagon for Oreb, Mi'kal found an old rusty sword lying near his place on the table. The sword must have come from one of Oreb's secret caches, but Mi'kal was as pleased as if it were fresh from a Roman armory. Susanna was smiling, and Oreb gave him a congratulatory pat on the back.

"Practice while I am gone, and use it if you must to protect my precious wife."

"That would be about the only way I would use it! But thank you for teaching me."

"You've done well. Learn to move a little faster—and watch your back. If the flat blade comes down on your neck, you've had it."

When Aziz came with the wagon hitched to Moses, Mi'kal renewed his acquaintance with the gray mule by rubbing his long ears.

Susanna insisted on putting in an extra cloak and a basket of food. She was trying to stay cheerful, but her eyes kept filling with tears. Oreb wrapped her in his arms, and they stood in a tight embrace. Then he climbed into the wagon and picked up the reins. He motioned for Aziz to hop in. "I'll drop you off at the stable."

Susanna and Mi'kal stood by the gate as the wagon began to move. One of the wheels squeaked slightly as Moses plodded down the lane leading to the main road. They stood watching until the wagon was out of sight, but even as Mi'kal closed the gate, he could still hear the squeaking wheel.

Susanna was sitting on the bench under the sycamore, swaying back and forth and moaning. She looked up, and there was terror on her face. "Oh, Mi'kal, we must pray! We must pray! I know how much danger he is in. He never wants me to know, but I do. And I love him so!"

In the wagon, as the wheel started to squeak, Oreb looked at Aziz. The boy lowered his head.

"I'm sorry. I'll grease it now if you have the time."

"No, but you better do it the first thing when I get back."

243

Perhaps a squeak wasn't too bad, Oreb thought. Few Roman patrols would believe that an enemy of the empire would be foolish enough to call attention to himself with a noisy wagon.

For the rest of the morning Susanna busied herself in the kitchen, and Mi'kal let her cry in secret. He occupied his time by practicing with his sword. His arm was getting tired, so he was glad when the gate bell jangled and he had a good reason to lay the sword aside.

The visitor, impatient, jangled the bell again.

Susanna came from the kitchen as Mi'kal swung the gate open. Aziz was there, a grin covering his excited face. Behind him stood a curtained wagon hitched to a pair of powerful grays. A tall, muscular man jumped down and opened the flaps by the rear steps.

Mi'kal watched as a woman stepped through the curtains. For one second he stood as if made of stone, and then he gave a shout and bounded forward.

"Mother!" His joy equaled the joy of those who had welcomed Lazarus back from the dead. "Mother!"

"O Mi'kal!" Her breath was soft against his cheek as he embraced her.

He held her away from him and gazed at her with hungry eyes, trying to get used to the miracle. Tears mingled as they kissed, and then as if one miracle wasn't enough, he heard a remembered voice speak his name.

The driver reached to help her, but Mi'kal pushed him aside and raised his arms. As Leyla tumbled into them, he found her lips and kissed her.

She pushed him away, blushing furiously. "Mi'kal! Stop it."

Tears choked his voice as he tried to speak. "I thought you were dead. I was sure you were both dead! Leyla, how did you get here?"

"Mi'kal, it will take hours to tell you everything. For now, just accept the fact that we are here. Now meet Silvanus. He has been our escort from Damascus."

Mi'kal gripped the man's hand. Silvanus was muscular and taller and older than Mi'kal. His skin was slightly dark and his face oval, but Mi'kal knew he was not an Arab. He was no ordinary wagon driver either. His clothes and his countenance suggested an educated man.

"How did you know where to find me?" The wonder of it was still too much for Mi'kal to comprehend.

Silvanus smiled and pointed to Aziz. "This young man told us. We were watering the horses and—you tell them," he urged Aziz.

"Mi'kal, I was out on the Jerusalem road by the watering trough. Sometimes I stand there and if anybody looks like they need help, I tell them about the stable. His horses were drinking and your mother was asking anybody who stopped if they knew anything about somebody called Mi'kal."

Leyla interrupted. "We've asked at every well or watering trough between here and Damascus."

"And then she asked me." Aziz pointed to Quintira. "I said if the Mi'kal she wanted had sort of shiny hair and green eyes, I knew where he was. And after I told her, she kissed me." The words were accusative.

Susanna had stayed silent, but now she stepped forward to be introduced. "I know you are tired. Would you like to freshen up a bit before you explain everything?" She turned to Silvanus. "Bring in all the baggage. There is a room for each of you. And hot water for a bath."

Leyla sighed with happiness. "Oh, joy divine!"

Mi'kal couldn't keep his eyes away from Leyla until she and Quintira went into the house with Susanna. She was as beautiful as she had been the first time he saw her step into the Syrian sunshine. Today she wore a soft lavender garment with a cape of deep blue, and her hair, loose and tied with a ribbon, shone against the dark fabric. The sight of her had made his pulses race. He was anxious to tell her how much he had missed her. Surely the excitement he was feeling must be love.

As Silvanus began to unload, Mi'kal helped him lift down several hampers and bags. Finally, Silvanus released the team and wagon to Aziz to take to the stable. "Give them proper care, young man. I expect them to be ready for me in the morning. And if you clean the wagon, sudden prosperity shall be yours."

Silvanus picked up the heaviest of the hampers and went into the house. Mi'kal picked up two of his mother's bags but lingered as she came back into the court after leaving her traveling cloak in her room.

"Susanna is one of the most beautiful women I have ever seen," she said.

"No more than you."

"Aziz told us about her wedding the other night. He said everybody was surprised because they didn't even know Oreb."

"You'll like Oreb. He brought me into Galilee. They fell in love the minute they met. Today Susanna told him she thinks she has conceived already."

Quintira's dimples danced. "Sometimes it happens that way, doesn't it?"

"Mother, do you know about the raid on our camp?"

"No. What raid?" Her voice showed quick concern.

"Muktar attacked Raaschid."

She put her hands over her face. "Oh, no. Think of the children. Why did he do it, Mi'kal? Why?"

"I don't know." He told her what he had heard from Aurans about the raid. "When I heard that Raaschid had taken Ne'ma as his wife, I thought you were either banished or killed."

"The Lord bless them both," she said softly.

"Now, Mother, you must tell me what happened to you and Leyla."

"Our good fortunes are due to the purple scarf and Grandfather's *bulla*." He looked puzzled, and she went on. "But right now, Mi'kal, you must excuse me. I need to rest." He scolded himself as he saw the weariness on her face. Susanna had come to the doorway, and she took Quintira by the arm. Mi'kal started to follow, but Susanna motioned him away.

Mi'kal began to wonder about Leyla. Why hadn't she hurried back to see him as his mother had done? Was she lingering somewhere with Silvanus? Was she interested in him? Was that why she hadn't been as excited to see him as he had been to see her?

Silvanus and Leyla came into the court, laughing and holding hands. Mi'kal felt a stab of something he recognized as the sharp pain of losing his first love.

He left them to their conversation. There was something his mother would want to know even if she were dead tired. How was it possible he had not yelled it out the minute he saw her?

He knocked lightly on the doorpost of her room and pushed back the draperies. Quintira was lying across the bed, fast asleep. She had not taken time to bathe or even remove the combs from her black hair. Mi'kal removed them without disturbing her. He kissed the white locks that rimmed her forehead and tiptoed from the room, closing the draperies after him.

There would be time enough when she awoke to tell her that the call of his Green Bird had led him to her Messiah.

CHAPTER THIRTY THREE

The hanging lamps were lit as they gathered in the courtyard under the stars where Jesus and his disciples had gathered a few nights before. Quintira, bathed and rested, glowed with happiness. Mi'kal had told her earlier about Jesus—all he had heard and seen—and the candles in her eyes had burned like sacred flames. Then Susanna had shared more wonders of Jesus with them throughout the evening meal.

Now Susanna and Mi'kal were waiting to hear what Quintira and Leyla had to tell them of their journeys from the Syrian desert to the wilderness of Judea.

Quintira was swathed in a cloak of soft rose embroidered with red pomegranates. She had given Susanna an equally beautiful wrap with a border of white swans.

"I have many things to share," she said as Susanna protested. "You have been kind to my son. My father-in-law has provided me a great amount of money and many clothes."

So Leyla and Quintira began to talk about King Aretas of Petra, of Herod Philip, the tetrarch of Caesarea Philippi, of the palace and courts of Lysanias, governor of Syria. They shared the stories of miraculous escapes and unbelievable good fortunes.

Leyla told of her rescue by Kwa and the death of Duag at the spring. They wondered what had happened to Kwa in his quest for freedom. Had he gone to the coast as he had mentioned he might?

Susanna listened with a rapt look on her face as Quintira told of Raaschid's judgment to banish her to the desert, the horrifying thistles in her hair, her rescue by the Old One, and his amazing disclosure of his royal heritage.

Susanna and Mi'kal didn't miss a word as Leyla spun her tale of the fabulous entertainment at the palace. She told how she had passed the piece of purple scarf to King Aretas and how he had invited her to come to him the next day. He had believed her story, and then they had seen Quintira and the Old One waiting to see Herod Philip. Aretas had taken Quintira into his heart immediately.

Susanna seemed especially enraptured with the tales of the Old One. "Where is he now? Why is he not here with you?"

"Herod Philip arranged for his passage to Rome," Quintira explained. "He has gone to claim the villa and the trust fund that is supposed to be there from his father, Antony. Then we are to visit him, and Mi'kal can travel and see all the things he has longed to see."

Mi'kal smiled and knew his dream had faded. He no longer cared if he saw the Sphinx with the human head and the lion claws. The Old One had been right that day so long ago when a small boy boasted of seeing all the wonders of the world. Grandfather had said maybe yes, maybe no; the choice would be his to make.

"Did Herod Philip think it safe for Grandfather to return to Rome?" Mi'kal asked. "I would think—"

"The tetrarch is a worthy man. He would do nothing that would cause harm to anyone," Quintira assured him.

"I agree," Silvanus said in his deep voice. "But his secretary is something else. I work in an office next to his, and I have my misgivings. He is a loyal vassal to Tiberius, but we can hope for the best."

Leyla explained that Silvanus was Aretas's chief scribe. The king had sent him with Leyla and Quintira to find his grandson in Galilee or Judea. "I had told him that if we found Jesus, we would find Mi'kal."

Susanna turned to Mi'kal, and she was smiling. He was glad to see the tears had gone since the arrival of his mother and Leyla. "I can hardly wait to tell Oreb you are a prince of Petra. He knows you as the son of a lesser desert chieftain—but, grandson of Aretas!"

"Please don't," Mi'kal said. "I didn't tell him because I have no intention of—"

"He thinks of you as a boy he pulled out of a ditch."

"A ditch?" Quintira looked up in surprise.

It was time for Mi'kal to tell his story.

The moon had finished its descent behind the far hills as they went to their rooms, but the stars were brilliant. Mi'kal sat on the edge of his mother's bed and watched her brush her hair. He spoke briefly of many things, as he had often done in the tent. He spoke of the Zealots and of the controversies surrounding Jesus.

"I am learning to use a Roman sword—just in case."

Quintira shook her head. "Our prophets have said that when the Messiah's kingdom comes, we will turn our swords into plowshares and our spears into pruning hooks."

Finally, he told her how he knew his search for the Green Bird was over. He told her about the sign in the sky over Lazarus's empty grave and the sunset wings spread over Jerusalem. She took his hands and kissed his palms. "So my little prince has fulfilled his dreams. I am happy for him."

Before saying goodnight, he told her of the family in Papyron. Of Zeus and Dannah, and of Hosea, who was not quite right in the head.

Quintira watched him closely as he spoke of Zeus, and a small light twinkled in her eyes. "Darling, does it hurt too much about Leyla?"

"Not too much. Something like a bee sting to my pride."

"The Old One and I saw it happening. We were on the road several more days than necessary. I wanted to see Sepphoris, where I was born. There is a mass grave there where they buried many of those who died during the raid. And, of course, I wanted to see Grandfather embark. He was to sail within hours of boarding."

"I have learned something," Mi'kal said as he rose to leave. "A boy can *think* himself into being in love at least for a few minutes. Next time I will not be so foolish."

"Tomorrow you must tell me more about your friend, Zeus. Is that really her name?"

"No. But I wouldn't dare tell you what it is. I like her a lot, but she makes me angry sometimes. She makes me feel foolish because I never know what she is going to do next. She flits around like a horsefly. And she thinks she knows it all."

"Apparently she knew enough to help you with the wagon after the ambush. And she was there to pull you out of the river."

He laughed and kissed her. "It's time for you go to sleep."

"First, let us give thanks to God for his wonderful goodness."

After the prayer, Mi'kal had too much to think about to sleep, so he sat in the luminous courtyard. Silvanus came out and dropped his dark robe from his shoulders.

"I like to feel the night air," he said. "To me, it gives the spirit cleansing." Muscles rippled on his bare shoulders and chest. "Leyla and I are leaving for Damascus tomorrow. King Aretas plans to return to Petra sometime soon. We will go with him. We intend to marry, but I want to make sure that she is sure. In some ways she is so young."

"I am sure she loves you."

Silvanus stretched, and he saw Mi'kal's admiration. "You admire my body. I admire your mind and your destiny. You Jews know who you are in God's plan. Your mother talked to us, all the way here, about God's love for Israel. She had a wise proverb or a psalm of praise for every broken axle or deceptive mudhole."

"She wanted to be a rabbi."

Silvanus's laughter was deep and pleasant. "And now—about this man you call the Messiah. I will keep my eyes and ears open about him, too. Our talk at the table tonight was thought provoking."

Early the next morning, as Silvanus and Leyla prepared for their return to Damascus, Leyla cornered Mi'kal. "You don't hate me for falling in love with someone else, do you?"

"No. I like Silvanus very much."

"At least he hasn't thrown away any straw dolls."

"I shouldn't have done it."

"I'm glad you did. I was very frightened after Duag caught me. I told your God if he would save me, I would believe in him and never have another idol. Your mother has been teaching both of us, and Silvanus wants to know all about your God, too."

Later, as Silvanus started to help Leyla into the wagon, Susanna said,

"I am sorry Jesus was not here to talk to you. All men, of all nations, should hear what he has to say."

"We will consider all we hear about him," Silvanus said. "If it is true—as you believe—that his doctrines bring salvation to all men, I will be his disciple."

Susanna and Quintira gave them a basket of fruit and kissed them both.

Before Silvanus picked up the reins, he dropped several coins into Aziz's hands. "You did a good job on the wagon." The small brown face beamed.

Mi'kal handed up the whip.

"God go with you, Silvanus," Quintira said.

He smiled at them. "I should tell you—I like for my dearest friends to call me Silas."

"Good fortune, Silas!"

Mi'kal grabbed Leyla's hand. "If the first one's a boy, name him Mi'kal."

Her face flamed with the color of an oleander blossom. Mi'kal grinned. Served her right.

CHAPTER THIRTY-FOUR

The next few days were peaceful in some ways and troublesome in others. Quintira and Susanna became close friends, and Mi'kal enjoyed hearing them talk quietly in the kitchen or courtyard. But talk of food and flowers could not hide the acute awareness of the nearness of Passover and the growing danger to Oreb and Jesus.

Every moment her husband was away was agony to Susanna. She would often go to the open gate and stare down the lane, lifting her head to listen. Each time she came back through the court there were tears on her cheeks.

Once Quintira held her and said, "Susanna we must wait on the Lord. Your husband is as eager to get home as you are to see him. I, too, am eager to meet him."

Susanna tried to smile. "I think I'll know when he's coming. Something in here will tell me." She touched her breast. But as the Sabbath before Passover came, nothing could ease Susanna's restless trips to the gate.

Mi'kal was glad his mother was there. He had promised Oreb to take care of Susanna, but Quintira's cheerful helpfulness and calm faith was what Susanna needed.

Mi'kal suffered, too. Oreb might never be home again if a patrol caught him with a wagon full of weapons. He found himself listening for faint sounds of battle. How stupid of him! When the real fighting started, everyone in Ephraim would know. The cries of "For Israel and the temple" would rebound from hill to hill, from mountain to mountain.

If the Zealots lost to Rome, the crosses would sprout on the hills again. Even if the Zealots did not revolt, Jesus was in danger from his own religious leaders. Mi'kal remembered the feeling of dread as Mary of

Bethany had shown him the burial ointment and said it was for Jesus. She had been saying something else when he left the room, but he had been too upset to listen.

He picked up the lyre and touched the strings. Where was his faith? Why should he feel despondent? Nobody, including Caiaphas and the Romans, could do anything to Jesus without the consent of God. God's Son would be surrounded by more heavenly chariots than Elisha had ever seen.

He could smell red beets boiling and freshly sliced onions. His mother was humming. Perhaps she had persuaded Susanna to lie down and rest. Quintira continued humming, and he tried to match the lyre to her tune. She heard his notes and came to the door singing.

"Praise the LORD.... Praise him for his acts of power.... Praise him with the harp and lyre, praise him with tambourine and dancing, praise him with the strings and flute.... Let every thing that has breath praise the LORD."

Susanna had not been asleep; she came out to listen, her worry forgotten for a moment. "Mi'kal, you do so well. Jesus would be pleased with you." She offered him a small spiced beet from her fingers.

"Enough to make me a disciple?" Part of the disappointment he had felt when Jesus would not take him to Galilee showed in his voice as she wiped red juice from her hand with a kitchen towel.

"He has his chosen twelve, Mi'kal, but anyone who loves him can be a disciple."

He had just laid the lyre aside, and the women were deciding which flowers to cut for the supper table when they heard the sound of hooves in the lane. They rushed to greet Oreb, but instead Aziz rushed through the gate.

"Mi'kal, you've got another visitor!" he yelled.

Mi'kal looked beyond Aziz and saw a stocky man dismounting from a white stallion that reminded him of El Gamar. The man wore a plain wound turban and was clothed in a short common garment.

Mi'kal heard his mother gasp. Her hand gripped his shoulder. "Mi'kal, it's your grandfather!"

King Aretas? How did you greet a grandfather you had never seen? One who was a king? He felt his knees tremble.

Susanna greeted the visitor. Aretas bowed as he introduced himself. Then his face lightened as Quintira and Mi'kal stepped toward him. She started to kneel, but he stopped her and drew her hand to his lips. "God's grace upon you, my daughter."

Susanna offered hospitality wine and then excused herself, whispering to Quintira that the king would probably prefer to talk to them alone.

Aziz was hunched like a small bird on the edge of a flower pot. Aretas tossed him a coin. "Take the horse for a rubdown. Water and feed him and bring him back. His name is Pegasus. You may ride him if you wish." The permission to ride sent Aziz flying.

The chill of nervous tension eased.

Aretas lifted Mi'kal's chin and stared into his face. Mi'kal, in turn, noticed eyes as dark as charcoal, facial lines inscribed by kindness and strength.

Then the king stepped back. His eyes measured Mi'kal's height, the width of his shoulders, the square corners of his face, and length of the red-gold hair and beard. What he saw caused his face to crumple and his arms to go around Mi'kal.

"Oh, son of my son! Would that my Mumtaza could be here." For a moment he could say no more.

Mi'kal too was struggling for speech. "You really believe Leyla and my mother? You really believe I am your grandson?"

"Seeing you is like seeing my son in a mirror. You are Myndus over again. Besides, I have proof."

He pulled Quintira's portion of the purple scarf from his girdle and handed it to her. "I intended to give it to you in Damascus. I simply forgot. As I explained to you, I have the other half at my home in Petra where his mother always kept it in her secret box."

Quintira pressed the scarf to her cheek. "How did you find us?"

"Through Silvanus. He managed to send me reports regularly. When he was sure he was close to finding Mi'kal, I mounted and came. I passed them this morning as they were returning, and they told me you were here at Ephraim. I inquired at the stable to make sure that I was near the right home."

"I have grown fond of Leyla," Quintira said. "Will she do well to marry Silvanus?"

"He is an excellent fellow in all ways. Never afraid to look for and accept the truth whether it be pleasant or unpleasant. A man who could well sing in calamity."

"I'm glad," Mi'kal said—and meant it.

"My daughter," Aretas began, "the main reason I am here is that I want both of you to come and live at Petra. You will be given all the honor a prince of Petra and his mother should have."

Mi'kal and his mother looked at one another. He couldn't read his mother's eyes, but he knew what his heart was saying. He shook his head. "Grandfather, I have never wanted to be a prince—in the black tents or anywhere else. I am just an ordinary man."

The king smiled. "Ordinary? Most unlikely! Maybe you both should think on it for awhile."

Quintira lifted a hand. "My Lord, I would not be happy in a palace. I have lived too long in the black tents. I need a much simpler life, and I have been invited to stay here to meet our Messiah and his disciples. I am looking forward to helping with a baby when Susanna's son comes."

"I, too," said the king, "could have been content in a black tent with my beloved 'Taza. But when you are a prince, you have to do many things you do not wish to do. I have a nation depending on me."

"There is no one depending on me," Mi'kal said. "Your Nabateans do not know I exist. If I give my allegiance to anyone, it will be to Jesus of Nazareth."

"But you *are* a prince in your own tents," Aretas reminded him. A touch of judgment in his voice.

"Raaschid was not my father."

"But he thinks of you as his son. He is sorry for his misjudgment of you. I know, because I have spoken with him."

Quintira moved suddenly. "You have seen Raaschid?"

"Yes. I went to his camp immediately after talking to Leyla. I rode a racing camel so I could more quickly slay the man who had slain my son."

Quintira paled. Mi'kal felt a flash of anger. "You wanted revenge after so many years?"

"It was my intent. His mother never quit grieving over our son's murder. But when I found the camp, I could do nothing but pity him."

Quintira was puzzled. "Pity Raaschid?"

"He is confined to his couch. An arrow took him in the spine. You do know there was a blood feud?"

"We heard," Mi'kal said. "But I don't know the reason brother came against brother. Did you hear why?"

Aretas told then as much as he knew. Raaschid had gone to report the murder of his son, Sa'ad, and to comfort the girl he was to marry.

"The quarrel started when he discovered it was his nephew who had committed the murder."

"Zauf?" Quintira said in horror. "Why would Zauf kill his cousin?"

"The camp wasn't talking much about it. The only thing I know for sure is that he confessed, and Raaschid cut him down with his sword."

"You mean he didn't wait for Muktar to judge his own son?" Quintira asked.

"No."

"Then that is the reason for the feud," she said.

Mi'kal held his mother's cold hand and asked, "Is there anything left in the camp?"

"Many of the tents were burned, and I saw many burial cairns. The livestock is gone. But I understand the flocks are still in the hills."

"Who is in charge?" Mi'kal asked.

"The young wife is doing what she can. She is plain but strong and is devoted to the chief. I heard an older wife perished in the fires."

Quintira shivered. "I am sorry about Gutne, but I am glad for Ne'ma. She has loved him for a long time."

"There is affection on both sides," Aretas said. "She takes good care of him, and his eyes follow her. She boasts she is carrying twins."

Mi'kal smiled. "That I can believe."

When Aziz brought the stallion, Aretas rose. He made one last plea for one or both of them to promise to come to Petra.

"Grandfather, your Nabatean blood runs in my veins, and for that I am glad. But as I said, I am only a common man."

257

The king lifted Quintira's hands to his lips. "Let him say what he will. We know he has all that is required in a prince, don't we?" He untied a heavy pouch from his waist and pressed it into her hands. She protested, but he insisted.

The white horse pawed the ground as Aretas took off a signet ring and gave it to Mi'kal.

"Keep it. Use it. Anything you sign will be paid for or done. No one will turn you down, unless it is Herod Antipas." Scorn and hatred crossed his face. "My daughter Thalia killed herself with charcoal fumes after Antipas sent her home with divorcement papers when he brought his brother's wife home with him from Rome." He paused, his hands on the pommel. "Believe me when I say that someday he will pay for it." He vaulted into the saddle and held the stallion steady.

"I almost forgot my other message. Warn your friend, Alexander Helios, it will be dangerous to go to Rome. Gryphus, the liaison between Philip and Tiberius, has sent a swift messenger to the emperor and probably plans to act on his own. If I know either of them, your friend will be in danger. Don't let him sail."

Mi'kal saw his mother go pale. "But he is already gone! On the *Medusa*, out of Caesarea bound for Miletus. Philip advised him to take the first available passage."

Aretas settled into the saddle, draped a cloak in front of him, and loosened his sword. He laid his hand on a heavy loop of chain that hung near the saddlebag.

"Let us hope I am wrong. But remember, whatever happens, Philip had no part in it. He is one Herod who is honest and good—the only one." He turned the horse and looked down at them.

"Pray I get safely out of Palestine. There is something brewing here. I felt it in Galilee and even more so here in Judea. I am like a war horse who can sniff the smell of battle. Be careful."

As Aretas and his white stallion disappeared at the bend of the lane, Mi'kal stood for awhile before letting the gate click shut. When it did, he knew it had closed on an important pathway of his life.

CHAPTER THIRTY-FIVE

Mi'kal picked up the lyre and struck the strings. The morning promised a beautiful day. Perhaps he would take his mother for a short ride if Susanna didn't mind being alone for a little while.

He laid his head against the tree trunk and began a tentative melody, singing what he could remember of one of his mother's favorite Scriptures. Mi'kal had always liked it, for it gave him confidence.

Though the fig tree does not bud and there are no grapes on the vines, though the olive crop fails and the fields produce no food, though there are no sheep in the pen and no cattle in the stalls, yet I will rejoice in the LORD, I will be joyful in God my Savior.

God my Savior? What did it mean? Saved from what? Certainly not from want or ill fortune. Habakkuk, the writer of the praise, must have gone through deep adversity.

"You sound at peace with the world," Quintira said as she came into the court wearing a robe as blue as the flax flower. Susanna came too, looking a little pale.

"Mother, when Jesus calls me to be a disciple, I will have the same powers the others have, won't I?

"The Twelve are something very special, according to Susanna."

Mi'kal seemed not to hear her. His hands were behind his head and his face glowed. "Imagine being able to heal the sick or even raise someone from the dead."

"Son, your pride is showing." Her voice was unusually sharp.

Susanna spoke from the doorway. "As a believer, Mi'kal, you will have the power to do something more important than healing bodies. Jesus does the healing to glorify God and to prove he is the Son of God, but you will be able to tell men and women how they can have forgiveness of sins and everlasting life."

Quintira sat down beside him. Her voice had softened. "Before any of us can help other people have their sins forgiven, we must ask God to forgive ours."

He stared at her. "What makes you think I'm such a big sinner?" There was an uncomfortable silence. Then Quintira ran her fingers through the hair over his ears in a way he had always remembered.

"Mi'kal, you have always been a good boy, but you have never been without sin. Sin came with you when you were born because you are of Adam's race. I have explained to you how he brought sin into the world. Susanna says she believes Jesus has come to remove that sin. His very name, Jesus, means savior from sin."

"But Mother, I have always tried to sin as little as possible."

"Big or little—it makes no difference," Susanna said. "If we break the least of the laws we have broken them all."

"You mean because I ate a crayfish with Zeus and let her steal me a pair of sandals I am guilty of everything—murder and blasphemy and all the rest?"

Susanna started to answer, and then her face changed color. She threw her hand over her mouth as she rushed away.

Mi'kal tried to remember if he had ever seen a Bedouin woman suffering from morning sickness. He also wondered what Susanna would say about Oreb's sins if he told her about the soldier in the Jerusalem alley.

But maybe he shouldn't mention Oreb. Susanna seemed a lot less worried today. Maybe her stomach sickness was taking her mind off her worries—or maybe Oreb was on his way home. She had said she would know.

When she returned, looking wan, Mi'kal said, "If you get to feeling better, I'd like to take Mother for a little ride. Maybe as far as the river?"

"I'll be all right." She smiled. "Oreb will be home soon. I feel it in here." She laid her hand on her heart, then went pale again.

Quintira followed her. "Have you tried chewing on some of your unleavened bread?"

Mi'kal laid the lyre aside and put on his sandals. He went to the kitchen door and told his mother he was going to rent a cart from Hiram's stable while she prepared a jug of water and food. Susanna called for him to be sure to get one with quiet wheels.

Mi'kal could smell fresh straw and manure before he reached the stable. The smell reminded him of the horse corral at the desert camp. The stable was a low, sprawling affair with one wide door at the front and an open side where Hiram had his forge. At the back were living quarters. Hiram was working outside at the sawhorses. Aziz was spreading fresh straw in the stalls.

Hay and straw bales were stacked high. There were several empty stalls; only three mules and a horse were still in the stable. A gray donkey that looked like Astarte was tied by the door. Several small wagons and two wheeled carts took up what space was left. Aziz harnessed the smallest of the mules to one of the carts. Mi'kal asked if the axles were greased.

"Oreb's wagon was squeaking like a gaggle of geese," he said.

Hiram showed consternation. Aziz looked ashamed. "Father, I'm sorry. I neglected to tend to it."

"We will make amends when he returns. But it must not happen again. If we grow careless, we lose customers. If we lose customers, we go without shoes and bread." Then he smiled and laid his arm about his son's shoulders.

Aziz insisted on sending Quintira a straw hat. It was woven much like the ones the Old One made from palm leaves.

Mi'kal set the food and water near his mother's feet and put his sword under a pile of old grain sacks in the bed of the cart. He was not sure why he was taking the old weapon, but he felt more adequate with it.

As they went, Quintira exclaimed about everything. How blue the sky! How green the fields! How bumpy the road!

Mi'kal scarcely listened. He was thankful she was alive. He began to chant praises. "O LORD...how priceless is your unfailing love!"

Quintira joined him. "Shout for joy to the LORD, all the earth.... Know that the Lord is God. It is he who made us, and we are his people.... Give thanks to him and praise his name. For the LORD is good and his love endures forever."

There were large stones in the road, and Mi'kal concentrated on driving. He remembered how hard he and Zeus had worked to pull the Romans to the tollhouse. He tried to visualize her. Wide shoulders and soft gray eyes. Tight red curls like the image on a Caesar coin. A spirit as free as sea breeze.

What did he know about sea breezes? The Old One was the one who knew. Was he riding a galley such as his father had taken into the ill-fated battle of Actium? Was the Old One in danger, as Antony had been?

A crow flapped in undulating flight ahead of him. Was it an omen?

After Mi'kal and his mother left, Hiram and Aziz went back to work. The blacksmith laid a strip of tin across two sawhorses and began to cut strips of metal to repair wheel rims.

They were startled when three mounted Roman soldiers stopped. Hiram greeted them with calm pleasantness, which darkened with apprehension as two of the men swung down from their saddles. One bearded man, evidently in command, barked some orders.

"Search the place," he said to the one who was dismounted. To the other, "Stay here and keep your eye on him."

Aziz started out of the stable but stopped beside the donkey hitched by the door. The soldier brushed past him. The soldier on the horse ordered Hiram to sit on the ground with his legs spread and both hands flat on the earth. The mounted man used his army pike to enforce obedience.

The soldier in command yelled to the one in the stable. "Find anything, Rex?"

"No weapons. But the wagons are well used. Too well used for such a village." He came out leading the two mules and the horse.

"Leave them alone," Aziz yelled.

"Take them to the main road," the bearded one told the soldier with the pike. "Put them with the others we've collected. Rex and I will finish up here. Take care of our mounts, too. No sense in advertising our presence."

The horses and mules were tied together and led away. Rex turned to the donkey. "What about this flea bait?"

"Finish him off."

Rex aimed the sledge hammer and the donkey dropped without a sound. Aziz threw himself at the soldier, screaming and crying. "I wish I was big enough to kill you!" The soldier knocked him aside.

Hiram struggled to stand and the leader pushed him down with the tip of his sword. Then he changed his mind and prodded Hiram to his feet. "Let's get both of them into the stable out of sight. Then we'll see if he's willing to tell us who uses his wagons, and why."

Inside the stable, Hiram protested. "Nobody uses my wagons except for ordinary work hauling grain and manure and charcoal or fire brush. See for yourselves."

"We will." The sledge hammer hit the bed of a wagon and planks cracked. Spokes splintered. Wagon tongues split.

"I hope you die," Aziz screamed. "I hope the next time you turn a corner somebody kills you."

Above his screams he heard the squeak of wagon wheels. Hiram stiffened and Aziz's face paled. The Romans heard it too.

"One of your dung wagons no doubt," Rex said as he forced Hiram and Aziz down behind a horse stall. The bearded soldier took a position inside the door. The squealing came nearer, accompanied by a cheery whistle.

Hiram touched Aziz and motioned toward a large ax head lying in the straw. It usually was used to hold down the canvas over the hay bales.

Aziz inched it slowly toward his father who read the fear in his son's face. He shook his head slightly. His gaze went to the piece of tin lying across the sawhorses outside the door. He motioned for Aziz to stay down, but he rose swiftly and heaved. The ax head landed on the tin with the resounding roll of thunder.

263

The sound of squealing wheels and whistling stopped.

"We've lost him," the man in the doorway yelled. Then turning in anger he yelled, "Take care of that Zealot lover!"

Rex didn't hesitate. He lifted his sword and brought the flat blade down hard on the back of Hiram's neck. The blacksmith rolled lifeless against his son.

Aziz screamed and screamed until the soldier lifted him like a pitchfork of manure and tossed him to the top of the hay bales. He landed on a rolled up canvas used to tie down hay or straw and screamed again.

There was no further sound from outside. "We will have to look for him. He can't be far," Rex growled.

"He isn't," said a low voice behind him. Aziz had been the only one to see Oreb coming through the door of the small room attached to the back of the stable. He had on the helmet and the Roman belt, but he didn't look ridiculous with the broadsword in his hand. He saw Hiram lying dead and heard the frantic screams of Aziz. Anger, like a flame, lit the Zealot's face. With a wild cry, he reached the Roman. One thrust and the soldier was down.

The bearded man was faster and kept away from Oreb by leaping from feeding trough to watering buckets, from hay bales to grain sacks. A fallen bridle caught Oreb's foot and sent him sprawling. His sword spun out of his hand.

As the Roman rushed him, Oreb scrambled to his feet and grabbed a pitchfork. The heavy sword broke the handle and knocked the fork from Oreb's hand. He slipped on fresh dung and went flat on his back. The fall stunned him long enough for the Roman to straddle him. Aziz screamed for him to get up. The Roman raised his sword with both hands for the thrust. He hesitated for just a second, as if waiting for the thumb-down signal.

Above him, Aziz gave the rolled up canvas a heavy shove. The canvas dropped as the blade descended. The full weight caught the Roman across his head and one shoulder and sent him sideways. His sword missed Oreb's chest and tore into his left arm and shoulder.

The soldier struggled to his knees, fighting the heavy canvas. Oreb grabbed the tines of the fork with his right hand and thrust them upward with all his might into the face of his enemy.

The Roman fell backwards, blood spouting. His hands grabbed at his face. He died while Aziz pulled Oreb out of the stable. He was too heavy for Aziz to lift, so he made a ramp of broken boards and pulled him up into the wagon.

Aziz was shaking and crying too hard to drive. He laid the reins on Moses's rump and the mule understood. The wagon moved quickly down the lane.

CHAPTER THIRTY-SIX

i'kal planned for them to eat lunch near a ford where the shore was sandy. As they approached the river, Quintira laid a restraining hand on his arm. They could hear jumbled and anguished voices. Mi'kal slowed the mule, but they were out of the concealing growth of tall rushes and small oak trees before Mi'kal realized he had driven into trouble.

Three Roman mercenaries were shoving frightened men and women about and tying them up like shocks of wheat. A fourth soldier splashed and cursed in the river, trying to round up several oxen and donkeys struggling in their traces. The carts and wagons were overturned and debris floated away. On shore, beyond the quivering victims, piles of rakes, scythes, and forks had been confiscated and piled up.

Mi'kal pulled to a quick halt. "Sit still, Mother. Don't do or say anything."

A dark, swarthy soldier came forward, sword in hand. Mi'kal felt a rush of anger against the hireling. Who was this barbarian that he should come into Abraham's land and mistreat God's people?

He jumped down and tried to keep his voice calm as he spoke to the soldier in common Latin.

The soldier grunted and stared at Quintira. He lifted the straw hat from her head with the tip of his sword. She didn't flinch.

"The boy speaks in Latin but you are definitely a Jew." He sneered and dragged her from the cart. "Every Jew hates Caesar's guts."

Mi'kal started to protest and a second soldier laid a heavy hand on his shoulder. Quintira said, "Never mind. I'll be all right."

The first soldier pushed her out of the way and began to examine the

266

cart. He lifted out the jug of water, shook it, then unstoppered it and took a long drink. He handed the jug to his friend while he set the basket of food aside.

"Nothing else here," he said to the soldier holding Mi'kal. He sounded disappointed. Then he let out a hearty "aha" as he lifted the grain sacks under the seat.

He called to his companion. "What do you make of this?" He held up Mi'kal's sword.

"Wouldn't cut butter. With weapons like that Tiberius has nothing to fear." He chuckled and gave Mi'kal a shake.

The swarthy soldier dropped the sword back into the cart. "But how many sharp ones has he smuggled to the enemies of Rome?"

"I carry that for protection against thieves," Mi'kal said. "That is all."

"We know nothing about rebellion," Quintira said. "We are lately from Syria."

She lifted her head and smoothed her skirts. Fear for her added to Mi'kal's anger. With her high color and her shoulders lifted, Quintira was beautiful.

The angry farmers screamed and tore at their ropes. The soldier in the river, still trying to right the carts and release the animals, yelled at the three on shore.

"Shut them up. I can't do a thing with these beasts as long as they keep screaming."

The soldier herding the prisoners grabbed an old man who had escaped his bonds and was trying to retrieve one of his shovels from the shallow water. The farmer made a feeble effort to hit the Roman, but the soldier yanked the shovel from him and tossed it aside. The shovel just missed Quintira.

"Why can't you Jews ever learn?" he growled, as he drew his sword.

"Don't hurt him," a woman begged. "He is an old man. We have no quarrel with Rome."

The soldier holding Mi'kal said, "Go ahead. Kill the Jewish dog. We have seen too much of this the last few weeks."

"No!" the old woman screamed.

Mi'kal closed his eyes. He could hear Oreb saying, "Reach for the gut." He heard the thud and then the sickening sound as the sword was pulled out.

"You filthy murderer!" he heard his mother shout.

He opened his eyes in time to see her picking up the shovel that had fallen at her feet. She poked the handle hard into the crotch of the soldier who had held her and then brought the iron scoop down hard on the killer's head. He doubled up as he fell, and a cheer went up from the victims. She grabbed up a sickle and began to hack at their bonds.

The soldier in the river shouted a warning and pushed through knee-deep water toward the shore. The soldier she had hit with the shovel handle limped toward her. She faced him with sickle swinging.

The soldier holding Mi'kal was not prepared for Mi'kal's sudden jerk. He lost his hold, and Mi'kal sprang for the sword in his cart.

Behind him, the farmers freed of their bonds armed themselves with pitchforks and rakes. They rushed out to meet the soldier in the river.

Mi'kal slithered across the bed of the cart and grabbed the old sword. The Roman poked his face over the sideboards. Mi'kal raised up and pushed for the man's throat. The point of the blade caught the soldier beneath the chin strap and went in. Blood gurgled as he fell backward.

The last soldier seemed unaware of what had happened to his comrades. He was mocking Quintira, laughing at her as he side-stepped her sickle and threatened her with obscene indignities. His expression changed when he saw Mi'kal. No more cat-playing-with-a-mouse look, but an insulting smirk. Mi'kal knew he could not equal the man's strength or skill, but something inside steadied.

David had fought a giant and won. He would fight as Oreb would expect him to. He started forward with a shout. "For Israel!" The shout brought a dozen more shouts.

Cliffs across the Jordan echoed and multiplied the cries. As Gideon's men were impelled by their shouting, the farmers and their wives were encouraged. They came with scythes and rakes and forks already bloodied. The Roman went down.

Quintira had vomited, and Mi'kal was dizzy from delayed fear. They held one another to stop their shaking.

The farmers washed their hoes and rakes in the river; the water ran red. Mi'kal saw Quintira's hat and picked it up. It was crushed and sodden with blood. He gagged as he tossed it away. Above him a crow laughed, and he knew why. In spite of all his proud boasting of victory over Death, he had become Death's servant. He, Mi'kal of the black tents, had done Death's dirty work.

Quintira asked no questions as she watched him throw his sword into the middle of the river.

Mi'kal worked with the farmers to right their carts and soothe the draft animals. They put the old farmer's body in his cart, and Quintira covered it with her light cloak.

While they worked, Quintira and Mi'kal heard much news of Jesus and Jerusalem. Jesus had been led into the city on the first day of the week by a procession of men, women, and children waving palms, shouting praises, and calling him Son of David and King of Israel. Jesus had returned to Jerusalem the next day to teach in the temple and do miracles on the porches and in the gates. Although it was known that Caiaphas wished to bring Jesus before the Sanhedrin and Pilate with charges of blasphemy and treason against Caesar, no hand was laid on him. Rumors said that more of the Sanhedrin and priests and scribes believed in Jesus than were willing to admit.

Some of the farmers spoke of murder and unrest in the lower city. Barabbas, a man known for his violent hatred of the Romans, had been led away in chains after a fight outside an inn. He was charged with killing several of Rome's men with an ax handle after they mistreated an old shopkeeper.

Mi'kal was troubled by the arrest of the southern Zealot. What would it mean to Oreb and the men under Neophron? Surely with the loss of Barabbas, the revolt could not go on.

One of the farmers told him they had expected no trouble at the ford. Things had seemed quiet in the villages as they started for the wheat and barley fields in Galilee, but Roman soldiers seemed to be everywhere. Patrols were on all the roads and in the hills searching for Zealot sympathizers and caches of weapons. The emperor had sent word that if there were any more skirmishes, the roads would be fenced with crosses.

The common people took the threat seriously. Many of them remembered, as did Quintira, when Archelaus, brother of Herod Antipas, had crucified thousands of rebels during the time of Judas of Galilee.

When Mi'kal and Quintira reached the fork of the road that led to Ephraim, the old woman who had lost her husband climbed down from her wagon and kissed Quintira's hands. She offered to give back the robe that covered the body of her husband, but Quintira refused. Mi'kal helped the widow back into her wagon. She patted his hand. "We really are farmers. We had no thought of weapons."

But Mi'kal found himself thinking of Oreb. Oreb did have weapons, and he had been gone for a disturbingly long time. Susanna had seemed confident enough that he would be home today, but what if he wasn't? What if some Roman squad had stopped the wagon with the squeaking wheels?

As the small mule plodded on, the day that had started so peacefully had no joy or beauty left.

Quintira began to cry. "I did not mean to kill," she said. "Suddenly I was eleven years old, and I saw my mother die and my father lifting the shovel and—"

"You have no need for shame. He deserved to die."

"Even the stones looked wet, as though it had rained—like that morning in Sepphoris."

"They were wet from the river water." As the cart jolted over a large stone, Mi'kal tried to smile. "Life is rather like this road, isn't it, Mother? Sometimes we need to be jolted out of our complacency. I have condemned my good friend, Oreb, for killing. And yet, today I have killed."

Quintira's hand closed over his on the reins.

As they entered Ephraim, Mi'kal decided they would leave the cart at the stable and walk down the lane to the big house. Everything seemed as usual as they drove around the slight bend toward the stable. Then he saw the sprawled body of the donkey and drew the mule to a sudden halt. There was no sound or movement from inside the stable.

He leaped down. Quintira would have followed him, but he motioned for her to stay. He walked rapidly, calling for Aziz and Hiram.

He came out with tears coursing through his beard and carrying Oreb's bloody sword.

"Mi'kal what is it? What's happened?"

"The stable owner has been murdered. Everything is wrecked. The animals are gone."

Quintira's face went white.

"There are two dead soldiers. I don't think Hiram killed them. I think this killed him." He held up the bloodied sword. "It's Oreb's. Mother, do you know what this means? Oreb is wounded too. He would never leave his sword. He must have come in while the Romans were here."

"What about Aziz? Is he...?"

"No. He might be with Oreb. They're probably at the house!" He swung into the seat and cracked the whip. The wheels bounced as the cart careened past the borders of roadside flowers.

Mi'kal saw Moses and the wagon outside the gate, and his heart lifted. Then he saw the bloodstains on the wagon planks and on the stones. He helped Quintira down, and both of them rushed through the gate. Aziz was slumped by the sycamore. His garment was stained with blood. His eyes were large in his stricken face. When he saw Quintira and Mi'kal, he pointed dumbly toward the house.

They found Susanna working frantically over the unconscious Oreb. His blood was everywhere. Quintira pulled her away and began to give orders. She forced the jagged edges of the wound together and wrapped them tightly with her head mantle.

"Is he going to die?" Susanna whispered. Tremors shook her.

"Not if we can stop the bleeding. Is there a doctor in this village?"

"Not a very good one."

"Any of them can sew up a sword cut. Mi'kal, take Aziz and find him."

In the court Aziz looked up through tears "After we get the doctor, can you help me bury my father?"

"Of course."

As they went, Aziz spoke very low, his head lowered. "I wanted to have a stable just like my father."

"You can." Mi'kal fought for something to lighten the boy's grief. "Right now you have two wagons and two mules. Matthew took one each to Capernaum. Remember?"

"I promised you a donkey."

Mi'kal put his arm about the small shoulders and thought of Kaleb. "We'll get another donkey someday."

When they went to bury Hiram, they discovered someone had taken the bodies of the soldiers.

"There was a third soldier in charge of the horses and mules they were stealing," Aziz said. "He probably came back."

They found a few pieces of smoldering charcoal from the forge in a pile of wet straw.

"They're not going to keep me from having a stable!" Aziz said angrily as he scattered the smoking straw.

Later, as the boy came into the darkened room where Susanna sat with Oreb, she took his hand in hers. "Aziz, I want you to stay with us...as our boy. If my husband lives, it will be because of you."

CHAPTER THIRTY·SEVEN

Everyone in Ephraim expected Oreb to die. The doctor had done all he could do. He had stitched the wound and wrapped the shoulder with a mess of maggots to clean the putrefaction. But as the hours passed, the poison caused a deadly fever.

At times Oreb breathed loudly, with heavy movements of his chest. At other times his breath came so quietly that Susanna had to lay her head against his heart to be sure it was still beating.

The second day had dawned when Quintira woke Mi'kal from his exhausted sleep in a chair. She whispered his name and shook him gently. He opened heavy eyes and saw her bending over him. "What is it? Is Oreb—"

Her finger went to her lips. "He still breathes, but we dare not wait any longer. You must go for Jesus."

"But, the Passover...the Sabbath. What if he won't come?"

"He may have partaken of the Passover Supper last night. And Susanna says Sabbath rules don't seem to bother him. He will know he has to come. If we lose Oreb, we may lose Susanna and the baby."

Mi'kal struggled to his feet. "I'll go."

At the stable, while he hitched Moses to a cart, Aziz insisted it was going to blow up a storm. He laid a heavy badger skin in the cart as protection against wind and rain.

Mi'kal looked up at the sky before he climbed into the cart. Aziz was probably right. The clouds hung low and ominously gray.

He started off at a good pace, and the fresh air was a welcome change.

He tried to relax by snapping off the heads of the wayside weeds with the whip Aziz had put in at the last moment, in case Moses grew contrary. Each time the whip cracked, Moses would flick his ears. Mi'kal was certain he was wearing a mule smile. Well, no need for both of them to be eaten up with anxiety.

Overhead the sky changed to a disturbing mixture of gray and black, lacquered with yellow. Clouds moved in from the south on a fast wind. Wispy at first, they joined one another and rolled like windblown sand shrubs. High overhead, they gathered into masses of dingy plumes.

The rain began slowly with large spatters. Mi'kal flicked the gray rump with the whip and apologized. "Sorry, Moses." He draped the badger skin over his head and shoulders.

Blackness came down in sections, like curtains in the goat hair tents. Rain began to fall in torrents. The mule's hooves made slopping sounds in clay that would soon become sucking mud. Above the sound of the hooves he thought he heard someone yelling. He pulled to a halt and listened again.

"Wait up, will you? I need a ride." A drenched figure appeared alongside the cart. His heart came up in his throat. Even through the pouring rain he recognized her. Her wet hair looked almost black. Rain beat a tattoo on the copper pot.

She didn't recognize him until he rolled the badger skin back, and then she screamed with delight. She dropped her backpack to the cart floor. "This is a change. This time you're rescuing me." She threw her arms about him and began to laugh. "You were driving like Jehu. What's the rush?"

He shared the skin with her as he told her about Oreb and the need to find Jesus. "Do you know where he might be?"

She gave him a wide-mouthed grin; rain drops rolled off her nose. "Haven't we gone through this before?"

"Zeus be serious for once."

"I'm sorry. I guess I'm just so relieved to get a ride. I don't know for sure where he is. I haven't been in Judea, but I think he was planning to have the Passover supper in a home in Jerusalem. A friendly lady invited the Twelve to her home, but it was to be a secret so Caiaphas and the others couldn't grab him."

"If it was a secret, how do you know?"

"I keep my eyes and ears open. Anybody could do it."

"Oh, no. There is no one else in the whole world like you."

His admiration was honest. She looked up at him, the raindrops sparkling on her lashes. "You really think so?"

A sharp flash of lightning and an extended roll of thunder covered his reply. The thunder rolled beyond the hills where it met other thunders and came rolling back with increasing waves of terrifying sound. Darkness came, thick and impenetrable. The road disappeared in front of them.

"What should we do? I don't have any lanterns."

"There's an old wooden bridge right ahead," Zeus said. "If we stop there we can get under the cart and we won't be in the mud."

Mi'kal heard the wheels hit the timber and stopped. They jumped down. "Stay, you son of Beelzebub," Mi'kal said, hoping he sounded as tough as Oreb. Under the cart Mi'kal wrapped the badger skin about them.

A crack of thunder shook the bridge. Zeus moved closer and Mi'kal put his arm about her. Lightning struck a tree near them and sent it crashing down. They could smell the burnt wood.

The creek under the bridge began to roll, tossing water against the boards and splashing them. Zeus shivered with cold and excitement. "I love storms, but I've never heard one this bad. God must be angry about something."

The bombardment of lightning and thunder continued. At times when the world lighted up, they could see every blade of grass and every crack in the wooden bridge. The wind rocked the cart. The mule brayed.

"Stay, Moses!" Mi'kal yelled again.

Zeus pressed closer to him and his arm tightened. She began to giggle.

"What are you laughing at?"

"I don't know. I guess it's just the excitement of—"

"Being with me?" He tried to see her face between flashes of lightning. Suddenly the whole bridge cracked and heaved and kept on heaving.

Zeus grabbed for him. "Mi'kal, it's an earthquake!"

The love of the storm was gone; stark terror was in her voice. He steadied her tremors as she pressed against him. He felt her frightened breath under his chin.

She became aware of him and tried to move away, but he held her. This was something he wanted to remember. This was much, much more than the feelings that had caught him during Leyla's dancing.

"Mi'kal! Let me go!"

"No! Zeus, don't you know I love you?" The admission surprised both of them, but he knew he had never meant anything more in his life. He began to kiss her, as he had seen Oreb kissing Susanna. Her cheeks were wet and cold, but his kisses warmed them.

"Stop it. Stop it!" Panic shattered her voice.

He leaned over her, holding her face between his hands. "Zeus, I love you."

Suddenly her lips went to his and she was quivering. "I'm glad. Glad. Because I love you, too." And in the kiss Mi'kal felt the promise of the lifelong love of his mother's purple scarf.

Her voice filled with wonder. "O Mi'kal, think of it. Our first real kiss in the midst of thunder and lightning and an earthquake. Mi'kal, promise me you will always love me."

"I will—always, Zeus. Always." He released her for a moment to untangle the heavy badger cloak about them. The bridge swayed with a motion almost as terrifying as the bridge over the whirlpool. The timbers heaved under the cart, and Moses pulled forward. Zeus rolled loose and went sideways over the edge. She screamed as she landed in the rushing waters.

A series of crackling lightning bolts showed her face, white and terrified, above the rushing current. The flood waters were carrying her away. She tried to grab the roots of the trees and heavy shrubs along the shore, but the current, like an angry bull, tossed her over and over.

Mi'kal leaped in, yelling her name, but the current swept him off his feet. He grabbed a board that had been ripped from the bridge and tried to keep afloat. His feet hit an outcropping of rocks and he struggled to get to the bank. He crawled up on slippery clay. A lightning strike nearby sent needles through him.

The rain pelted his face. Zeus's screams had ceased. The endless flashes of lightning came again, a long shuddering series of bolts. One vast plume of light illuminated the sky from one horizon to another.

He saw her. She had reached the bank and was dragging herself out of the current, trying to get to her knees. For one moment he saw her as plain as if it were daylight. Then a blazing bolt hit a large tree near her. Zeus went backward into the water as the tree fell.

Thunder boomed. The earth shook. Darkness descended. Mi'kal screamed for her until he was hoarse.

Again the horizon lit with forked lightning. Then, as if there was no more damage to do, the storm was gone. The thunder retreated beyond the hills. Light began to creep in below the darkness like dawn coming in under the tent curtains.

Mi'kal forced his way through the sodden shrubs, the fallen trees, and patches of flattened grasses to the place he had last seen Zeus. There was no sign of her. The waters roared against the trunk of the fallen tree. How far had those waters carried her?

He sat down in the mud and wept.

Zeus had wanted to fall as a cedar of Lebanon—and she had. He would leave her to the world she loved. Let the hills bow as she went by; let the willows weep as they had in Babylon; let the birds sing her requiem.

He must do what he had come to do. He must get help for Oreb. He fought his way back to the cart, finding it hard to walk, blinded by tears and with mud-soaked sandals and a wet tunic binding his legs. Ahead of him, the road and the bridge were bathed in the innocence of midafternoon sunlight.

He breathed a prayer for the soul of Zeus and the life of Oreb as he lifted the reins. "Good boy," he said to Moses, for Oreb's mule had remained steadfast under the shaking of the earth.

As they headed for Jerusalem, the mule picked his way carefully through the mud slides and the debris, as if he knew his driver was not

277

fully aware of the desolation.

Little by little, as they neared the city, Mi'kal came out of his daze.

In spite of the peace after the storm, the traffic moved slowly and seemed overshadowed with gloom. Had something disturbing happened in the city? Had the holy temple been damaged by the earthquake and storm? Many Jews believed if anything happened to the Holy of Holies, Israel would be destroyed.

He stopped the next family group and spoke to the father. "Sir, did the storm do damage to Jerusalem?"

The man stared at him with dazed eyes. "The veil of the temple is rent! God save Israel. We will perish! Everything is lost. Everything." He shoved his family on.

Mi'kal tried to stop him. "Sir, I wanted to know if—" The family moved on.

Mi'kal saw an old woman and a young girl coming near. He jumped from his wagon to stop them. "Woman, can you tell me, was Jesus of Nazareth in Jerusalem today? It is important that I know. A friend is dying and—"

She uttered a shrill wail and pulled the mantle over her face. The girl answered him. "My grandmother cannot answer you. She has not spoken since noon."

"Did the storm harm her?"

"No. She grieves because of Jesus, sir. They put him on a cross on top of that ugly hill. They killed him, and he was her friend."

She lifted her hand in a little wave and went on.

Mi'kal pulled Moses to the side of the road and sat with the reins loose on his knees.

Crucified! Jesus of Nazareth crucified? No! The Messiah could not die! He who promised eternal life to others surely could not die.

Mi'kal lifted the reins, and the hooves pounded a refrain in his head. Something else was banging an accompaniment to the hooves. Mi'kal looked on the floor of the cart and saw the backpack, the blackened copper kettle, the small shovel. He grabbed at the pack, anger against God bursting inside him, and flung it as far as he could throw it.

It bounced and clanged. The shovel spun away. A bevy of frightened quail, hiding in the grass beside the road, rose with a whir of wings. Then Mi'kal was out of the cart gathering all of it up, holding it close. As his mother had kept the purple scarf, he would keep the copper kettle.

CHAPTER THIRTY EIGHT

By the time Mi'kal drew rein at the foot of the crucifixion hill, there were no more denials in him—only pain. He was like a child trying to understand a punishment he had not deserved. It was a pain like he had not experienced since his mother had punished him for getting into her precious box and wearing her purple scarf.

Only one other living person was on the hill—a Roman centurion striding around in a water-soaked red cape and wearing a helmet adorned with a horsehair plume.

Two of the crosses still held their horrible burdens. The middle cross was empty. An executioner had broken the legs of the two men with a mallet so they could no longer press themselves upward to breathe. Something about the smaller body caught Mi'kal's attention. Perhaps it was the hair which was drying in the sunlight and showed a touch of gold even through the dark perspiration of death.

The man had a placard over his head: Murderer and Thief. Mi'kal looked into the dead, agonized face of the victim. A memory stirred. This was the Zealot Oreb had recognized in the line of captives in Jerusalem. The boy the soldier had brutally kicked.

Mi'kal wondered if the older victim, with a similar *titulus*, might be Barabbas. The farmers had said the most notorious of the rebels had been taken prisoner during a fight in the streets.

What had the Zealots thought when they saw their expected Messiah nailed to the cross between them?

He raised his eyes to the center cross. The sign banged against the upright. It was written in Aramaic, Latin, and Greek: Jesus of Nazareth, King of the Jews.

Mi'kal wanted to beat on the upright and scream, but he kept his voice low. "Jesus, you said you were the Green Bird. I believed you. You said you were the Messiah, and my mother believed you. You said you were the Son of God, and Zeus believed. If you had been any one of the three, they could not have killed you and broken your legs and—"

"There wasn't a bone in his body broken." The centurion stood near. He held his helmet in the crook of his arm. His hair was black. Blue-gray eyes, red from the dust that had preceded the storm, squinted at Mi'kal from a strong face. "There was no need. He just lowered his head and cried out, 'It is finished,' and was gone."

Mi'kal could no longer hold his angry grief. "But he was not supposed to die! He promised me—all of us—if we believed in him we would live forever. In a world down here just like this!" Disappointment choked him.

"I would continue to trust him," the centurion said quietly. "Faith is most important during the things we cannot understand."

"He could have called down a multitude of angels and—"

"I believe it. The whole thing is past my understanding." The centurion showed honest confusion. "We free a man guilty of sedition against Rome and crucify a rabbi."

"Who took him away? Where?"

"Two men from the Sanhedrin, with proper orders from Pilate. I understand there is a tomb in the garden below here. A few of his friends helped. Three or four women and a man called John."

"But there should have been many. Unless…" His eyes sought those of the officer. "Unless they decided he had fooled us all."

The Roman placed his helmet over his short hair and adjusted the cheek straps. "Do not judge him hastily. This is a day Rome will never forget. We have not heard the last of this Man."

His gaze went to two men climbing the hill carrying a litter. "They have come for the thieves. Now I can leave. At least your Jesus will not be consumed with lime and fire." He started to stride away, and Mi'kal stopped him.

"Centurion! Can you tell me where to look for his disciples? I must talk to someone. I cannot settle this by myself."

"Evidently they went into hiding. I would have recognized some of them, but there was none except John."

The captain strode away. Mi'kal descended the hill with his mind in a turmoil. The Roman centurion was exalting Jesus as a man to be reckoned with even though he was dead. And those who had been chosen to follow him were frightened and ashamed.

As he climbed into the cart he hesitated. Where should he start? At Bethany? Even if he found them, would any of them be able to help? Would they still have the power? And even if they did, was Oreb still alive? He doubted if any of them had faith enough to bring a man back from the dead. Mi'kal closed his eyes and prayed.

Then he turned the cart toward Bethany.

Moses was straining against the muddy ruts on the hill when Mi'kal noticed a man walking ahead of him, close to a portion of broken wall that had once enclosed a large olive press. At the same time, he saw the furtive movements of another man in the midst of the olive grove. He wasn't sure why he felt the second man was plotting mischief against the first, but in the desert he had been taught to trust his senses.

Then he sat up straight, every nerve alert. The man in the road was slender and wore a wheat-colored tunic! Lazarus had worn such a garment in the hours following his resurrection. Mi'kal remembered news had been brought to Ephraim that Lazarus had been added to the men Caiaphas wanted to be rid of.

The man in the grove could be an assassin!

Mi'kal saw Lazarus leave the wall and head for the middle of the road. His head was bent, and he was concentrating on missing the water-filled ruts.

The man in the grove left the shelter of the trees and changed direction, too. He stepped lightly over a pile of fallen stones in the wall and lifted a knife from his belt.

Mi'kal struck Moses with the whip and shouted, "Lazarus! Look out!"

The assassin cast one look at the cart hurtling toward him and lunged toward his target. Lazarus turned, threw up his arms to protect himself, and slipped on the mud. The attacker leaped forward, ready to strike. His dagger flashed in the sun. Mi'kal grabbed the mule whip, stood up in the wagon, and snapped at the dagger as he had snapped at the flowers. The leather thong wrapped itself about the assassin's arm. The dropped dagger fell almost at Lazarus's feet. He pressed it into the mud.

Mi'kal jumped from the cart and raced toward the man who had managed to untangle his arm from the whip. Mi'kal grabbed the neck of his garment with his left hand and hit him hard with his right fist. The man went down. Mi'kal bent over him and hit him again. The sound of his knuckles hitting bare flesh did something good for the anger and grief inside him. He wanted to hit and hit and hit.

"Mi'kal, let him go. Let him go." Lazarus grabbed him by the shoulder.

Mi'kal stood up, jerking the assassin to his feet.

"Get out of here," he said. "Get out before I kill you."

As the assailant backed up against the low wall looking dazed and licking at the blood in the corner of his mouth, something inside Mi'kal changed. He didn't take time to analyze it then, but later he knew. He had gained confidence in himself. He was capable of taking care of himself and giving orders. Perhaps he was even mature enough to accept whatever it was Jehovah willed for him.

He picked up the dagger and dropped it in the wagon. "Get in," he told Lazarus. "Why did you want me to let him go?"

"If my Lord can pray for forgiveness for those who were crucifying him, I can accept this."

The man still lingered, cursing under his breath and rubbing his bruised jaw. Mi'kal yelled at him. "Go back to the Pharisees and the priests and tell them you failed!"

"Yes," Lazarus added in a quieter voice. "Go! Tell Caiaphas to order in sackcloth and ashes, for in three days all of Jerusalem will know he crucified their Messiah."

The man spit in contempt. "At least Judas got his man," he yelled as his hand closed on a loose rock from the wall.

The cart was moving. Mi'kal turned to Lazarus. "What does he mean—Judas got his man?"

The stone caught Mi'kal a savage blow behind an ear, and he slumped on the seat.

After Mi'kal left Ephraim to find Jesus, the pall of impending death fell over the house. Oreb had lost too much blood, and the poison was spreading rapidly.

The village doctor changed the compress of bloated maggots and gave him large doses of painkilling medicine. But he admitted there was little hope for a recovery.

Quintira was in constant prayer that Mi'kal would return quickly with Jesus or any of the disciples empowered to heal the sick.

A blustering wind rose, bruising the purple blossoms on the wall and scattering the yellow petals of the roses by the door. The shutters banged until Quintira fastened them, and then the house filled with shadows and oppressive heat.

At noon, reverberating thunder rolled in the Jordan valley and lightning laced the smoke-colored clouds. The rain pounded the stones of the courtyard. Quintira knew that wherever Mi'kal was, the storm would delay him.

She begged the doctor to do more…something…anything.

The doctor became angry, picked up his bag, and stalked away through the wet courtyard repeating there was nothing anybody could do. "You might as well get used to it. If we could do the impossible, the cemetery would be empty."

Quintira stared after him, unable to believe that any physician could walk away from a patient.

When early stars appeared in the pallid sky, a few of the Ephraim neighbors came in quietly bringing dishes of food, small loaves of flat Passover bread, and an abundance of loving sympathy for Susanna.

With the sympathy they brought the news of the crucifixion. Some had been in the Holy City. Some had family members who had been there. They told her of the casting of the lots, as it were, for the two men presented on Pilate's porch. Barabbas to be released! Jesus to be crucified!

"To the shame of Israel," one woman said, "the high priest paid many of the people to shout for Barabbas's freedom. The murderer is now free in the hills."

"How could they?" Quintira asked as she visualized the terrible scene.

"He prayed for his enemies the first thing," a younger girl said.

"Surely only a merciful God would do that," her mother added.

Between them all they relived the terror of God's anger in the thunder and lightning that chased everyone from the hill and many of them from the city. They told her of rain so heavy it washed away many homes and of the earthquake that shook the temple.

"Some say the earthquake opened the Holy of Holies. Anyone can go in."

Quintira shuddered.

Through it all they kept their voices low. Susanna must not know that Jesus was gone.

When the gate closed behind the last of them, Quintira felt numb. There was no Messiah! Yet she had been so sure. She had rejoiced when she believed the Messiah had come. But Mi'kal's faith in Jesus surpassed her own. Only not faith, perhaps, but rejoicing. Jesus had been the fulfillment of his childhood dreams.

If he had found Jesus crucified, what would he do? Would he control his hurt and disappointment enough to fetch a physician? Or one of the Twelve with power to heal?

Quintira fell to her knees by the bench. She looked up through the tree. Darkness had come, but she could see only a few stars through the leaves. She moved out from the shadows. The bowl of heaven was lighted with a million points of light, like a Syrian camp full of Bedouin fires. Perhaps it was so with faith. One must move out from the shadows. "O Lord, give me such faith," she whispered.

She heard a soft knock on the gate, then a click as it opened. The neighbors had not thoroughly shut it. She jumped to her feet. "Mi'kal?"

A man stepped forward. "Do not fear. I have not come to harm you." His voice was Galilean. The full moon broke through a cloud, and she could see him plainly. A slender man, no taller than herself, with a closely clipped black beard and dark eyes under slim brows.

"I'm not afraid," Quintira said. "But I must tell you we have grave illness here." She kept her voice low.

"That is why I am here. I am James, from Capernaum. Half-brother to Jesus." He also lowered his voice.

"His brother?" she doubted her ears.

"I went with my mother to share Passover with a friend in Jerusalem. When we learned of Jesus' arrest and Pilate's order to crucify him, my mother insisted on going to the hill. I offered to take her, but she went with my cousin John."

"The neighbors have told me he was the only disciple there."

"Yes. I felt sorry for Jesus when I learned all his disciples had fled. One had actually betrayed him to his enemies. I decided to join my mother, and then the storm came. By the time I reached the hill, almost everyone was gone except those who had been crucified. I saw a centurion looking up at Jesus. He took off his helmet and knelt. I could scarcely believe it. I heard what he said. It still rings in my heart like a bell."

James lifted his head and the moonlight struck him full in the face. There was a glow on his countenance. His voice sounded like a muted trumpet. "'Truly this was the Son of God!' That is what the Roman said. But in my heart I heard another voice, one saying, 'This is my beloved son in whom I am well pleased.' And everything I had doubted through jealousy and disbelief vanished. I accepted my brother for what he was—the Son of God. God heard your prayer, and his Spirit came upon me and sent me here. I am to pray and anoint the wounded man with oil. He will be healed to the glory of God the Father and our Lord Jesus Christ."

There was no doubting him. Quintira struggled to keep back the joyful and relieved tears.

"Then come. Come quickly." She grabbed his hand and stumbled over the doorsill in her haste to get him to Susanna.

The room smelled of putrefaction. Some of the wicks in the lamps were smoking for lack of oil. Oreb was suspended somewhere between heaven and earth by a thin thread of breath. Susanna looked at them with blank eyes, not recognizing a stranger.

"Fetch me a bottle of oil," James told Quintira.

When she returned, he lifted his hands and began to pray. The prayer became fervent. Sweat stood out on his forehead as he poured the oil over Oreb's head and chest.

The lamps flared sharply. The oil made tiny rainbows on the black beard and chest. Oreb's breathing became quiet but strong. He moved. He opened his eyes. Susanna let out a soft sigh, too weary to rejoice. She laid her head against Oreb's chest. He used both arms to hold her close.

CHAPTER THIRTY-NINE

The heavy-set man with the bushy gray brows had been running for hours. He had fallen into muddy ditches, been slapped in the face with tree limbs, and prodded in the legs with the sharp edges of broken shrubs.

Freedom, after four days in the dungeon of the Antonia, was too precious to take chances lingering around the Holy City. Pilate's guards had turned him loose outside the gates and warned him to get going. He read the threat in their voices. He, the guilty, was free—for a little while.

Maybe they had released him to please the public. Then again, they might be expecting him to run right back to the Zealot hide-out below Bethlehem. If so, he had fooled them, for he was heading for northern Galilee by way of Perea. He would find the little tributary—the creek that ran down from Ephraim, through the gorges and into the Jordan—and he would avoid the popular crossing at Jericho. After the storm it would be impossible to wade across the creek. He would have to find a way to cross it before he reached the falls. The southwestern side was impossible to descend. The cliffs came up straight from the gorge.

In times of high water, the ford below the falls was still possible for a strong man. But pursuing horsemen or heavily armored men could never cross. Somewhere near, to the west of him on the main road, he knew there was a wooden bridge that went over the creek. But the storm may have washed it out. Besides, there would be unwelcome traffic.

After fording the Jordan, he would go north through Perea to the Hornet's Nest and confer with Neophron. Now that Jesus was crucified, the plans for the uprising sometime during the seven or eight days of Passover were useless. They would have to give up hope for a Davidic kingdom—at least for now.

Early this morning he had been convinced that the Nazarene was not the Messiah. Jesus had been scourged, mocked by the Romans, and led out like a common criminal on Pilate's porch. The people had been given a choice as to which of the two men should go free, and they chose him— a notorious rebel—rather than a righteous rabbi from Galilee.

If Jesus had indeed come to be King Messiah, then God's plans had gone awry—or the world had taken a wrong turn, which was much more likely.

The man was breathing heavily as he stopped plowing through the mud and wet grass and sat down on the cover of an old well. He should be relatively safe now. The storm had given him opportunity to get out of or around places that might have been dangerous for him without darkness or rain. He had never trusted the Romans, and certainly not Pilate.

He ran his hand through his stubbly gray beard. His mind had been working as hard as his legs.

Just when had he realized that God had done something big that morning? Something more significant than Israel had ever seen before? Had the revelation come when they stood on Pilate's porch together? Was it when the choice was made—not entirely by the will of the people but because of the coins passing from the hands of the high priest's servants to those who would choose?

This was a ritual as old as Mosaic law: the casting of lots for the choosing of the scapegoat and the goat for the sin offering. One to live. One to die.

Although it was the custom to release a prisoner at Passover time, Pilate would never have ordered *him* up to the porch as the alternative if God had not planned it so. Why not the young, inexperienced Zealot with the reddish hair? The public might feel sorry for him. He was too young to die.

No. He, the most wanted rebel of them all, had been given the chance to go free. He had the feeling the chance had been selected for him by God according to plans made an eternity before.

Somewhere inside him, his spiritual eyes had been opened. Jesus was to die in his place! A sin bearer, not only for him, but for the whole world. The time of the Messiah had not yet come, but the world was in need of a Savior. Henceforth, he was a new man—free of the Romans but forever bound to Christ. A wood spider ran across the top of the well and the man rose. The rest had done him good.

Ahead, he heard the sound of swift waters. He had reached the tributary.

The creek was boisterous, throwing up foam and tearing large batches of vegetation from each bank like a rowdy child. Soon it would plummet over broken ledges and rush through the narrows to meet the Jordan. There it would become peaceful, like someone in old age, and drift quietly to the Salt Sea where its life would end.

He had not searched long before he found exactly what he needed—a tree that had fallen across the creek. Walking the lightning scarred trunk was no problem. He was still light and sure on his feet. He was jumping to the ground when he saw her, partially hidden by the soggy branches of the tree.

The furious waters must have carried her past the tree just as it fell. Branches swept her to the bank and leafy fingers held her there, away from the falls. The waters had receded from under her, but the tree limb held her firmly to the ground.

She appeared to be dead, but he felt for her pulse and was sure the faint beat came from his own finger tips. Her arms and legs were exceedingly cold.

He lifted her into the crook of his arm and put his ear to her mouth. He shook his head and laid her down. Such a pretty thing. So young to die. Maybe he should take time to cover her with stones.

Above him he heard strange whisperings in the trees. Small yellow birds began to sing. One of the birds fluttered down and landed lightly on her breast. He sat without moving. Still singing, with its head lifted, the bird moved toward the girl's shoulder. Then it crept closer to her ear. The man sat transfixed with childlike wonder.

He became aware that another bird had lighted on his shoulder. The big man known for his violence against those who hated Israel—the man some would hate because he had gone free and Jesus had died—sat with a yellow bird singing on his shoulder, as if knowing it was as safe with him as with its mother in the nest.

He scarcely breathed.

The light wind through the leaves of the trees made crying sounds. Small creatures came from the grasses along the bank. The trees and the small ones were grieving over this girl, this child with the virgin breasts. The birds were singing a requiem.

The man laid her gently on the ground and started to lift her hands to lay them across her when one of her fingers closed on his.

He jumped with surprise. He slapped her lightly on both cheeks. "Wake up," he said. "Wake up!"

It was as if he had called up the dawn. She opened her eyes. They were large gray eyes, startling in their beauty but still dazed. He saw now that her hair must be red under the mud that coated it.

She reached for his face and tried to form a word. A name? She tried again but no sound came. A frightened look passed across her face. She stared up at him.

He could read the questioning panic in her eyes. *What has happened to me?*

She tried to sit up, and he helped her.

"You have been through a terrible experience. Don't worry about anything." He was not sure she could hear him. "Trust me. What is your name?"

He felt relieved when she tried to answer. The chords in her neck tightened. Her fists closed and her hands thrust out from her face as if by force she would bring forth speech.

"Take it easy," the man said. "You were probably shocked with lightning. Your voice will come back. Give it time." He groaned to himself when he saw her panic. He hoped to God he was right.

She wanted to stand and he steadied her. She swayed, closed her eyes, and started to fall. He caught her.

"Are you sick?"

She shook her head rather carefully, closed her eyes, and made circling motions with her hand above her head.

"Your head's going around?"

She nodded.

"The water has made you dizzy. You should be at home. Where do you live?"

She pointed south. He shook his head. "I can't take you south. I have just been released from prison in the Antonia. I don't think everyone approved of Pilate's decision."

Her gray eyes looked at him with lively interest but no fear, asking for an explanation.

"Today Pilate released a prisoner in honor of the Jewish holiday. The people had a choice—Jesus of Nazareth or me, Barabbas. They released me and crucified him."

She pushed away, staggered, and sat down hard on the half-dried mud. She buried her face in the dirty garment over her knees and broke into tears.

He waited until her crying was over. "You knew him?"

She wrapped her arms about herself in a gesture of love. Then she pointed upward. An awed, worshipping light spread over her wet cheeks.

"You loved him and you think he came from heaven to love you?"

Her nod was emphatic.

"Was someone with you when the water washed you away?"

She gave herself another hug and a flush covered her cheeks. She tried to say his name. Her face contorted with the effort. She gave up with her lips quivering. She pointed upstream, made the love gesture, and laid her arms across her breast as she closed her eyes. Then she made other gestures and wiped imaginary tears from her eyes.

"You were with somebody you love, and you think your friend will believe you are dead?"

She nodded.

"You would be if this tree hadn't caught you."

She showed surprise and wonder as she looked at the fallen tree. She began to smile and talk with her hands again. She put her hand to his mouth and hers and patted her stomach. She folded her hands under one cheek and closed her eyes.

"Where can we eat and rest? Don't worry. I'm going to take you to my sister's house in Lodebar. She and her husband make locks and keys." Barabbas smiled. The skin above his grizzly beard crinkled. "I think I recognized one on my cell door."

Zeus looked down at her ruined garment and ran her hands through the tangled mop of red, stiff with drying mud. Her eyes questioned him again.

"You'll get clean things when we get to Eunice's."

He invited her to climb onto his shoulders. He grasped her wrists in strong, hairy fingers and began to descend the ledges, past the noisy rapids to the quiet river below.

Lodebar was a small, whitewashed village sliding over the slopes of a barren hill in a land that had once been part of Gilead. The village had never been of much importance, for even the name meant "nothing of much worth."

Only one village craft had gained wide popularity over the years, the locks and keys of Hamad the Persian and Eunice, his wife. Very few of the villagers noticed or cared who came or who went unless they were wealthy merchants stopping to order locks or bring in their prized keys for repair.

Today a few, sitting in their doorways, saw a big man carrying a girl on his back. Her arms and legs were streaked with mud. They saw him enter the door under the large wooden key hanging from a crossbar with "Hamad" carved on it.

Inside, Barabbas bellowed, "Eunice!"

She came running. Eunice was a large woman with gray hair pulled back tight from her face and held by a woven cord. She wore a working man's tunic and a leather apron. Her hands were large and calloused; her fingers darkened with wood stains and paint. Barabbas deposited his burden on a bench and then embraced his sister.

The girl watched them, and her face grew bright with curiosity as she looked about the cavernous room. Well-worn planks covered the floor.

The room smelled of new wood, sawdust, turpentine, paint, and forged metal from what must be a workroom at the rear.

The walls held a miscellaneous collection of keys. Some were small enough to hide in a hand, others so large it would take two men to handle them. There were keys made from iron and bronze and polished wood. A few of the finished keys were ornate, with inlays of ivory, or were heavily scrolled. One had a bronze cow head, perhaps ordered by the priests of a heathen temple. Another had the head and horns of a satyr. Some were as plain as the homes they would protect. Others as lavish as the villa the customer owned. A narrow shelf below the keys held the corresponding locks and door grooves.

A large table was covered with work in progress. A smaller one held jars and bowls of small metal parts, pumice stone, both solid and ground, and cruses of finishing oils. Sheets of papyrus with designs and rolls of parchment with drawings and measurements covered most of the space.

"Hamad!" Eunice yelled, and her husband came from the inner room wearing a blacksmith's apron. He was smaller than she, but his arms were muscular. A beaked nose dominated his face. He bore a full, black curly beard, and similar curls circled his bald head.

When they started to talk about her, the girl stopped staring at the fascinating array of skilled craftsmanship. Eunice started to say something to her, but Barabbas interrupted. "She can hear but she can't talk. She can't walk either. She gets dizzy when she moves her head. She must have been stunned with lightning and then almost drowned in the flash flood."

The woman's voice was heavy but kind. "Girl, do you remember being struck?"

No, the head said.

"Could you talk before the storm?"

Yes, Zeus nodded.

Eunice noticed each time the girl moved her head her eyes would close for a moment. Evidently each head shake brought on dizziness.

"Barabbas, do you have any idea where she lives?"

"She wanted to go south at the ford. We crossed below the falls."

Eunice began to call off the names of villages with no success. She reached into her pocket and brought out a small piece of slate and a marking chalk. "Write where you live and your name, and we will see that you get home."

The girl's hand closed on the chalk, then she made angry childish scribbles on the slate.

"Barabbas, she can't write! I might have known."

They were interrupted by a customer. He took the lock with the satyr key. Well pleased with his purchase, he paid for it with an Egyptian tetradrachma and refused change.

After he was gone, Barabbas said, "Eunice, I have to go on north for my own safety. Can you take care of her until she can take care of herself?"

"Of course. But I can't spend too much time with her. We have orders for two dozen locks for the new fortress on the Trachonitis border. Malichus ordered them, and you know what he does if things don't go as he plans."

"I remember very well the time you were burned out."

"Yes, and threatened with worse."

The girl tried to get to her feet, as if to leave, but she staggered and sat down. A look of stubbornness and determination crossed her face. She slid from the bench and began to crawl toward the door. Eunice put her arms under her and lifted her up.

"None of that! You're going to stay right here until we find out why you are dizzy. Then you can go home."

"We have a doctor who comes through here three times a week," Hamad said. "After you get over your shock, you'll probably be able to talk again."

"The first thing is a bath and a decent garment," Eunice said. "Come on. I'll steady you." She picked up a lock of the red hair and crushed the mud. "I have an idea this will be something to see when we get the dirt out. After that we'll have to give you a name. We can't go around calling you Girl."

Hamad was passing the silver coin to Eunice when the girl smiled and reached for it. Eunice looked puzzled but gave it to her. One side had the half-smiling profile of an Egyptian ruler, a Ptolemy. The reverse side had the engraving of an eagle. She held out the coin and pointed to the eagle.

"What are trying to tell us?"

The girl pointed to herself.

"Your name?"

She nodded. Eunice and the others tried to guess. Bird? Silver? Rome? Egypt? Each time one erred, the other two grunted in amusement. The girl showed frustration.

Barabbas turned to his sister. "You make all kind of symbols and likenesses on your keys and locks. Think of anything or anyone you would connect with an eagle."

Eunice bit her lip. Her fingers played with the corner of her apron. "Rome mostly. Sometimes the god Zeus—"

The girl tossed the coin to her and clapped her hands. Yes, yes, the red curls said.

Hamad stared. "Your name is Zeus?"

A smile broke across her face. Eunice thought, how beautiful she will be when she is clean

M i'kal opened his eyes to a fresh dawn. He was on a couch at the back of Martha's house, under a lattice of blue morning glories. The sky had a pink glow, and small white clouds reminded him of almond blossoms.

He was aware that Martha and Mary had taken turns caring for him through the night. He knew they had called in a physician who looked into his eyes with a lamp and murmured something about a concussion.

He remembered babbling on about Jesus and the hill, about Zeus and the storm, and about Oreb and the need for a miracle. He couldn't have been making much sense.

He thought he remembered Martha kissing him because he had saved her brother from the enemy. But mostly he remembered the wonderful feeling of slipping into oblivion after swallowing the doctor's sleeping potion.

He swung his feet off the couch and stood up. For a moment his head swam, and he steadied himself against the pillar of the porch. The morning glories hung like a drapery before him. He stretched out his hand and touched one of the closed blue and white blossoms that would soon open to the morning sunlight.

He had never been so close to morning glories before, and he remembered his mother had told him she used to enjoy squeezing the unopened blossoms and hearing them crack. He squeezed and smiled. Then he heard soft laughter and turned to see Mary sitting on the well outside the porch. A pail, wet with dripping water, was beside her.

"I hope you don't mind. My mother told me she used to—" He felt a little dizzy and laid his hand on the lattice.

"Everyone with morning glories does it. How do you feel?"

"As if I've been hit on the head with a shovel." He frowned. Memories came with that word. Ugly, nasty. "Mary, did Lazarus take care of my mule?"

"Of course—yesterday, while the doctor was here. He is in a stable in Bethphage, very near to us."

"I am grateful to all of you." His hand went to the bandage on his head. He moved to sit beside her in the sunlight on the well.

"We can never do enough for you. You saved our brother's life. He would be here this morning to thank you again, but he has spent the last two nights from midnight until dawn in Jerusalem. He wants to be one of the first to know when Jesus comes out of the grave. Many are doubtful, but how could he not believe?"

"Were you there when he died?"

"Only Lazarus. Martha wanted to go, but he said there was no need for us to see his suffering." She leaned toward him as if trying to make him understand. "You see, we *know* that he will be coming back to us in just a few hours on the first day of the week, as he told us more than once. How can we look at Lazarus and not believe? We can have patience and wait."

"Last night I wanted to ask Lazarus something—but I don't think I did. Just before that fellow threw the rock, he was taunting us. He said, 'At least Judas got his man.' What did he mean?"

"He meant that Judas betrayed Jesus and caused his arrest."

Mi'kal stared at her. "How? Why?"

"He knew Jesus and the disciples would go to the olive garden to pray after the Passover Supper, and he led the temple guards and the mob to the garden. No one understands why he did it. But we know the high priest paid him. Lazarus says Judas did repent and tried to give the money back, but the priests laughed at him. Later, he hanged himself in the Valley of Desolation. The poor soul. I grieve for him."

"So do I," Mi'kal said sadly. There were things about Judas he had liked.

She looked at him. The morning sunshine shone on his red-gold hair and beard. The boy from the black tents whom Zeus had brought to the house on the day Lazarus was raised was now a man. A handsome man. He had grown taller and broader, and his green eyes held a determined glint. Then, as she watched, they filled with sorrow.

"Mary, I too am guilty of betrayal. I lost faith in him for a little while on the hill. The centurion had more faith than I, for he said the world would never forget what had happened there that day."

"Mi'kal, you are an infant in the faith. One does not censure a small child for stumbling. His chosen Twelve have followed him for three years, yet one betrayed him and ten fled. Jesus understands our weaknesses. In his humanity he has felt all things that we feel."

"But Mary, I shouldn't have failed him. I loved him. Zeus would have been ashamed of me." He sat down suddenly, his face pale. The pain was coming back again. "Mary, last night when I was babbling, did I tell you about Zeus?"

"Yes, and we are sorry. But perhaps she is still alive."

"I'd like to think so. Oh, how I would like to think so!" His voice was desperate. "I will go back and look for her again, but—" He shook his head. "Mary, I feel empty. Part of me is gone forever. Can you understand? Nothing will ever be as beautiful as it was before."

"I know." Mary said it in such a way that Mi'kal wondered about the someone she must have loved.

Martha spoke from the doorway, "Mi'kal, you shouldn't be up. The doctor said you should not move around too much for a couple of days."

"I can't stay here, Martha. No one knows what's happened to me. My mother will be worried sick. Oreb is probably dead. I don't think he could have survived another night. And if he is lost, we may lose Susanna and the baby too."

"I've known Susanna for a long time, Mi'kal," Martha said with assurance. "She is a strong woman. They can't blame you for the delay. They know there was a terrible storm, and on top of all that, your injury. But if you insist, we will see what the doctor says." She left them and returned to her duties.

Mary took the bucket of fresh water to the kitchen. If it hadn't been for Oreb, he would stay until the resurrection morning. When he saw the cross, he had forgotten that Jesus had power over death. And he had promised resurrection for all who accepted him.

He stood to his feet again. There was no need to rush back to Ephraim. Oreb was surely dead. Quintira was with Susanna. He had to forget about the folks in Ephraim and do what his heart told him to do. He would start at the bridge and search the creek as far as he could go before running into the cliffs that formed the gorge. If Zeus had gone over the falls, her body might be carried to the Salt Sea.

How was it possible he had come to love her so much, so suddenly? But his mother and Myndus had fallen in love in just a few hours. So had Susanna and Oreb.

Perhaps that was the way it was with those predestined to meet and love.

Yes, he had to go, but without an argument with the good Martha. He would pick up Moses and the cart at the stable in Bethphage. He unwound the bandage and laid it aside. The bruise on his head felt as big as an ostrich egg.

At the well, he drank from a gourd of water Mary had left. He passed the vineyard and walked toward the road.

On any day but the Sabbath, the vineyard would have been crowded with pickers singing as they piled the baskets full of grapes in colors to rival Joseph's coat. Today there would be little traffic on the highway. He didn't look like a Jew. No one would throw angry looks at him for using the cart.

At the miller's, he told Gideon about the loss of Zeus. Gideon expressed his sympathy and promised to get word to Dannah and Hosea as soon as he could. He and Dannah were betrothed and would be married in a year.

Mi'kal promised that if he found any trace of Zeus at the creek he would let them know. "But until I get there, tell Dannah Zeus died in a way that she had wished. She told me once she wanted to fall like a cedar in Lebanon or an eagle plummeting from the sky. She had her wish."

Mi'kal led Moses across the little bridge. Many of the planks were gone. The side railings trailed in the water. The current ran heavy, but the water, like a subdued child, was content to stay in its accustomed course.

Signs of yesterday's rebellion were everywhere. Debris of all kinds littered the bank. Broken crates and swollen bodies of drowned animals, domestic and wild, floated among the bobbing bird nests. Carrion birds, rats, and other animals were feasting on the produce washed away from shoreline gardens.

Mi'kal stepped down among the supports of the bridge and went into mud up to his ankles. Wet clay made him stagger and slide. The grasses were soggy; the clumps of bushes twisted and treacherous. He had to climb over or walk around roots of fallen trees. Many were old and gnarled and perhaps glad to have their struggles ended.

Mi'kal knew the exact spot where he had last seen Zeus. He went slowly, looking for any clue. The large tree he had seen hit by lightning was arched across the water. Part of the bark was stripped off, and burn marks showed the fury of the lightning. He crossed on it and saw where someone else had crossed, probably the day before. The muddy footprints were dry. He walked to the edge of the ledges; the rapids still roared. He could go down the tumbled rocks to the river below, but he knew there was no use. By now Zeus's body would be in the Salt Sea, unless someone had pulled her out and covered her with rocks.

He looked down and imagined that he could see her going over. Her arms outstretched like the wings of an eagle. He sat down on a rock and pounded his fists against his knees.

Suddenly he was seeing Zeus again. Her red hair flamed in the sun. Her gray eyes were angry. They had been talking about sin, and he had grown hostile when she said he needed to see himself as a self-righteous sinner and ask Jesus to forgive him.

"My sins?" he had blurted back in anger. "What about your sins? You eat all kinds of forbidden things and run about half naked and sleep wherever you want to sleep and do all kinds of men things. Who knows what all you have done?"

Her face went white. Such hurt he had never seen in anybody's eyes.

God forgive me, he groaned as he remembered. Oh, Zeus. I am sorry, so sorry. He fell to his knees.

"O God, where is the goodness and mercy that David wrote about? Nothing but evil has followed me. If the fault is in me, cleanse me, Lord. Make me willing to accept your will, as your Son was willing to bear the iniquities we laid upon him. Forgive me my sins and use me." Mi'kal stayed on his knees for a long time, and when he rose he knew his soul was clean.

Before he returned to the cart he heard them—yellow birds singing in the trees. He saw them flying from one side to another across the creek. "Zeus, Zeus," he murmured. Could he believe she had sent the birds to comfort him?

Warm sunlight poured over him. Not a blasting heat such as in the desert, but a penetrating warmth that stirred his pulses. He closed his eyes and felt the warmth moving across his eyelids like the fingers of a lover. Some of the burden was being lifted from his heart. Somehow, someway, God was going to make it all turn out for good.

Mi'kal heard the whistling before he reached Susanna's gate. He stopped to listen. To be sure. Yes, it had to be Oreb! He broke into a run. Quintira was radiant as she rushed to meet him. Oreb was watering the flowers. He set the watering can down as Mi'kal embraced him.

Later that night, when his sorrow would not dim their joy, he told them about Zeus. His mother wrapped her arms about him and said, "Beloved, there is hope. Until we know for sure, there is always hope."

"Even if she is gone, Mother, I think I can bear it. When Jesus rises from his grave, I will know Zeus is happy. She believed in him. Somewhere she is roaming celestial hills. And I can be happy because she is."

That evening Oreb also told them the time had come again for him to don his "idiot" postures and heavy sword and ancient helmet. It was time to signify what Roman caravans would be sacked or what arsenal or warehouse burned. The big uprising was forgotten, but the hornet stings would go on.

Oreb confessed that since his healing, his thoughts of the Messiah-King had changed, but he was still a Zealot and would continue to fight for the freedom of Israel.

"I was restored to life to be a Zealot. Israel has always had men of God who fought for the freedom of the nation. How else can I show my complete love for the Lord? If it were not for Israel, the knowledge of our God would vanish from the earth."

The following morning in Bethany, Mary and Martha woke early. This was the third day! Lazarus had gone into Jerusalem before dawn, for if Mary was right, Jesus would fulfill his promise to rise again.

Gradually the sky changed its cloak of gray for a robe of flaming colors. The colors melded together making one great splash of apricot across the sky. Yellow birds in the cages began to sing. Lavender hyacinths in the corners of the court flung their fragrance about like profligate revelers.

Above the singing of the birds, the sisters heard their brother's footsteps. His face was shining but there was a sadness in his voice. "The Lord has risen! He lives! I have seen the grave and it is empty! But don't expect the world to rejoice. The Sanhedrin is already denying it. And even the disciples are doubtful. Our world prefers to sit in ignorance."

The sisters soon discovered their brother was right.

CHAPTER FORTY ONE

E unice stood watching Zeus at work at the polishing table. The girl was wearing one of Eunice's garments, altered to fit a younger and more slender figure. The red hair was clean and blazing. The locks were growing longer and thicker.

Fortunately the doctor had been in the village the day Barabbas had carried her in. The physician watched Zeus try to walk. Then he washed out her ears and put in some warm drops of medicinal oil.

"There is nothing to worry about. She has an infection inside the ears. She may have trouble for a few days, but the dizziness and the blackness when she moves her head will vanish. As to her voice, I think the same. She suffered a shock from the lightning and the flood. Sometimes our systems cannot take so much at one time. It may take awhile—or even another good shock." He smiled, but Zeus looked serious. He patted her shoulder, accepted his fee, and departed.

Zeus was depressed after he left, but after watching Eunice rub down a piece of scrolled wood, she reached for the pumice and picked up another unfinished key.

Eunice smiled and showed her how to hold it. "I will be glad to have your help. We have lots of locks to finish for a very mean man. I would as soon tickle the belly of a mother bear while her young are sucking as to disappoint him."

Zeus laughed.

Eunice used the ear drops for three days with no noticeable improvement in Zeus's ability to walk without staggering. Something had to be done. Eunice could hear her crying at night. Barabbas had said that Zeus had been swept away from someone she loved. From his account of the storm and the flood, Zeus's family and friends had every reason to believe she was dead.

Eunice talked it over with Hamad. "I've got to get her well. Though to tell the truth, I would love to keep her forever."

He understood. They had never had children, for she had been past childbearing age when he married her and she had joined him in the shop. She did the fancy scrolling and finishing; he did the iron and wood-work according to her specifications.

He put his arm around her and gave her one of his rare kisses. He was not an affectionate man, but he knew she was his life. She knew it too.

Zeus was aware they were discussing her as she worked with a pair of tweezers to get a splinter out of her thumb. Today she had worked too fast smoothing the wood, but this particular key had the motif of a crow. Mi'kal hated crows. He said they reminded him of evil. She had argued just to see his eyes flash. Yes, crows were brash and sassy and bossy. But they knew what they wanted and refused to be scared away in the face of many difficulties. The flecks of green and black in Mi'kal's eyes had flashed as he told her she should have called herself Crow instead of Zeus. She laughed at his anger, which made him angrier still.

Now she knew they quarreled because neither of them wanted to admit they were falling in love. The admission had come with the kiss under the cart.

She tried to keep the memory of the flood away. Sometimes when she moved too fast and the blackness came, she heard the roaring waters and felt herself tossed over and over as she rushed past rocks and fallen trees.

She remembered trying to crawl up the bank. She remembered her struggle to get to her feet. She remembered Mi'kal screaming her name. But she could not remember falling back into the water. If the big tree hadn't caught her, she would have plunged down the rapids and into the river. There was little chance that she would have been alive when she hit the Jordan.

When storm memories became unbearable, Zeus concentrated on the kiss under the cart. *Mi'kal! Mi'kal!* Her mind kept repeating his name. She tried to form his name with her lips, but no proper sound came.

She gave the tweezers a yank and the splinter came out. She looked at it with disgust. Such a ridiculous thing to cause such pain. Maybe love was like a splinter. Whatever it was, it hurt. Hurt because she had no one to give it to.

If only she had been able to write. She had never really missed it until now. Maybe Mi'kal would teach her. Maybe he would understand how stupid she felt when Eunice handed her the slate with the chalk.

She could be home now—with Mi'kal, with Dannah and Hosea—if she could write. Or walk. Even if she could walk a little she could find a wagon going south and eventually make her way home. Maybe, if she saw some of the hills she loved, her voice would come back.

She stood up, holding to the edge of the table. She took a step away from the bench, then swayed as things went black. She grabbed for support and sat down hard on the bench. The ear drops weren't helping. She laid her head down on the key with the image of the crow and let the tears come quietly.

Eunice had seen it all from the doorway. She went back into the workroom where Hamad was making a lot of noise with his hammer and chisels. "I've got to find some way to help that girl! She has to get home."

Mi'kal sat under the sycamore in Susanna's courtyard. He had been very quiet for several days. Now and then, either Susanna or Quintira would look out at him and return to the other shaking her head.

"He is grieving over Zeus," Susanna said.

"Maybe not. He may be thinking. Always as a child he grew silent when he was trying to think."

"He hasn't practiced the lyre for days."

"Perhaps if I took it out to him," Quintira suggested. She dropped her knife by the bowl of dates she had been stoning and washed her hands. She had taken over many of the kitchen duties during her stay. The regular kitchen maid had taken time off to be married and get settled in her new home.

Mi'kal lifted his head and smiled as his mother came with the musical instrument. "Susanna says you have done very well with this."

He nodded. He could remember the day Jesus had laid his hand on the strings and asked them to cooperate with the boy who wanted to sing about the Green Bird. That day he had received confidence when the strings did as he wanted them to do, and confidence inspired continued practice. Would it be that way all his life? First faith, then practice?

"Mother, I have been thinking..."

"I know. Susanna thinks you have been grieving. Something besides Zeus is making you sad? Can I help?"

"Mother, I do not even dare think about her. I believe my heart has picked up a message from God. Jesus has risen from the dead. This we know because Lazarus sent us word. But there is so little said of it...so little notice taken. Lazarus said that Jesus met with his disciples in a house in Jerusalem, but he knows little about it except what some of the disciples have said. Jesus told them that they should carry the message of forgiveness of sins and life everlasting to all the world, starting with their own brethren. I think I want to do that."

She sat on a stool near his feet and wrapped her arms about her knees. The wind sent a purple blossom from the vine to her lap. Her dark eyes were on him with the same proud, adoring look he had known all his life.

"There is no quiet place of the boulders here Mi'kal, but I will listen if you want to talk."

"Mother, I think he wants me to go back to the desert. Since the raid, our people are as sheep without a shepherd. Burned tents litter the valley. Children are hungry because they have no fathers who can hunt. There is little milk because the goats and the camels were stolen. Ne'ma is growing large with child. Raaschid lives with pain, unable to leave his couch. They must soon dismantle the camp and return to the red sands of Arabia, and there is no one to lead them. I must go back and help them. The sons of Ishmael and Esau need Jesus as much as the sons of Isaac and Jacob."

"Mi'kal, this is no surprise. But what about the world you have always wanted to see?"

"The Old One told me it would be my choice."

"He knew you were born to be a prince of the black tents."

"I have never wished to rule, but a prince must do what a prince must do." He seemed to be hearing the voice of Aretas.

Her hands closed over his. "You know I cannot go with you. I would never enter Raaschid's world again. I will stay here and be a grandmother to Susanna's children. She has been begging me to stay. When will you go?"

"I don't know. I must be sure this is what God wants me to do. I think it is, but"—he smiled—"I will put out a fleece."

"Like Gideon?"

"Yes."

"If he approves," she said slowly, picking her words carefully, "you will need help."

"I know. I have thought of it. I will pray for a man."

"I mean other help. You will need to take a wife."

"Yes, but I will never love anyone as much as I love Zeus. Mother, we kissed during the storm—before she drowned. No one can ever mean as much to me as she did then."

"You can't take someone without love."

"I'll be good to her. Give her all honor and—"

"Those things are not enough. You must love her."

Their talk ended as it usually did, with an embrace or her hand on his while she quoted or sang some of her beloved Scripture. This time she sang from the wisdom of Solomon. Susanna came to listen.

Trust in the LORD with all your heart
 and lean not on your own understanding;
in all your ways acknowledge him,
 and he will make your paths straight.
Do not be wise in your own eyes;
 fear the LORD and shun evil.

Mi'kal spent most of the night in prayer on the bench under the sycamore. Had God really spoken to him? Had he told him to go to the Bedouin who had left the worship of the God for the multiple gods of the heathen nations?

"Into all the world." Surely the black tents were part of the world. Yes, he would put out a fleece.

"Lord," he prayed, "send me a companion. Send me a man. Moses had his brother, Aaron; Joshua his friend, Caleb; David his commander, Joab. Send me such a man to help me. One who knows the nature of the desert and those who dwell there."

As he finished his prayer, a feeling of confidence or faith came over him such as he had felt when he plucked the strings and sang for Jesus of the Green Bird.

Now he wanted to do a far greater thing. Surely Jesus would understand, as he had understood that day under this same sycamore tree.

Oreb was surprised to find Barabbas at the Hornet's Nest. For hours there had been only one topic of conversation: the arrest and crucifixion of Jesus and the release of a Zealot.

Later, as they ate roasted hares, Neophron planned the next series of deadly stings. He told Oreb what he should look for in Damascus and Palmyra as well as in the warehouses along the way. And he wanted him on his way by dawn. Most of the men had bedded down when Oreb and Barabbas stepped outside. The wild asses were braying in the hills. They stooped at the spring for a last drink of water.

"Tell me," Barabbas said, "it's probably a fool's question but—do you happen to know any red-headed girl in Judea or roundabout who calls herself Zeus? If you do, maybe you can help me."

CHAPTER FORTY TWO

Quintira had been snipping yellow nasturtiums when she answered the gate bell. The black man standing outside smiled widely, showing filed teeth. An embroidered cap covered his hair. A fine garment fell to his knees. A necklace of ivory crocodiles hung about his neck. Quintira gaped at him and then gasped in joyful surprise, "Kwa!"

She took him by the hand and the gate closed behind him. He set down a woven bag he was carrying and spoke with affection. "My good lady, I am almost as surprised to see you as you are to see me. For many weeks I thought you were dead."

"I would have been if it were not for the mercies of my God and the Old One. Raaschid judged me guilty for protecting Leyla and Mi'kal and banished me to the desert."

"They were never guilty. I tried to tell him."

Mi'kal and Susanna came out as they heard voices. Mi'kal took one look at the visitor and grabbed his hand. "Kwa! Leyla said you went to the coast."

After acknowledging her guest, Susanna left the court and returned with a pitcher of cold water and slices of melon on a tray.

"My prince, Leyla and her husband send greetings to both of you. I saw them in Damascus a few days ago. I was inquiring about you. I thought she might know where you were."

"Me?"

"I caught her just in time. They were ready to leave for Petra. She told me you were here at Ephraim. I left my camel at the stable." His white teeth gleamed. "I don't think the boy has handled many camels. He thought one bucket of water was plenty."

Mi'kal laughed. Susanna arranged some chairs for them.

"We are grateful to you for saving Leyla," Mi'kal said. "And I am glad she and Silas are safely married."

"They seem happy. She said he works for the king of Petra."

"He does. Now tell us everything that's happened to you since you left Leyla with the slave boys."

As Kwa talked, they ate the melon sprinkled with fresh mint. He told them he had been working on the docks at Caesarea where he had pledged himself to the overseer for seven years. He had been loading crates of Galilean salted fish on the *Medusa* when the Old One boarded the vessel.

"I knew him even though he didn't look like the stake-maker of the tents. He knew me, too. We talked awhile. He seemed to have money. I thought he had made it at gambling. He said he was going to Rome. He wanted me to go with him. He said I reminded him of the happiest years of his life. He bought me back from the dock steward." Kwa paused.

Something in the silence troubled Quintira. She put her hand on his knee. "What did you really come to tell us?"

"I have something I knew you will want to know." Again he paused.

Mi'kal felt a chill. "Something about the Old One?"

"Yes. I am sorry." He fingered his necklace. "There is no easy way to say it. Your friend is dead." Mi'kal stared at him. "He was murdered one hour before the *Medusa* was to sail. He was walking on deck, and he was stabbed in the back."

"Why?" Mi'kal asked, swallowing his tears.

"Tiberius ordered it done," Quintira said, her face angry. "King Aretas told us we should not trust Gryphus or the emperor. Oh, Grandfather!" The anger crumbled with the onslaught of grief. She covered her face with her hands.

Kwa looked puzzled. "Why should Tiberius...?"

"Tiberius must have thought he would be a threat to his throne," Mi'kal said. "The Old One was not a desert wanderer. He was the long-lost son of Marc Antony and Cleopatra."

Kwa spoke slowly, with primitive fury. "I am happy to tell you that Tiberius's man did not live long enough to collect his pay. I saw the murder from a distance, but I caught him before he left the dock."

Kwa rummaged in the bag he had set down by the gate and pulled out a square of parchment. He handed it to Mi'kal. The writing was in Latin.

This is to certify that I have redeemed a certain black worker called Kwa, from the overseer of the wharf at the moorings of the *Medusa* in Caesarea. I hereby give him complete manumission. He is to be no man's slave from this day on. Signed and dated by Alexander Helios, son of Cleopatra, last of the Ptolemys.

Later that night, Mi'kal sat with Kwa under the sycamore tree and talked about his future.

"Kwa, you are a free man and can choose your own course. But I'd like for you to work with me. I am going back to our camp. Muktar brought a blood feud down on it. My people need help."

"Raaschid would beat me with rods."

"No. I will be prince of the camp. I am sure Raaschid will agree. He was injured in the raid and can no longer walk."

"Gutne would want me punished."

"Gutne is dead. Raaschid has married Ne'ma. She is with child, perhaps twins. Sons, I hope. And until they are grown, I am going to take charge. I need a man like you. You have come as an answer to prayer. Will you help me?"

The black man could not resist the pleading in the green eyes. "I will go. As a free man, I will go."

Mi'kal's heart filled with thanksgiving. God had verified his call to the black tents.

The next morning he began to make plans for his return to the desert. Neither of the women tried to make him wait. Oreb might have tried, but he had gone north to the Hornet's Nest. They did remind him that he would miss the two great events the disciples were anticipating in the next few weeks. Jesus was going to go back to his Father from the slopes of

Bethany, whether in a cloud or in a fiery chariot, no one knew. And a few days after that he had promised to send the Spirit of Comfort and Power who would abide with each of them and enable them to do greater things than he had done.

Peter was certain that when the Power came they would turn Jerusalem upside down and on its ear. Rome and all her foundations would crumble.

But Mi'kal shook his head. No, he could not, would not stay. There was much to be done. And Jesus could send his Spirit to the believers in the tents as well as to the disciples in Judea and Galilee.

Quintira listened to him and Kwa making lists of what they would need, and she suggested he buy more of everything. Aretas would not want him to be miserly with less than he needed.

"Mother, I will get only what we must have. Our sheep were safe, but I will have to get camels and goats for milk. Our people know how to work; they know how to suffer and do without. I will suffer and do without with them. I do not intend to rule from a velvet couch. They must never know I carry Aretas's seal."

On the second morning, Mi'kal and Kwa walked to the stable to rent a wagon. Aziz offered to close the stable and give Mi'kal the mule and wagon Matthew had returned if he could go to the desert with them.

"Susanna needs you as part of her family," Mi'kal said. "And it would not be good for Ephraim to be without a stable. You must stay so no one will ever forget your father." After much persuading, Aziz finally agreed.

Mi'kal and Kwa left for Jerusalem early, taking the stable's largest and strongest wagon and the two mules. They would spend several days finding and buying or ordering all the things they needed.

The first thing Mi'kal did was to use King Aretas's signet ring to arrange for money and credit at a bank. He had approached the bank officials with embarrassment and doubt, but after a quick search for the cylinders that carried the replica of the royal seals, he was treated courteously and efficiently. His grandfather evidently was a man of standing in the financial world.

He and Kwa bargained furiously for two days inside and outside

Jerusalem, looking for baggage camels. Kwa's knowledge of the beasts was far superior to Mi'kal's. And Kwa's wharf experiences with commercial warehouses was indispensable. He knew where to find the black goatskin in the tentmakers' street. They would need much of it for patching the tent roofs and curtains. He found the best place to order jars of oil and lanterns and lamps.

Mi'kal was given addresses, farther along their route, where they could find ridge poles and tent stakes and milk goats.

They spent the first night in a caravansary where Mi'kal heard of a horse auction to be held the next morning in the Jerusalem theater. The theater and the gymnasium had been built by Herod Antipas in spite of violent objections from the Jews. Mi'kal told Kwa he intended to buy a stallion. He was in need of a strong horse for the trip back to the tents. And they could use him in breeding the mares.

Mi'kal found what he wanted. He knew it instantly when the large gray horse, speckled with black and white and with flowing black tail and mane, was led out for the buyers to examine and appraise. Broad of chest and slender of nose, with intelligent eyes and delicate legs, the animal stood a hand's-breadth higher than any other. The auctioneer called the horse Titan. Mi'kal liked the name. Bidding was high, but Mi'kal was determined to own the magnificent beast. He knew his grandfather would want him to persist until he did.

At the same sale, Mi'kal bargained for a bridle, saddle, and saddle blanket from one of the horse dealers. He also ordered a wagon with a strong team. He decided on dark brown horses with white hocks. They were not available for a few days, so the pair would be delivered to the stable in Ephraim. Kwa had loaded Aziz's wagon, but many other purchases were to be delivered.

Before they headed home, Mi'kal said he wanted to visit Papyron. His Bethany friends would want to know about his decision to return to the desert in response to the command to "go into all the world." During the trip, he and Titan could become better acquainted. Kwa could stable the mules at Bethphage and stay in Bethany with Lazarus while Mi'kal went on to Hosea's home.

Lazarus and his sisters were glad to see Mi'kal and they admired his horse. He introduced Kwa and they welcomed him, saying that Quintira had mentioned him several times. Lazarus was doing a poor job of repairing a wall that had been cracked by the earthquake. Kwa watched for a moment and then began to help with the mortar and the stones.

Mi'kal ate a bite, accepted a water skin, and started down the Jericho road. Before he reached the river, affection had been established between himself and the gray. The horse was sensitive to the slightest heel or knee pressure.

Mi'kal tried to prepare himself for the sight of the little house. He knew that when he saw the river he would have to open the door to his grief and share the pain with Dannah. Already there was a lump in his throat the size of a boulder. His eyes misted when he saw the mulberry tree and the bench.

Dannah met him with a rush. He asked about her father and she shook her head. "He isn't aware that she won't be back. Every morning he asks about her, and then he forgets. He is concerned only with his cabbages. Gideon is helping him plant today. The storm ruined his garden."

They sat on the bench and she took his hand. "Mi'kal, did she ever tell you she was in love with you? She was, you know."

"Yes, Dannah. We had crawled under our cart to get out of the storm. I had my arm about her and I kissed her. She told me she loved me. We were so happy, Dannah. And then the earthquake came and the bridge heaved. I let her roll into the water. God help me, I had taken my arms from around her and—"

"Mi'kal, she wasn't afraid to die."

"I saw her on the bank climbing out, and then the lightning struck. A tree fell, and she fell with it."

Dannah held Mi'kal's head against her shoulder. "It was just the way she wanted it—if it had to be. She would have hated to die in bed."

Later, when Gideon came from the garden to join them, he heard about Mi'kal's decision to return to the desert.

"Stop at my father's mill in Bethphage. Explain to him about the camp, and he will double the measure without charge. He does it all the time. His heart is as big as his millstones."

Once again Mi'kal ate at Hosea's table and slept on the kitchen floor with Gideon. Once again he saw Hosea bathe in the Jordan and read the Scriptures at night. He felt the presence of Zeus—so near, as if he could reach out and touch her.

In Lodebar, the few villagers had quit speculating about the young girl working in Eunice's shop. They were content to sit in the shade, as little as it was, while their dogs slept and their goats grazed. Nothing much moved in the village except when the customers came to Hamad's shop.

Common gossip said the redheaded girl was dumb, unable to speak or hear or walk. Poor thing. But they all believed Eunice would be good to her.

Inside the dusty workshop, Zeus was applying small dabs of gold gilt to the center of some carved water lilies. Eunice came in carrying a towel and a steaming bowl of water mixed with vinegar. The acrid smell of the vinegar blotted out the smell of gold paint. She moved the work material aside and sat the pan down. Steam curled about it.

"Come on," Eunice said. "You're going to sniff vinegar. The doctor isn't doing you any good."

Zeus questioned her with her eyes.

"My mother used vinegar for everything. If she wanted to have a baby she drank it; if she didn't want to have a baby she'd bathe in it. I've used it for everything. Now we're going to try it on your ears—or whatever it is that's keeping you from walking."

Zeus shook her head and pushed the steaming pan away.

"Do as I say or I'll dump the whole thing over your head. Which reminds me, my mother used to rinse my hair with it, too."

Eunice pushed Zeus's head down over the pan and covered it with the heavy towel.

"Now sniff."

Zeus sniffed. Her nose burned. She tried to lift her head, and Eunice's big hand came down on it.

As the water cooled, Eunice came with another steaming kettle.

When her patient was allowed to sit up, she made a funnel from thin papyrus paper and began to wash out Zeus's ears.

"Four times a day we are going to do this. If the doctor comes in while we're doing it, I will charge him for my prescription."

Four times they did it that day, and four the next. Then, to the delight of everyone, Zeus walked a short distance from table to door before staggering. The blinding black flashes diminished.

She hugged Eunice. She tried to say, "I'm getting well." She failed, but her confidence was returning. Maybe she would be able to go home soon. The thought made her heart rejoice.

Mi'kal arrived in Bethany the next evening, full of praise for Titan. Martha was equally pleased with Kwa's repair work on her wall.

When Mi'kal spoke again of his intent to leave Palestine as soon as possible, Martha tried to persuade him to stay in Judea—at least until Jesus met with them again.

"Surely you can stay a few more weeks. The disciples say Jesus will be teaching them for forty days. Then he is coming back to Bethany to ascend to his Father. Surely you want to see him before he leaves us."

Mi'kal shook his head. "I can't linger, much as I desire to see him again. But I know that where I go, he will go. In a few months we will have to fold up our tents. The migration to Arabia is a slow and tiresome thing. We have lost many horses and camels, so the women and children will be traveling on foot. If we linger too long, the snows catch us. We must have time to rest and let our stock graze. I will have to use my sheep for food and clothing. There is much to do and I have few men to do it. No, I must go now."

During the evening, Lazarus asked many questions about life in the desert. "I should go with you," he said. "My life will never go back to normal here in Judea. My students want to touch me and watch me eat. They ask me what I saw when I was dead. In the city, I am still the target for murder. Would you have any place where I could be useful to you?"

Mi'kal bit his lips and shook his head. Hands rather than minds were what his camp would need for several months to come.

Lazarus smiled. "It was just a thought."

As the stars came out, Mi'kal acknowledged his weariness and followed Kwa up the steps flanked with blooming geraniums. Shadows from the morning glory vine, attached to the shutters, made mosaic patterns on the floor.

He was in the room where the resurrected Jesus told his disciples to go into all the world and preach the gospel. His pierced feet had walked this floor. Perhaps his hands with the nail prints had touched the morning glory vine.

Mi'kal closed his eyes and felt the Divine Presence. Jesus was pointing to the tents and saying, "Go!"

Kwa was already deep in sleep. Mi'kal found it hard to think of this man, who was so ready to help, as a murderer. He was finding it true that all men were a mixture of good and evil. No man was completely blameless, though he might think so in self-righteous pride, as he himself had done.

Mi'kal reached through the shutter and put his fingers on a cool, closed blossom. He thought of the days ahead. He would have to push his people long and hard. He cracked the blossom and tried to relax. Perhaps things at camp were not as bad as he imagined them. Perhaps some of the horses had been out to pasture when the raid came. If so, some of the mares might be carrying foals of Centaurus and El Gamar. Perhaps some camels had escaped capture and were in the process of calving.

But the clan needed more than material comforts. He would attempt to establish peace with his uncle's clan and eventually reunite the broken tribe.

One thing was certain—there would be no more raids on clans or caravans. He would bring down the standard with the rapacious jackal and put up another, one that would honor the two women he loved. A purple flag with a yellow bird.

He lifted his face to the night wind, took a deep breath, closed the shutters, and lay down. He was pulling the blanket over him when he thought of a way Lazarus could be of great use in the black tents.

The next morning Mi'kal explained that in his rush to supply his people with material needs, he had forgotten his biggest responsibility. He must get the message of eternal life and forgiveness of sins to all of them. Who could represent the life-giving power of Jesus more than Lazarus? Who knew how to teach those who would be as children in the faith more than a man who had been a teacher of children? Lazarus could do more than that. He could teach the children to read and write.

"Not only the children," Lazarus said.

Mary was equally excited at her brother's joy. "I believe it is God's will. Sooner or later, as the disciples start to preach, the animosity against Lazarus will increase."

Martha appeared doubtful. "What about your health, Lazarus? The extremes of heat and cold will be hard on you."

"When I am too warm, I will rest. When I am cold, I will work."

Martha finally agreed. "You are right, Sister, as usual. When Peter and the others start to preach, all of Satan's power will be used against them. Yes, it is best for Lazarus to go."

CHAPTER FORTY-THREE

As Oreb left the Hornet's Nest, he had sharp stabs of regret. He had not been able to ask Neophron for time to go to Ephraim and tell Mi'kal that Zeus was alive in Lodebar. Even if he had asked for the time, Neophron would not have been agreeable. He had been in short temper over the time it had taken Oreb to go to Jerusalem and confer with Barabbas and report back to him.

Oreb tried to make him understand that a man should be allowed at least a couple of days to fall in love and get married. Even though he had supplied several depots with a wagon load of weapons since then, he didn't think Neophron would agree to another delay. In fact, their leader had been pretty surly with the notable Barabbas over the street riot, practically blaming him for the abandonment of the coup.

All things considered, Oreb decided he had better get his reconnaissance done and then find Mi'kal. He eased his conscience by telling himself that Zeus needed a few more days to get well.

At times during his ride to Palmyra his conscience roused and growled at him, but he tried to pacify it by swearing at the patient Moses. Then his guilt would double, for he knew the healing prayers of James had done more than restore his arm. The old Oreb had died, and the new man should not swear at a faithful old friend.

All of those in Susanna's house, as well as many of her neighbors, were tired when the eve of Sabbath came. They had spent hours packing Mi'kal's hampers and saddle bags. At sundown they accepted the Sabbath day of rest with gratitude.

Mi'kal planned to leave Ephraim at dawn on Sunday. He and Lazarus had already shared one period of tearful parting. At Bethany, the sisters had helped Lazarus select the things he would need in his new life in the desert. They swung between sorrow and joy.

Martha gathered up his cloaks and sandals and set them aside for Mi'kal to pack into the already overloaded wagon. Mary collected his books and writing materials. They embraced one another each time they passed. None of them knew what lay ahead.

When it came time for the wagon to leave for Susanna's, Martha clung to Lazarus as she wept. "God go with you."

Mary hugged him with a joyous face. "Serve the Lord with gladness."

Lazarus's face was wet with tears as he turned to wave to them. Mi'kal rode alongside the wagon. "You will see them next year. I have promised to return for Dannah and Gideon's wedding."

The six camels Kwa had bargained for in Jerusalem had been delivered to Aziz's stable and tethered in a field. All but one were females. Two of them were pregnant. One had recently calved and the young one came with her. She would be the source of milk for their return.

Aziz and Kwa spent one morning picking names for the camels, for Kwa told him that all the Arabs had a name for each of their beasts. The calf was named Aziz.

Kwa exchanged the camel he had ridden into Ephraim for one of the new ones—a fawn-colored female with long eyelashes. He named her Maha in honor of the staunch little beast that had carried him and Leyla to safety.

The big wagon and team of brown horses were delivered from Jerusalem. Ephraim men loaded the wagon with tent materials, jars of oil, clay lamps packed in sawdust, lanterns to hang from the ridge poles, and boxes of common medicines beyond the natural ointments and compresses the camp women knew how to prepare.

Gideon had been right about his father's generosity. On the day they left Bethany, the Bethphage miller had loaded Kwa's wagon with two barrels of flour for each one Mi'kal had paid for.

All of Ephraim became involved with Mi'kal's caravan. They insisted on bringing in things they felt he would need for his Bedouins. Baskets and blankets, dried fruits and dried fish, packets of spices, bags of salt, and jars of honey. Some brought flower seeds to make beauty in the camp.

Children brought gifts for children, wooden toys and cloth dolls. Women did not forget women. They brought soft slippers, bolts of dark cloth, and needles and bright thread for embroidery. Men came with strips of leather for sandals and heavy cord for latchets. And they did not forget tools, including axes and hatchets. Each time Mi'kal was handed a love offering, he embraced the giver and his eyes filled with tears.

To Mi'kal the whole thing was incredible. How wondrously God had blessed him, and yet...

He was beginning to have misgivings. What kind of reception would he have in the camp? The scouts would know hours ahead that he was coming. Would his people welcome him with cheers or with stones? Would they still blame him for Kaleb's death? Still wonder about him and Leyla and Sa'ad?

If they accepted him, he knew what he intended to do the minute he was under the banner at the long tent. He would kneel at Raaschid's feet, kiss his hands, and call him Father. He would respect Ne'ma as if she were his mother, and love her sons as if they were his brothers.

But the biggest question was, would Raaschid be glad to see him and appoint him prince of the clan? Something inside of him said yes.

Of one thing he was sure. Lazarus, as teacher of the tribe, would sit on the judgment rug with him. They would work together to replace the Bedouin hearthside gods of wood and stone and straw with a living God—a God who could not be seen but whose mercy and majesty were visible with every rising sun and every lighting of the stars.

Mi'kal found himself singing as his mother would have sung. "The heavens declare the glory of God; the skies proclaim the work of his hands." Tears stung his eyes. How he would miss her! And Zeus! His heart would carry a double pain.

At dawn on Sunday, Kwa ordered the couched and loaded camels to rise. He mounted Maha. Lazarus climbed into the wagon behind the brown team. He had never driven horses, but he was anxious to learn.

The villagers gaped when Mi'kal came out wearing the regular tunic and flowing *aba* of an Arabian prince. Quintira insisted he should pass through the desert into Raaschid's camp in proper garb. His white head-piece was tied with a golden cord.

At the last moment, Susanna came with the lyre, and Quintira handed him her folded purple scarf. He protested, but she insisted. He tucked it into his embroidered girdle and kissed her.

Aziz came running to cling to his neck. "I will never forget you. Never. And the next time you come I will have a donkey for you."

Mi'kal held him close. Finally, he loosened the boy's clinging arms and mounted the stallion. He could ride in the desert this time with confidence.

The moon would be just a scimitar for several nights, but with Kwa there was no danger of getting lost. If they left now they would have full moonlight by the time they crossed the worst parts of the desert. And with Kwa he hoped to avoid the tortuous hills of gravel and flint, the dried gullies where his red stallion had died, and open desert where the sandstorm had terrified Leyla and him.

All who gathered to see them depart were in tears. Mi'kal's deepest regret was the absence of Oreb. There had been no word from him.

When the last embrace was given, Mi'kal rode to the front of the caravan. The sun shone on his golden beard. He turned and lifted his arm. Lazarus picked up his reins. The wheels turned and the wagon creaked. Kwa tapped the neck of his mount, and the line of camels began to move.

Behind them Quintira began to sing. "The LORD bless you and keep you; the LORD make his face shine upon you and be gracious to you; the LORD turn his face toward you and give you peace."

None of the villagers returned home until the dust of the caravan faded from the lane. Mi'kal couldn't look back. Another gate had closed on another pathway of his life.

As each day passed in Lodebar, Zeus grew more determined to walk and talk. She had continued with the steam treatment, and the heavy swirling darkness in her head was diminishing. She was able to stand without swaying. Although she could feel no improvement in her ability to speak, Eunice encouraged her to try.

Hamad found her an apt apprentice. In the workroom, she was doing more than polishing. She was learning to use small chisels to groove out the part of the lock that fit into the side of the door and to smooth the iron or wooden pegs used in the locks and keys.

Eunice was pleased with Zeus's interest because it benefited both of them. Zeus forgot her troubles for awhile, and Eunice had more time for etching or engraving.

Today Hamad's workroom was full of heat from the forge. The smell of staining oils and paints in the finishing room was almost overpowering.

Hamad and Eunice were open in their anxiety to get the locks ready for the ill-tempered Malichus. Zeus was curious, so Eunice told her of a time Hamad had been unable to deliver an order as promised because of a delay in a shipment of iron from the hills near Gerasa. Malichus had stormed at Eunice, then pulled down many of the finished keys in the salesroom and commanded his attendants to smash and burn them.

"I have continued to take his orders because the pay is good and Hamad prefers making the larger locks."

Zeus was finishing a bolt and decided to ask Hamad about an unevenness in one set of pegs. She rose from the table, stood for a moment to be sure she had her balance, then took two faltering steps toward his bench. She wasn't staggering and there was no swirling heaviness in her head.

Hamad held out his hands to her, and Zeus grabbed them. She laughed with joy. He called for Eunice, who was in the kitchen. When she came, Zeus began to move across the floor and back again. Eunice clapped her hands.

"Great God of us all be praised! Any day now you will be able to talk, too. I know it."

Zeus choked with happiness. She could go home! With two good legs under her she could walk or beg a ride to Judea. She could find Mi'kal!

That evening she communicated her intentions to leave for home the next day. Eunice argued that she should wait another day or so to see if her speech would return.

"Tomorrow is the Sabbath and there will be less traffic than usual. Less chance for a ride."

She tried to explain she would take a chance on finding rides. Many of the drivers weren't Jews and cared nothing at all for the Sabbath.

"To tell the truth," Hamad said, spreading a thick layer of butter across his hunk of bread, "neither of us want you to go. You've become like a daughter to us." He lowered his head and applied himself to his plate of lentils.

Zeus made gestures of love for both of them but showed she was determined to go. They accepted her decision.

The next morning as Zeus came into the kitchen, prepared to leave, Eunice was packing a small basket of food. Her hair was loose and hung about her face. She was quiet and moved slowly.

She is sorry I am leaving, Zeus thought. *I must show her I will never forget her.* She put her arm about Eunice. She was burning up with fever.

Zeus took her by the hand and led her to a chair. Hamad came in with a bucket of goat milk.

"I know she's sick. She was up all night. She's going to lie down as soon as you leave."

Eunice protested weakly. "We have to get the order finished."

She began to gag and Hamad reached for a basin. Zeus dipped a cloth in cold water and handed it to him. The vomiting was making her ill, but it also made her realize how much she cared for these two friends who had done so much for her.

Her return to Papyron would have to wait. The keys had to be finished. She owed Hamad and Eunice that much, and more. Mi'kal would still be there, somewhere among the disciples. Zeus pushed the basket aside and pointed to herself and the workroom.

"No," Eunice said shaking her head.

"You should go," Hamad said. "These attacks never last long. Seeing your family might bring your voice back."

The red curls shook violently.

Eunice gave her an apologetic look before the sickness came again.

Neither Hamad nor Zeus had expected Eunice's sickness to last almost a week. In spite of herself, Zeus was growing increasingly anxious to get home. She was feeling an anxiety that was not natural to her as she stood in the doorway looking out at the bleak village of Lodebar.

Flat topped houses, in need of whitewash, were surrounded by parched trees and scraggly flowers. Thin and mangy dogs slept in the streets. Lodebar was indeed a place of little importance, except for the legend that a king's grandson had once taken refuge there.

Eunice had told her that in ancient days one of King Saul's grandsons, Jonathan's son, had lived here in obscurity in order to escape David, who had ordered his men to kill all of Saul's family. Years later, when King David heard about Jonathan's son, he sent men to fetch him to the palace. There he was given a seat of honor at the king's table because David remembered the devoted friendship he had enjoyed with Jonathan.

She wished her own stay in Lodebar could end as happily. She wanted nothing more than to be eating at Prince Mi'kal's table forevermore. But for several days she had felt as if she were getting farther and farther from him.

Today the uneasiness should be lifting. She was free to go. Eunice had eaten a little this morning, and she was much stronger. The order for the fortress locks was completed.

Why was she lingering? She should hail the very next wagon heading toward Jericho. But first she must finish oiling the beautiful little box Hamad and Eunice had made for her.

She was about to return to her worktable when a cart approached, pulled by a small mare. A large, red-and-white-striped umbrella shaded the driver.

A wizened man looked up at the sign above her and stopped. He gave her a toothless smile, and she smiled back. He stepped down and asked for the locksmith in a quavery but strident voice. She beat lightly on the door jamb. Hamad and Eunice both came.

The man introduced himself as a steward for a wealthy estate near

Magdala. He was returning from a business trip to Jerusalem. He had stopped to look at the locks and keys for a new gate his master wanted to install at his villa near the Galilean sea.

Eunice engaged him in conversation as he looked at the keys. Zeus was pleased when he selected the crow's head.

The customer was chatting about his trip into Judea. Zeus began to listen when he spoke about a small but heavily laden caravan that pulled out of the Ephraim road ahead of him several days before. The camels had caused him to pull his horse to a halt, and he had exchanged a few words with the rider of a magnificent gray horse. The young fellow was dressed like an Arab prince and was evidently the owner of the caravan.

They were carrying tent materials and supplies and heading for some camp in the Syrian desert. Since both were traveling the same direction, he had joined them. He had enjoyed the companionship and the protection until he left them several days before. They had gone on to reach the Antioch-Damascus-Palmyra road. He had crossed over into Perea and stopped to visit friends.

He probably never would forget the young fellow because he didn't look like an Arab. His hair and beard were bright, like a piece of burnished brass.

Zeus drew a sharp breath. The old man looked at her with curiosity as Hamad took the money and handed him the lock and bolt that went with the key.

Eunice had heard her, too. She was quick to understand. "Zeus. You know him? The man on the horse?"

The red curls bobbed. Her face became radiant. She made other motions. She wanted to know more.

Eunice spoke to the customer and pointed to Zeus. "She cannot talk, but she wants to know more about the man on the gray horse."

He shrugged. "I can't tell you much. I gathered he was returning to a camp somewhere in the Syrian desert. The cameleer was black and wore an ivory necklace that he refused to sell. He was a desert man. Probably from Egypt. The fellow driving the wagon was unpracticed. Great looking horses, but he directed them as if they were children in a school room."

Zeus made frantic gestures. Eunice understood. "One more question. Where would that caravan be by now?"

The man shrugged again. "Who knows? They said something about stopping at some custom post on the Damascus road. Seems the Arab knows the fellow in charge." The old man flashed a toothless grin. "Friend or not, they will sock him double for his pregnant camels."

They watched as the customer climbed into his cart and adjusted the striped umbrella. He lifted the reins. "Thinking about it, I'd say that caravan is in the desert by now."

Hamad was perplexed as Eunice gathered a quiet Zeus into her arms. Eunice could read the quiet tears.

"I'm sorry. If you hadn't stayed with me… Darling, you can follow him as soon as you can talk."

Zeus shook her head and continued to cry. She knew all about the hills, but she knew nothing at all about the desert.

CHAPTER FORTY-FOUR

By the time Mi'kal's caravan had passed through several customs posts, he was sharply aware of the heavy taxes required of everyone who traveled the Roman roads. Each axle on the wagon had a charge, and the pregnant camels were doubly taxed. Produce was examined and weighed. He praised God that Aretas's seal had been accepted as payment for the invoices without argument or disturbing curiosity. He felt certain other entries would be made before the debit slip arrived at the treasury in Petra.

Although his tax and travel permits would have allowed him to go straight through to Damascus, he inquired at Gaius's customs post for the captain. Gaius remembered him well. He asked about Zeus and expressed disbelief and sorrow as Mi'kal told him of her disappearance in the roaring water of the creek.

"By all the gods, I can't believe it! I can't believe anyone so full of life could be dead." Mi'kal, in turn, wanted to know if Gaius had heard from Aurans at the Jerusalem hospital.

"The last we heard," Gaius added, "he had been taken off active duty because of a bad limp."

"I'm sorry. He was proud of being a soldier."

"It's not all bad. I understand he's planning a furlough to Britain to see his family. A wealthy Jew in Jerusalem wants to visit the island to carry 'good news about the Galilean called Jesus,' whatever that means. He needed a companion for the ocean travel and offered to pay Auran's fare."

Mi'kal took a deep breath. "Captain, I think I can explain the good news. If you have time…"

Gaius listened.

"I find your story interesting," he said as Mi'kal prepared to mount. "I may inquire further of this Jesus if and when I get to your Holy City."

"You will find it to your eternal benefit."

The tollgates opened and Kwa led the caravan through. Mi'kal felt an inner warmth as they left the garrison. He had done his first witnessing for Jesus.

A short time later on the road, he tried to identify the ditch where Oreb had found him. He couldn't be sure, for the grass was higher now, the shrubs thicker.

As he rode between the encroaching cliffs where Quintillius was ambushed, there were no reminders of the carnage. He thought about the silver stallion that had bolted and patted the shoulder of his mount. Titan was equal in every way to either Centaurus or El Gamar.

He held the gray back as he looked up at the cliffs. The memory of Zeus was almost unbearable. She had come into his life from her hiding place somewhere in the shrubs above him. She had sat with her backpack and the little copper kettle, watching him make a fool of himself trying to prove he was a man.

How vehement she had been when she declared she would never fall in love because it might hurt. How right she was. Loving her and losing her was more torture than he could have imagined. But the kisses under the cart had also brought more pleasure than he could have guessed.

The unspeakable goodness of God was the only reason Mi'kal could ever give for his meeting with Oreb on the Damascus road. They might have passed one another if Oreb had not been whistling or if Mi'kal had not been trying to concentrate on something other than Zeus.

But Oreb was whistling, and Mi'kal saw him.

What other man wore such a ridiculous helmet or had a heavy Roman sword swinging from his left thigh? Mi'kal watched with amusement as Oreb passed the line of camels led by Kwa. Oreb had no reason to recognize a black man he had never met.

He grinned more broadly as the Zealot passed the wagon without recognizing the young teacher of Bethany. Lazarus had learned to wear a mantle about his head and face like an Arab.

But with his first sharp glance at the bearded Arab on the gray stallion, Oreb let out a yell. Their names met and mingled in midair.

"Mi'kal!

"Oreb!"

Oreb's exultant yell was followed by a quick second. "Zeus is alive! Hear me—she's alive!"

The words bounced inside Mi'kal's head. He reined in so hard the stallion reared.

"Alive? Where? How?"

"Barabbas found her. In the creek. Nearly dead. She's at his sister's house in Lodebar, at Hamad's key shop."

Full comprehension came, and Mi'kal lifted his arms and shouted. "Kwa! Lazarus! Wait up!"

Kwa pulled Maha to a halt. The brakes of the wagon squealed.

"Zeus was found! She's alive!"

The walls of the cliff echoed. Titan turned his head to look at him. Moses flicked his ears.

Mi'kal pulled closer to Oreb. "Where is Lodebar? How did you find her?"

Oreb repeated all that Barabbas had told him. He also told him what Barabbas had said about her inability to walk or talk.

Mi'kal brushed it away. "None of that matters. I love her."

He motioned for Kwa. Titan was skittish as the camel came near. "I'm going back to Perea. What do you think you should do with the caravan? Wait for me here or go on?"

Kwa's decision was to go on. They would leave the highway before reaching Damascus and cross the sands to the black cliffs the same way he and Leyla had come. Signs would be left for him to follow. They would bivouac at the base of the plateau where there was spring water and forage. A few hour's rest would be good for all of them.

Mi'kal turned to Oreb. "I'd like to travel with you, but Moses would make it seem like a forty-year journey." He adjusted the ties of his cloak and mantle. "Sorry old friend." He leaned over and patted the mule's nose.

"Don't apologize," Oreb said. "He's used to insults."

Mi'kal's throat filled with emotion. "I know you understand. I do not intend to eat or drink again until I find her." He pulled Titan's head up. "Oreb, one more thing. I trust you to get the news about Zeus to Gideon in Bethphage. He will carry it to her family in Papyron. Tell them I am taking her with me. We will be married. We will visit Papyron next year in time for Dannah's wedding. Give them our love." Happiness overwhelmed him. "Tell them I will cherish her always."

He felt the stallion trembling. His heels sent the message. Titan lunged forward. Mi'kal's cloak and head piece billowed.

Oreb let out an admiring whistle. The tollgates had better be open. If not, the Prince of the Black Tents would be flying right over them.

Zeus picked up the small ornamental box and held it to her cheek. The acacia wood was warm and fragrant. Hamad had made it for her as a surprise.

Eunice had made the design on the lid according to Zeus's desires. When asked what she wanted carved, Zeus had flapped her wings and pretended to soar, and finally Eunice understood. She wanted a bird—a bird in flight—and the colors she chose for it were green and gold.

The colors of Mi'kal's Green Bird.

All morning she had been working with polishing oils on it. Tears came into her eyes. She was ready to go home, but there was no joy. Mi'kal would not be there.

Those who sat doing nothing in the bright sunlight of the streets of Lodebar suddenly wondered if maybe something important was about to happen in their village after all. A young Arabian, in flowing robes and riding a gray stallion, made the dust fly as he galloped down the street yelling for Hamad's key shop. Someone pointed it out, and the rider brought the foam-covered horse to a rearing halt.

A few of them waited for what might happen next, but most of them closed their eyes. Whatever the reason behind the young man's rush, it was not worth interfering with their naps. They had slept through the thin trickle of news of the crucifixion and resurrection of the Nazarene called Jesus. If that hadn't kept them awake, why should they lose sleep now?

When Mi'kal stepped through the wide door of the shop, the sunlight coming in over his shoulders blazed on Zeus's red hair. He stood, transfixed with happiness.

Zeus saw a shadow fall over her table. She turned. The man, whoever he was, was in flowing robes, dark against the sun, except where the sun cast rays of light from a band about his head. She lifted a small mallet to strike the bell that would summon Eunice.

He moved toward her. Something caused her to get to her feet.

Then she heard her name.

It couldn't be. But it was. His voice. His arms about her! His face buried in her hair.

"Zeus. Zeus."

The sun no longer blinded her. She could see him. His eyes. His face. His love. Her throat felt renewed life. His name leaped to her lips. But there was no sound, for his lips were on hers, laden with love. Her knees grew weak.

"I thought I had lost you. Oh, Zeus."

She held on to him...tighter...tighter. Trembling.

"Don't worry," he said softly. "I don't care if you can't walk or talk. I love you." Her lips covered his. Then they moved and formed his name. He felt her breath and heard the whisper.

"Mi'kal, love me. Love me."

Her voice shook, and she lifted her head and cried out. She pulled away and ran with joy toward the little room in the rear.

"Eunice! Hamad! He's here. Mi'kal is here, and I can talk. I can talk!" She was almost hysterical with happiness as they rejoiced with her.

Zeus went back into Mi'kal's arms, and Eunice pulled her husband away. Mi'kal sat and pulled Zeus down into his lap.

"Darling, there is so much to say, but I have to know. Do you love me enough to marry me? I am going back to the black tents to be a leader of my people. Will you go with me as my wife?"

Her gray eyes held some of the old mockery. "You never wanted to be a prince."

"God changed my mind after the death of Jesus. You do know about it, don't you?"

Zeus nodded. "Barabbas told us about the crucifixion, and we heard from customers about his resurrection."

"There is much more you should know." He told her about the disciples meeting with the risen Lord. He told her of Jesus' command to go into all the world with the story of redemption and eternal life. He told her of his call to serve Jesus in the world of the black tents. Finally, he told her about Kwa and Lazarus, who had agreed to help.

"My faith in him failed the day I saw his cross. But now that I know he died for me, I must not fail him again."

Her hands went over the whiskers on Mi'kal's cheeks. She lifted his headpiece and ran her hands through his hair.

"You won't. He has given us eternal life. We need not fear death. I should never have laughed or argued about your desire to conquer death."

"But you were right. It is better to have your sins forgiven than it is to live forever. A sinner will live in eternal torment. I want to carry that message to my people. I want them to know I have found the Green Bird. But Zeus, I need you to help me."

Her gray eyes, alive with mingled love and laughter, lifted to his. She was twisting the golden hair at the neck of his robe. Her eyes filled with the mist of mysteries.

"I will go, Mi'kal, but I will miss the hills of Galilee."

"Zeus, the beauty of the desert is not like your green Galilee. But our desert stars are more brilliant. The flapping of the tent ropes and curtain make more music than David's harp. You will have your own racing camel and your own mare. You can ride where you will and cook in your little kettle. But I will be there beside you."

She slipped from his lap and knelt at his feet. Her hands gripped his. "As Ruth said to Naomi, Mi'kal, where you go I will go. I will go with you from the yellow sands to the red sands and back again. My old hills and rivers will never be forgotten, but I will love the sand dunes and the streams in the desert that I find with you."

She lifted his hands and laid them against her breast. He could feel her heart pounding. His heart pounded in return.

"Jesus lives, Mi'kal! He will be the real Lord of our camp." She looked up at him with her honest smile. A small flush spread across her cheeks. "Mi'kal, must we wait very long before we are married?" She hesitated and then rushed on. "I don't think I can wait."

"No?" The golden flecks in his green eyes mocked her, but adoration lit his face. He reached into his girdle and pulled out the piece of purple scarf. He unfolded it and laid it across her hair.

"I am as eager as you. The first night of the full moon I will take you as my wife under this, my mother's marriage canopy. Before Lazarus and Kwa, I will vow to love you forever, Zeus. Forever and forever."

Zeus folded the scarf and picked up her acacia box. She showed him the green bird with the golden beak and claws. "It's your Green Bird. Hamad made the box and Mother Eunice carved it for me. Mi'kal, I can never tell them how much I love them."

As she shut the lid over the folded scarf, she said, "I'm glad Lazarus is going with us."

"Why?"

"Someday I'll tell you."

Unnoticed, Hamad and Eunice had been sharing Zeus's happiness from the half-closed door of the workroom. Now Eunice pushed it shut.

"Hamad, did you hear?"

"Yes." He smiled as he touched her cheek. "She said she loves us."